H40 858 142 8

BEDFORDSHIRE

Checked
8/9/11

Hertfordshire
COUNTY COUNCIL
Community Information

2 5 JAN 2002

0 4 MAY 2002

1 7 AUG 2002

6.9.02

26.9.02

- 9 OCT 2000

1 7 DEC 2001

- 4 OCT 2002

2 2 DEC 2001

2 5 OCT 2002

1 2 FEB 2002

1 1 DEC 2006

2 0 NOV 2004

1 1 JAN 2010

29 SEP 2011

12/11

L32a

Please renew/return this item by the last date shown.

So that your telephone call is charged at local rate, please call the numbers as set out below:

	From Area codes 01923 or 0208:	From the rest of Herts:
Renewals:	01923 471373	01438 737373
Enquiries:	01923 471333	01438 737333
Minicom:	01923 471599	01438 737599

L32b

D1471979

Pimlico County History Guides
(General editor: Christopher Hibbert)

Already published:

Dorset by Richard Ollard
Norfolk by Tom Pocock
Somerset by Shirley Toulson
Suffolk by Miles Jebb
Sussex by Desmond Seward

Forthcoming:

Cambridgeshire by Ross Clark
Lincolnshire by Henry Thorold
Oxfordshire by John Steane

BEDFORDSHIRE

SIMON HOUFE

with a Foreword by Christopher Hibbert

A PIMLICO COUNTY HISTORY GUIDE

*In memory of my father, the late
Eric Houfe FRIBA (1911–93),
who lived all his life in the county*

PIMLICO

An imprint of Random House
20 Vauxhall Bridge Road, London SW1V 2SA

Random House Australia (Pty) Ltd
20 Alfred Street, Milsons Point, Sydney
New South Wales 2061, Australia

Random House New Zealand Ltd
18 Poland Road, Glenfield
Auckland 10, New Zealand

Random House, South Africa (Pty) Ltd
PO Box 337, Bergvlei, South Africa

Random House UK Ltd Reg. No. 954009

First published by Pimlico 1995

1 3 5 7 9 10 8 6 4 2

© Simon Houfe 1995

The right of Simon Houfe to be identified as the author
of this work has been asserted by him in accordance with
the Copyright, Designs and Patents Act, 1988

This book is sold subject to the condition that it shall not,
by way of trade or otherwise, be lent, resold, hired out, or
otherwise circulated without the publisher's prior consent
in any form of binding or cover other than that in which it
is published and without a similar condition including this
condition being imposed on the subsequent purchaser

Papers used by Random House UK Limited are natural,
recyclable products made from wood grown in sustainable
forests. The manufacturing processes conform to the
environmental regulations of the country of origin

Typeset by Deltatype Ltd, Ellesmere Port, Cheshire
Printed and bound in Great Britain by
Mackays of Chatham plc, Chatham, Kent

ISBN 0–7126–5339–2

Contents

Hertfordshire Libraries,
Arts and Information

H31 797983X

FARRIES   28.7.97

12.50

942.56

Acknowledgements

In researching this book I have received generous help from so many people who expressed great interest in their county, its architecture and its landscape. The journeys up and down the shire have resulted in the renewal of old acquaintances and the making of fresh friendships for which I have the county alone to thank!

I wish to thank Her Majesty The Queen for allowing me to quote from Queen Victoria's Journal in the Royal Library at Windsor, the Marquess and Marchioness of Tavistock for allowing me to look at documents at Woburn, and Lord Lucas for giving permission to quote from letters in his possession. I have also received advice on Melchbourne and Odell from the Hon. Hugh and the Hon. Arthur Lawson-Johnston and on Turvey from the late Sir Hanmer Hanbury and Lady Hanbury. Samuel Whitbread kindly gave me information about the Southill estate. The following have assisted me in my task: Miss Patricia Bell, Miss Anne Buck, Mrs Elsie Buck, Dr Stephen Bunker, James Collett-White, Councillor Mrs Dorman, Kevan Fadden, John Gaunt, Peter Inskip, Mrs Barbara Jenkinson, John Lunn, Baron Imré von Maltzahn, Phillip Miller RIBA, Mrs Ann Mitchell, Mr and Mrs Gordon Mitchell, Lady Reid, Nigel Temple, John Turner, Andrew Underwood, Michael Urwick-Smith, Miss Lavinia Wellicome.

The following clergy kindly showed me their churches: The Revd Ian Arthur, Vicar of Sutton, The Revd P. N. J. Jeffery, Rector of Turvey, The Revd K. Loraine, Vicar of Haynes and the Revd Roger Palmer, Vicar of Houghton Conquest.

I have consulted many libraries and public institutions where I have received invaluable help. Lastly, I wish to thank Miss Patricia Bell for reading through the first eight chapters of the book and for making useful comments.

Foreword

Although a visitor making a hurried journey through Bedfordshire by train or car would have little reason to believe it so, this county provides a landscape of surprising diversity. In the north the Ouse flows through a quiet countryside of spacious water meadows and stone villages. Elsewhere brick predominates, pastureland gives way to heaths and pinewoods, chalk hills to clay valleys, sheltered combes to windswept downs.

It is a county of contrasts, writes Simon Houfe who lives in the heart of it and knows it so well, 'borrowing a little bit of Northamptonshire here, a little bit of Hertfordshire there, a fen landscape from Cambridgeshire, a beech wood from Buckinghamshire'.

These contrasts of landscape are reflected in the remarkable variety of the county's churches. Several of the finest of these are thirteenth-century foundations, among them the churches dedicated to St Mary the Virgin at Felmersham and Eaton Bray, St Mary and St Helen in the charming village of Elstow, All Saints, Leighton Buzzard, the remotely isolated church at Chalgrave with its unrestored interior, and St Mary's, Luton, its splendid proportions dwarfed but not diminished by the industrial buildings which tower over it.

Bedfordshire is remarkable, too, for the diversity of its Victorian ecclesiastical architecture. It is, as Simon Houfe says, 'the extraordinary range of churches that impress one as one moves about the county. Towers by Clutton [architect of the magnificent Bath stone St Mary's, Woburn, completed in 1868], steeples by Gilbert Scott emerge from treetops, a tomb by Burges or a porch by G. F. Bodley will catch the eye and a medieval exterior will give place to a nave or chancel in rich Victorian clothing.'

Varied as both Bedfordshire's landscapes and churches are, the county remains resolutely itself; and this individuality, Houfe suggests, is even more marked in the people of the county than in their surroundings. Theirs is a 'forceful independent outlook absorbed by generations of yeomen small-holders and market gardeners, chapel-goers with a fierce belief in their rights. Their single-mindedness and openness of spirit made the county a centre for the Quakers in the early days and a nursery for missionaries in later years . . . This practical nature means that we have few important poets to our name and fewer novelists [though both Arnold Bennett and Joseph Conrad came to live here], non-conforming energy being channelled into good works rather than into the ephemeral life of an author.'

Certainly Bedfordshire seems to have produced or nurtured far more than one county's fair share of men and women renowned for their idealism. John Bunyan, the tinker's son, was born at Elstow and wrote *Pilgrim's Progress* in Bedford's town gaol, having already spent twelve years in the county gaol after his arrest while preaching in a farmhouse near Ampthill. John Howard, owner of an estate at Cardington and High Sheriff for Bedfordshire, devoted his life to the amelioration of the lot of prisoners, having seen for himself how cruelly they were treated. Samuel Whitbread, the son of a rich nonconformist brewer, was born at Cardington and, having been elected to Parliament as Member for Bedford in 1790, he soon became a renowned and influential opponent of all manner of oppression and abuse. These are but three of the most celebrated of Bedfordshire's worthies: there are countless others, from the rich and learned Lady Margaret Beaufort of Bletsoe Castle, founder of St John's College and Christ's College at Cambridge, and the Bedford merchant, Sir William Harpur, who became Lord Mayor of London and generously endowed Bedford School, founded in 1552, to Thomas Norton of Sharpenhoe, Protector Somerset's right-hand man and translator of Calvin into English, John Crook, whose great gatherings of Quakers at Beckerings Park drew George Fox into Bedfordshire, and Elizabeth, Countess of Kent, chatelaine of Wrest and patroness of John Selden, Samuel Butler and Ben Jonson's friend, the poet, Thomas Carew.

Appearing with these in Simon Houfe's illuminating pages are a host of other Bedfordshire characters as diverse as the landscape itself: the most ingenious clockmaker of his time, Thomas Tompion, born at Ickwell; the gardener and architect, Sir Joseph Paxton, designer of the Crystal Palace, son of a farmer at Milton-Bryant near Woburn; the unfortunate Admiral Byng of Southill, shot at Portsmouth after the loss of Minorca *'pour encourager les autres'*, as Voltaire put it; Dorothy Osborne of Chicksands Priory whose delightful letters give so vivid an impression of life in the 1650s; Captain William Peel RN, son of Sir Robert who owned an estate at Sandy, archetypal Victorian man of action, athletic, handsome and principled, recipient of the newly instituted Victoria Cross, hero of both the Crimean War and the Indian Mutiny; General Gordon's friend, son of the Rector of St Peter's, Bedford, the soldier, traveller, intrepid balloonist and brilliant linguist, Frederick Gustavus Burnaby, whose affectedly languid arrogance is brilliantly captured in the portrait of him, lying on a sofa and smoking a cigarette, by James Tissot; and the fifth Duke of Bedford, patron of art and agriculture, whose famous sheep shearings at Woburn are so charmingly commemorated in George Garrard's paintings, whose passion for farming is indicated by the ploughshare on which he rests his right hand in the statue of him by Sir Richard Westmacott in Russell Square in London, and whose fine collection of paintings included no fewer than twenty-four superb Canalettos, commissioned by his grand-father, which are still to be seen at Woburn Abbey.

Henry Flitcroft's reconstruction of Woburn Abbey on the site of the old monastic buildings was carried out for the fourth Duke of Bedford in the 1740s and 1750s, the three-thousand-acre deer park being laid out by Humphry Repton. Home of the Russells for over three hundred years, it is one of a sadly small number of grand country houses in Bedfordshire which have survived into our own day and are open to the public. Visitors may still go to see Chicksands Priory, Shefford, the former house of the English Order of the Gilbertines which, acquired by the Osborne family in 1576, remained their home until sold to the government in 1936. They may also visit Hinwick House, a handsome stone Queen Anne house on the Northamptonshire border, home of the Orlebar family since its completion in 1714; and Luton Hoo, in its fine park by Lancelot 'Capability' Brown, still contains the magnificent Wernher Collection, though the original house here, designed by Robert Adam for the third Earl of Bute, was gutted by fire and uninspiringly reconstructed in 1843 by Sydney Smirke.

None of Bedfordshire's great Elizabethan houses has survived except as remnants in later rebuilding, as at Hawnes Park and Melchbourne, Nor are there any ruins of medieval castles, other than the fragments of Lord Wenlock's at Someries, south-east of Luton. All that remains of the mansion which was built on the site of Warden Abbey are a few bits of brickwork, chimneys, crenellations and stone dressings, and the memory of the pear pies which were originally made by the monks here and which, to cries of 'Hot Baked Wardens!', were hawked about the streets for generations afterwards.

Houghton House, which was built for the blue-stocking Countess of Pembroke, Sir Philip Sidney's sister, and which, so it has been suggested, was the inspiration for Bunyan's 'Palace Beautiful', is now a shell. Wrest Park was rebuilt to his own design by Earl de Grey in a French Louis XV style between 1834 and 1839 with James Clephan as executive architect. Southill Park, remodelled by Henry Holland for Samuel Whitbread between 1796 and 1800, does, indeed, still stand and is still in the possession of the Whitbread family, but it is not open to the public in the general way, and we must depend on Houfe's word for it that its 'interiors remain intact and are probably the most perfect surviving rooms of the Regency, not merely in the county but in England. Here one can see the original silk curtains and pelmets in the windows, the original furniture by Marsh and Tatham and portraits by Gainsborough in the setting for which they were designed.'

Yet, while Bedfordshire comes very low down on the list of counties with interesting country houses to visit, it has treasures enough to offer. And no one who lives there or visits it would want to miss the remarkable Renaissance screen separating the chancel from the vestry in St Peter's, Dunstable, a church which incorporates the remains of the Augustinian priory where Cranmer pronounced sentence of divorce against Catherine of Aragon; nor the magnificent refectory at Rushmead Priory with its beautifully preserved timber roof; nor the thirteenth-century Chapter House at Elstow; nor the splendid fifteenth-century market cross in the attractive small town of Leighton Buzzard; nor yet the gabled sixteenth-century dovecote in the care of the National Trust at Willington with its honeycomb of nesting places for almost a thousand pigeons. Indeed, as Simon Houfe so ably demonstrates, Bedfordshire is a county in which to linger, not to rush through on a journey north, as Daniel Defoe discovered on his journey through England some three hundred years ago.

CHRISTOPHER HIBBERT

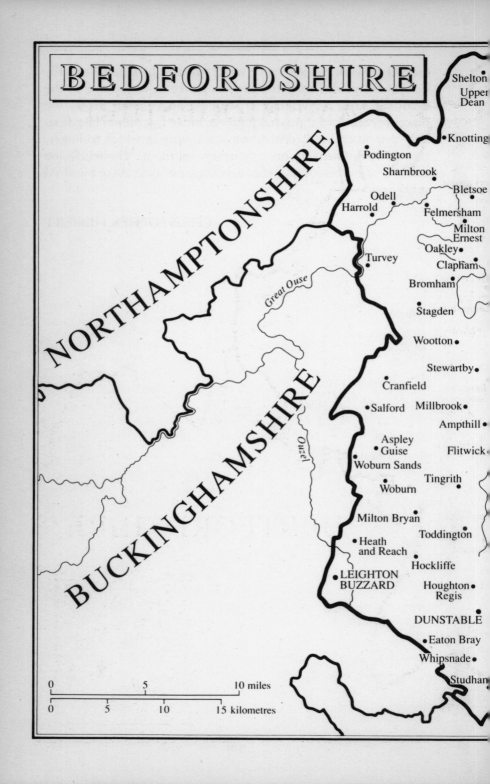

BEDFORDSHIRE

NORTHAMPTONSHIRE

BUCKINGHAMSHIRE

Shelton
Upper Dean
Knotting
Podington
Sharnbrook
Odell
Harrold
Bletsoe
Felmersham
Milton Ernest
Oakley
Clapham
Turvey
Bromham
Stagden
Great Ouse
Wootton
Stewartby
Cranfield
Salford
Millbrook
Ampthill
Aspley Guise
Flitwick
Woburn Sands
Tingrith
Ouzel
Woburn
Milton Bryan
Toddington
Heath and Reach
Hockliffe
LEIGHTON BUZZARD
Houghton Regis
DUNSTABLE
Eaton Bray
Whipsnade
Studham

0		5		10 miles
0	5	10		15 kilometres

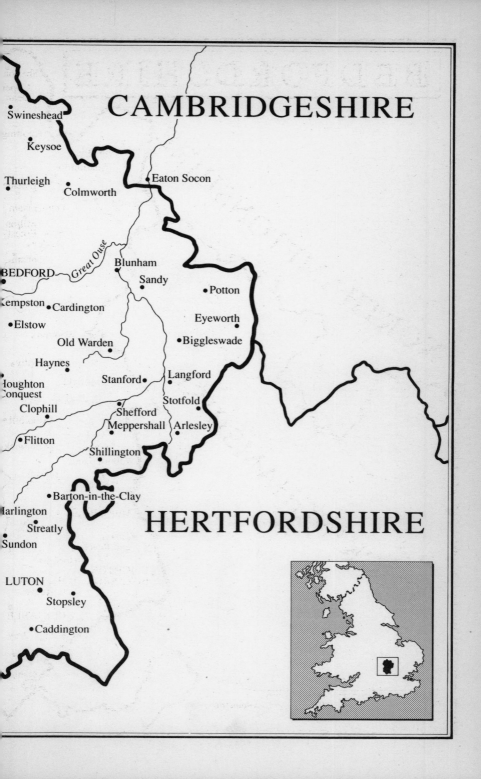

I

The Shape of a County

If you stand on the high road between the Bedfordshire villages of Carlton and Chellington on a winter's day, a great stretch of countryside spreads away northwards before you. There are the folds and undulations that lead down to the River Ouse which flows gently through this landscape, alternately watering the luscious green meadows or inundating the surrounding fields after a thaw or a deluge. The Ouse is very much the soul of the county, giving life and history to the villages it passes through, with rush beds and a watermill here and an ancient bridge and steep banks there. From our chosen vantage point we can see the stumpy tower of Carlton church slightly set apart from its village, the crenellations of Odell church in its knoll of trees and, near at hand, the graceful Decorated spire of Chellington, abandoned by its village and standing in the centre of good farmland. In the middle distance can be glimpsed the noble spire of Harrold with its attractive roofscape of village beyond.

On the further side of the Ouse, rising up from the river valley, is Odell Great Wood, a tangle of leafless brown trees presenting a phalanx on these northern borders of Bedfordshire. To the north-west is a larger concentration of wood known as Three Shires Wood where Bedfordshire, Northamptonshire and Buckinghamshire meet. It is in fact not Three Shires, but 'Threeshas', as a good hunting woman once told me with scorn in her voice.

It is noticeable how close all these communities lie together, clinging to the life of the river, and, in the case of Harrold, straddling its various tributary streams with little footbridges and walkways throughout the village. But there is another pointer that makes this landscape so distinctive. This is stone country: the farmhouses of Harrold, Odell and Carlton, and the cottages in the streets, are all of stone, making the area more like

Northamptonshire or a Midland shire than part of the Home Counties. Further upstream there is another handsome stone village at Turvey, its ancient stone bridge, mansion house and old mill facing northwards across the river into Northamptonshire. It is scarcely surprising that the inhabitants of these North Bedfordshire villages feel themselves to be apart from the remainder of their county, separated by the terrain, the architecture – almost by the culture – from those who live in the south. In researching for this book, it was difficult to persuade them that there was anything worth writing about south of the Ouse! The mutual antipathy between Bedford and Luton is well known.

The Revd A. J. Foster, the indefatigable Victorian clergyman who wrote many books about this county in the 1890s, divided the shire into three regions. The stone villages of the north, the sandstone villages of the central ridge and the chalk villages of the south. It is true that this view is somewhat simplified, he did not have to contend with the vast changes wrought by development and industry or the shifts of population, but his thesis largely holds good today. These three regions are now politically and administratively divided, as they were geographically in Foster's time, and to some extent they hang on to their traditions and loyalties.

If the north of Bedfordshire has the scent of Northamptonshire and the south has some of the feel of Hertfordshire, I would strongly argue as a man of Middle Bedfordshire, that this region of the greensand ridge that runs across the county east to west still retains its own distinct character. To the south of Bedford, the county town, there is a flat Ouse plain that sweeps from the rich clay fields of Marston and Wootton right through to the prosperous little town of Biggleswade in the east. Sharply divided by the river to the north and the greensand ridge to the south, this seems to me an area of large fields and windswept farms hiding behind small knots of trees, a country of no strong characteristics and no strong attachments. On its westerly side, the skyline is punctuated by the stark, pencil-thin chimneys of the brickworks, a strangely Lowry-like northern aspect; on the eastern extremities there are the homely vistas of market-gardening, together with the huge skyscapes that place these fields so firmly in East Anglia.

The greensand ridge which runs from Sandy in the east to the Brickhill woods in the west is one of the finest wooded parts of our county and has a beautiful and varied terrain. Although there is not the flow of a river as in the north or the drama of chalk hills as in the south, its hills are lofty, the views broad and expansive and the wildlife and vegetation rich and diverse. Deer roam these woods and the walker is surrounded by birdlife or the sudden delightful clearing of an ancient heathland with its unexpected outcrops of thin silvery sand. From the earliest times its terrain was perfect for country sports and it was partly for this reason that many of the county's famous houses and castles were ranged along its contours, adding much to its history. Three important monasteries were established here at Warden, Chicksands and Woburn, and though little of them remains, there are a dozen or more churches built in the local materials which are like beacons on these hills. They are not the fine churches of North Bedfordshire, they are more like castles with craggy towers and broken silhouettes, but any folk from these parts, suddenly set down by one of them, would instantly know to which locality they had been transported!

Still further south, we reach the chalk hills of the Chilterns; first the dramatic promontory of Barton Clappers, then the rounded and bare hillsides above Luton and the impressive line of the Dunstable Downs. Although both Luton and Dunstable are medieval towns, they are associated today with the nineteenth and twentieth centuries and industrial expansion in the south of the county. One has to remember that in this comparatively small county, shaped like a bunch of grapes, the stem in the northern villages is nearly seventy miles from London, whereas the lowest cluster in the south is barely twenty-five miles. The urban sprawl here is not so conducive to the selective historian, but if he treads carefully he can find rare and wonderful things. Just as the north is the region (not exclusively) of tall spires and limestone fronts, the south is the place for large churches with beautifully constructed walls panelled checkerwise in the flints of the chalk downland. Buildings like Eaton Bray and Totternhoe dominate the open landscape, where in other parts they would be hidden. The habitat here is as different from Odell or Old Warden as if it was another land, the chalk downs give rise to ash and beech, rare in other parts of Bedfordshire and which are best seen in such splendid settings as Whipsnade's Tree Cathedral.

Bedfordshire is therefore a county of contrasts, borrowing a little bit of Northamptonshire, a bit of Hertfordshire there, a fen landscape from Cambridgeshire, a beech wood from Buckinghamshire, but remaining resolutely itself. This individuality is, I think, more marked in the people than the country. There is a forceful independent outlook absorbed by generations of yeoman small-holders and market gardeners, chapel-goers with a fierce belief in their rights. This single-mindedness and openness of spirit made the county a centre for the Quakers in the early days and a nursery for missionaries in later years. At its best, this sturdy view is represented by the Bedfordshire diarist, Lord Torrington: forthright, questioning, not easily satisfied. At its worst, it is seen in the narrow parochialism of Eaton Socon's rejecting Sir Edward Elgar's music for its church!

The county's most famous sons, John Bunyan, John Howard and Samuel Whitbread II were men of crusading zeal and iron determination, visionaries perhaps, but visionaries who believed in plain speech for the benefit of mankind. This practical nature means that we have few important poets to our name and fewer novelists, that nonconformist energy being channelled into good works rather than into the ephemeral life of an author. The men listed above have a national standing and show that Bedfordshire has not looked merely inwards but outwards to its neighbours and far beyond. Its history fans out like a peacock's tail and touches many remote and unexpected points. Who would have guessed, for instance, that the great roof timbers of Ely Cathedral were grown in the woods of Bedfordshire at Chicksands? But it is all there in the chronicles of Ely of 1322–3, how the sacrist and Thomas, the master-carpenter, purchased not only prepared wood from Chicksands monks, but whole oaks and whole firs for their great undertaking. Conveyed to Barford, these huge timbers were floated down the River Ouse to Ely. Two hundred and fifty years later it was the turn of the Ampthill oaks to serve their country. These noble specimens were ideal for ship-building and between 1583 and 1598, two thousand of them were felled for Queen Elizabeth's navy and many must have found their way into those ships which defeated the Spanish Armada. Two hundred years after that, it was the osiers grown in the beds at Pavenham that supplied the hefty baskets for transporting produce at Covent Garden, and it was the firs from the ducal estates that made props for the trenches in the Great War.

The county has always been generous with its talents, sending people out to the four corners of the globe to preach, to fight or to govern. Richard Nicholls left his home to become the first English governor of New York in 1664, John Howard died while visiting the prisons of the Russian Empire and Colonel Burnaby was slain at the gates of Khartoum attempting to save his friend General Gordon. Seventeenth-century emigrés had the happy notion of carrying the county names into the New World, so Massachusetts boasts a New Bedford and a Woburn Center and Concord was founded by a parson from Odell.

But it is also a shire of paradoxes. Why, for instance, should a land-locked county produce one of the great tragic naval heroes, Admiral Byng? Who would have thought that some of the earliest experiments in steam navigation were carried out on the lake at Woburn in 1804–6 by Dr Edmund Cartwright, probably assisted by the American engineer, Robert Fulton? Is it a mere coincidence that this industrious puritan population should give birth to Thomas Tompion, the greatest clockmaker of his age, or that a market-gardening county should produce Sir Joseph Paxton, the greatest horticulturalist of a later period? The roadways are also paradoxical, for all the major routes bisect the county from north to south in opposition to those gentle divisions we have already mentioned. In fact, at the Chalk Cutting north of Dunstable, the terrain seems almost to defy the northward progress of Watling Street. Only the ancient Icknield Way does what is expected of it and snakes through the south of the county from east to west.

The direction of the roads is of course governed by geography and ours is a county that lies on a strategic route between London and the North of England. This has made us hospitable; we have always been a county of big inns and fat innkeepers, welcoming tables and groaning sideboards. Our country houses have taken in the traveller as a matter of course and many of our most distinguished visitors, whether they are Samuel Pepys or Celia Fiennes, Samuel Johnson or John Wesley, have been people in transit. They have noted our kindness, observed our peculiarities and passed on.

The trades although remaining largely the preserves of their traditional areas were also influenced by this passing throng. The straw-plait industry was long established in the south with its ancillary skills of decorative straw work at Dunstable and hat manufacture at Luton. Basket-making was important to the market-gardening industry at Biggleswade and further north at Pavenham. The cottage industry of lace-making was more widely spread, revived by the many village lace schools that grew up in the early nineteenth century. The craft was particularly favoured in the Ouse valley, in the greensand villages and in West Bedfordshire, which was known as 'the country of beautiful bobbins', examples being of boxwood, bone, silver, gold and pewter.

In the years before the Roman invasion, this part of Britain was populated by isolated communities living in farmsteads, tilling the land for cereal crops and holding small herds of cattle, sheep and pigs. It was a tribal culture, tribute being paid to the chief families, which in the case of South Bedfordshire were the Catuvellauni and in the case of East Bedfordshire, the Trinovantes. There was a mixture of Belgic settlers and descendants of the original Iron Age inhabitants. The most populous place was the fruitful valley of the River Ivel where a number of Catuvellauni burials have been found in the Shefford and Southill areas. With the Roman invasion of AD 43 and the gradual Romanisation of strategic positions, areas like Bedfordshire settled down to an agrarian pattern much as before. The most important Roman station was at Dunstable (Durocobrivis) on the newly constructed Watling Street. There were no other towns but there were a fair number of farmsteads and a few villas, though none of these were grand, the finest being on a site at Totternhoe where an extensive courtyard house existed with separate bathroom block and mosaic floors to some of the rooms. This may have been the country home of an official from nearby Verulamium. Sandy was also a small but wealthy settlement and the one at Ruxox near Flitwick may have been a temple. Water cults, which had been part of the native religion, were continued by the Roman occupiers and the discoveries of rings and fragments by springs at Chalgrave and Totternhoe may be the remnants of votive offerings.

Were there worshipping Christians at this period in our county? Probably, although evidence is slight. In the eighteenth century an intaglio ring was found at the Sandy settlement which had an image of the crucifixion, with a worshipping figure on either side. The inscription read *'In hoc signo vincas'*, or 'in this sign may you conquer', a quotation from a vision of the Emperor Constantine. Like so many of the earlier archaeological finds, this ring has been lost. [Simco, *Survey of Bedfordshire: The Roman Period*]

By the third century, the comfortable life of the Romano-British was beginning to be disturbed by northern invaders. There were attacks by Germanic tribes on the east coast and these were repelled by the Romans from time to time and order was stabilised for a while. The fourth century was a prosperous one for Britain and, despite threats, fine buildings like the Totternhoe villa were created. By AD 406, however, the situation was becoming serious, and by AD 410 the Empire could no longer defend its outer territories and the Romano-British were left to their own devices. The discovery of coin hoards at Luton Hoo, Podington, Flitwick and Cranfield, dating from this time, shows how unsettled life had become.

Saxon mercenaries had previously been employed to defend Britain against other German tribes and this may have continued in our area with increasing Saxon settlement taking place on a basis of coexistence. Slowly the balance of the population swung in their favour, the Britains moving westwards to the Celtic strongholds and the newcomers swamping the areas with their language and place names. The highly sophisticated European pottery associated with the Romans was replaced by the dark coarse ware of the Saxons, sometimes found on the Roman sites where they were probably squatting. The four hundred years of Roman influence were at an end, but their roads and town sites have remained to act as guides to those who came after.

The names that the Saxons gave to their new territory gives some indication of its appearance in those distant days. Much of it was low-lying and even marshy (Marston and Fenlake), although the settlers preferred the high ground of hills (Clophill,

Puloxhill and Ampthill) or cliffs (Clifton and Hockliffe). There were huge swathes of forest (Wootton, Bolnhurst and Gravenhurst) where the new inhabitants made clearings among the aspens (Aspley), the birches (Barford) or the willows (Willington). Eversholt and Everton denote the presence of wild boar, Cranfield of cranes and Crawley of crows. Names such as Limbury, Medbury and Upbury suggest settlements behind fortified stockades, and the 'worth' of Colmworth and Tilsworth suggests enclosed settlements. All of this gives us a certain picture, even if it is a little fragmented and indistinct.

By the seventh century, our region was absorbed into the powerful Midland kingdom of Mercia. The two most powerful kings of Mercia, Ethelbald (d.757) and Offa (d796) ruled in the eighth century when this part of England was peaceful and well organised. Christianity had established itself (the first traces were at St Paul's Bedford) and the parish system was beginning to evolve as need arose, but it did so in a haphazard and pragmatic manner. Under the king there were ealdormen, the highest nobles, followed by thegns who were the lords of villages where the free peasants lived, assessed as hides, the amount of land that could support a household. Within two generations of King Offa's death, his kingdom was crushed by the kingdom of Wessex and threatened by the Danes. The Danish invaders attacked the east coast, sailing up the rivers in their long boats and establishing temporary settlements. In Bedfordshire one has been discovered near the Ouse at Renhold. Like their predecessors they began to settle, creating an uneasy period of truce and skirmish for the original population. In 914, King Edward of Wessex moved against the Danes and forced Earl Thurcetel to give his allegiance at Buckingham. King Edward then occupied Bedford in 915 and created a new borough south of the River Ouse as a defence to echo the semicircular defences on the north side from St Paul's to St Cuthbert's. This new area had a moat constructed known as the 'king's ditch' which was visible until the nineteenth century.

The reorganisation of the country resulted in counties being created from the old Danish districts, each county being divided into hundreds. In Bedfordshire (not yet referred to by that name) there were nine: Stodden, Willey, Barford, Redbornstoke, Wixamtree, Biggleswade, Clifton, Flitt and Manshead. These hundreds had a court that met every four weeks. A diocese was established at Dorchester-on-Thames and a great deal of church building took place in the area. The finest extant examples are parts of the towers of Clapham, Stevington and Thurleigh, and the crossing tower of St Peter's, Bedford. These give little idea of the intricate beauty obtained by the Saxons in their art, but this can easily be seen in the remarkable cross base of Elstow, excavated near the priory about twenty-five years ago. Superbly carved with stylised ornament, it is now on display at the Elstow Moot Hall.

The county was first mentioned by name in the Anglo-Saxon Chronicle of 1011. Bedford became an important trading and religious centre and there was a small monastery here in the tenth century. From 1009, fresh waves of invading Danes bore down on the eastern counties and, approaching Bedford from the north-west, swept on to Tempsford. The monastery was destroyed but some semblance of order was restored under the Danish king, Canute. In 1042, the country gained an English king once again in Edward the Confessor and might have settled down to a period of peace and tranquillity, but Earl Tostig, who was a landowner in these parts, was also a troublemaker. Tostig was exiled and sided with the King of Norway, a dangerous alliance for the future of the realm. When King Edward died in January 1066, the hapless Harold (who owned the manors of Westoning and Arlesey in this county) was immediately chosen as his successor, but that autumn his sovereignty was challenged by both the King of Norway and by Tostig, who invaded the north and were soundly defeated by Harold at Stamford Bridge. Harold's depleted army then had to march southwards to meet the invasion of the Norman Duke William of Normandy at Hastings on 14 October 1066, when Harold II was killed. With this momentous event, the history of England, and of our county, was dramatically changed.

II
Castles and Abbeys

From the mists of these uncertain times, a pattern begins to emerge: the king and his feudal lords, the church and the beginnings of local government. From the Norman Conquest onwards the district that we know and cherish as Bedfordshire is a fully recognisable entity, its borders are roughly the same as our own, its place names and even its field names begin to have a familiar ring.

The Norman genius for organisation and documentation so clearly marked out in Domesday Book, soon had other opportunities to express itself in the tangible form of architecture and decoration. An occupying force, that was here to stay, was already raising castles in front of a subdued population, but the case of churches was rather different. The Normans, like the Saxons, were part of Christendom and shared common beliefs and common allegiances to Holy Church. The Danes had been regarded as heathens, but the Norman French were in reality Christian brothers, even if they did not behave as if they were. Before the Conquest there were already some Norman bishops in English bishoprics and these connections had always been close.

One of the first acts of the new conquerors was to alter the episcopal government of our area, moving the seat of the bishop from the ancient foundation of Dorchester-on-Thames to Lincoln. A bishop from Fécamp Abbey was installed there and the see was divided up into archdeaconries, one archdeaconry being created to cover the whole of the shire of Bedford. The country divided up the judiciary into secular courts to try lay cases and ecclesiastical courts to try church matters. Later Archdeacons of Bedford made regular visitations to the parishes to see that churches were properly repaired and to bring offenders against church law before the court, especially cases of marriage, bastardy and tithes. The archdeacons were all members of the cathedral chapter and attended there with the dean, precentor and chancellor. The canons of the cathedral had prebendal estates allotted to them and those of Biggleswade and Leighton were two in this archdeaconry. The royal manor of Leighton was given by the Conqueror to his bishop Remigius and it was later in the hands of Canon Theobald de Busar. So as not be to confused with another Leighton in the diocese (now Leighton Bromswold), the scribes added the prebendary's name to 'Leighton Busar' which developed into Leighton Buzzard.

At the coming of the Normans there were no surviving monasteries in Bedfordshire, although there were secular canons at St Paul's church, Bedford. The Norman lords were immensely rich from the possessions they had been given and they were naturally willing, for the good of the people as well as for their own souls, to build churches and found religious houses. It is hardly surprising that with the bishop coming from the majestic abbey of Fécamp on the Normandy coast, and the Norman kings from Falaise, Caen and Bayeux, that there would be a great tradition of building. The first foundation had come only ten years after the Conquest in about 1076, when Countess Judith, the Conqueror's niece, founded Elstow Abbey in memory of her late husband Waltheof. This was a Benedictine nunnery where the emphasis was on worship. Elstow's early abbesses were well connected Normans with names like Balliol and Morteyne.

The Norman builders, schooled in the tradition of their Continental abbeys like the Abbaye Aux Hommes and the Abbaye Des Dames at Caen, planned churches of size and scale. At Elstow they created an important Norman abbey of substantial size, with a long nave, a crossing with transepts and an apsidally-ended chancel. The structure would have evolved by degrees. It was usual for the church to be the founders' first priority, starting with the east end so that the rites could be performed from an early date. This would be followed by the cloisters and an eastern dormitory range for the nuns with further accommodation in a south range, the square completed by a cellarium (store) on the west side. There is some evidence that the nuns may have lived in wooden buildings to the south of the church until there were sufficient funds for completion. In any event, the monastery was an organic institution, continually adapting to new ideas and new needs; archaeological investigation has shown that Elstow was altered and expanded in the next four hundred years.

The surviving part of that Norman nave is now the parish church of St Mary and St Helen with a marvellous series of interior arches and arcades above, lofty and plain. They date from the early twelfth century and are the simplest of architectural elements with no decoration. Above the north door, however, is an arched Norman panel of c.1140 showing a Christ in Glory, with St Peter on the left and St John on the right. It is very French and derives from the School of Moissac.

It is not surprising that these links with France were so strong, for the Norman baronial families that ruled here had retinues and retainers who were continually moving backwards and forwards, the leading clerics were French, and the leading scholars came from centres like Bec. A few years later, there were even religious houses in the county which were direct offshoots of Arrouaise and Fontevrault, the superb cathedral where so many English kings were buried.

The autocratic rule of the first three Norman kings was followed by a very unsettled period during the reign of Stephen (1135–54) when no new monasteries could be founded. Perhaps the religious fervour of the First Crusade at the end of the eleventh century absorbed all the energies of the church just as the turmoil in the twelfth prevented growth. But the sixty years after Stephen were remarkable for during that time eleven more monasteries were added to the earlier foundation of Elstow. These included the Benedictine houses of Beaulieu (1140–6), Markyate (1145); the Cistercian ones of Warden (c.1135), Woburn (c.1145); and the Augustinian canons at Dunstable (1132), Caldwell, (1135), Newnham (c.1166) and Bushmead (c.1195). There was one monastery of the English order of Gilbertines at Chicksands, (1150), and the cells of foreign monasteries at Harrold and Grovebury, which have already been mentioned.

The Cistercians, or white monks, had two important houses here. They had come from France to Yorkshire under the rule of Bernard of Clairvaux, and their plain life and concentration on prayer led them to secluded and barren spots where their minds could dwell on God Almighty. This ascetic life attracted many educated young men and St Ailred of Rievaulx was one who fell under the influence of these men, joined them and eventually became their abbot. Walter Espec, the founder of Rievaulx, had lands at Warden in east Bedfordshire and founded a monastery here in 1136 under Simon, the teacher of the worthy St Ailred. The site at Warden was a desolate and windswept high ground of the kind favoured by the Cistercians, and described as 'Sartis', or a clearing in the woods, away from the village. As a matter of fact, a small village, Warden Street, grew up at the abbey gates but that settlement was fading at the Reformation and, like the abbey, has entirely disappeared.

About twelve miles across the county at Woburn, Hugh de Bolebec, another prominent Norman, gave land for another Cistercian house, an offshoot of the famous Fountains Abbey in Yorkshire. This secluded spot was in a cleft in the ridge about two miles from the parish church of Birchmoor, then the principal settlement in the district. After some years, a large village, Woburn, grew up at the abbey gates and eventually extinguished Birchmoor whose parish church and houses completely disappeared. Woburn village was provided with a chapel of ease and greatly benefited by the presence of a monastery across the fields, enjoying the trade and the visits of prelates from Fountains and other places.

The centre for the Augustinian canons, monks who were parish priests and therefore more involved with the community, was Dunstable. A small area which formed part of the old royal manor of Houghton Regis was used by Henry I to form a new market town at the crossing of the Watling Street and the Icknield Way. Henry I retained a royal residence there at Kingsbury and it was looked after by a housekeeper who was paid a penny a day. [Godber, *The History of Bedfordshire*, p. 60] Royal visits were frequent and royal envoys were received here by the sovereign, King Stephen, who spent Christmas there in 1137.

Into this town of growing trade, famed as a centre for tournaments and jousting, with a Jewish community and bustling markets, the king set up a monastery in 1131. The Augustinian house here was one of the largest in Bedfordshire and the surviving fragment of the Priory Church of St Peter at Dunstable is the grandest of its kind. Henry's loss of his son, Prince William, who was drowned in the Channel, was one of the reasons for the foundation. In his proclamation he states:

> Henry, King of the English, greeting to his Archbishops, Bishops, Abbots, Earls, Barons, sheriffs, and all faithful ministers, French and English. Know that, for God, and for my health, and for the soul of my son William and of Queen Matilda my wife, I have given to the church of St Peter of Dunstable (which I founded in honour of God and of his apostle) and to the regular canons serving God there, all the manor and borough of Dunstable.

St Peter's is characterised by a very wide nave of great semi-circular arcades, the inside shafts soaring into the gallery arcade high above. These giant shafts are cut only by the sills of the upper gallery which is more elaborate than that below. The lower arcades are decorated with zigzag hood moulds and each has a triple shaft and scalloped capitals. As the vanished east end would have been contemporary with the consecration, this surviving nave would seem to date from about 1150, the gallery being somewhat later. The whole ensemble of church, crossings, central tower and cloister buildings to the south would have been very impressive to the traveller passing along Watling Street, a place of hospitality and refuge as well as a place of great spiritual and aesthetic uplift. Pilgrims on their way to St Albans would have entered the church by the west door, a good Norman example of the twelfth century and the best surviving one in these parts. Despite its blocking by later builders and the insertion of a fifteenth-century door, the great semicircular arch, intricate carvings and delicate shafts give a good indication of the craftsmanship and majestic scale obtainable at this date. On the north side of the door is a fine piece of Norman intersecting arcade with a bobbin motif. Elsewhere in this fascinating building there is a Norman doorway on the north side with capitals containing carvings of a rabbit, a negro and a stag and hounds. The font is a bold and grand circular work of the Norman period with fine strapwork decoration to the rim. A fifteenth-century gateway still survives, and in the house known as the Priory in the High Street is a fine undercroft of rib-chamfered vaults which was originally the Hospitium.

The Augustinians also came to establish themselves in another urban setting at Bedford in the middle of the twelfth century, opening the houses of Caldwell and Newnham within ten years of each other. The small Caldwell Priory was probably established by a Bedford merchant, Simon Barescote, the leading citizen of the day, before a mayoralty had begun. The Newnham Priory developed out of the old college of canons at St Paul's. It was founded by the aristocratic Simon de Beauchamp, possibly as a result of one of the St Paul's canons murdering a man and creating a scandal and disturbance. This was one of the incidents that led to the rift between the saintly Thomas Becket and King Henry II. It was considered better for the church and the town that such brothers should live together in a monastic house away from the town centre under the rule of St Augustine of Hippo, and away from the crowded congeries of St Paul's parish, and so the foundation was eventually moved in the 1170s to Newnham, on the eastern edge of the town, then in the parish of Goldington. Bedford had obtained its charter from King Henry II in 1166, later confirmed by Henry III.

Simon de Beauchamp's mother, the Countess Rose, was involved in this Bedford foundation, but even more so in the coming of the Gilbertines to Chicksands in 1150. Countess Rose had been married first to Geoffrey de Mandeville, Earl of Essex, one of King Stephen's unruly barons, and then to the Bedfordshire Baron Beauchamp. De Mandeville had helped found Warden Abbey and so there was considerable rivalry between the two, to the extent that Countess Rose tried to prevent the body of her son Geoffrey being interred at Warden rather than Chicksands! An early visitor to Chicksands was Thomas Becket, who stayed there on his way south from the Council of Northampton in October 1164.

The Gilbertine order had been founded for nuns and canons by Gilbert of Sempringham, so that their monasteries were unusual in having two cloister complexes on the north and south of the church. The very domestic character of the order, with the two sexes in close communion, made them very popular although the 'Scripta' or code of the order was quite harsh. The life was based on humility, peacefulness and obedience and the rather ascetic approach to worship did not give much place to ornament. There was no music in their services and painting and sculpture were forbidden, even the number of lights permitted in the church was fairly restricted. The canons of the order wore the white habit of the Cistercians, their sisters the black of the Benedictines, and the two sides were screened from each other in church ceremonies.

It is known that Chicksands was the third largest Gilbertine house, with fifty-five canons and one hundred and twenty nuns. The surviving south cloister of the monastery which forms the main part of the country house today was probably for the canons, but nothing visible is of Norman date. The setting, by a tributary of the Ivel, a mile or so from Shefford, with well wooded ridges behind it, is one of the most attractive positions.

Other Augustinian monasteries were the priory of Bushmead, in the north-east of the county, about 1187 (mentioned later) and Harrold Priory, of 1140, between the church and the bridge over the Ouse, a strange site liable to floods. Nothing survives there, but the nave of the parish church is part of the original conventual church. Later arrivals in the towns were the Franciscan friars at Bedford in the middle of the thirteenth century and the Dominican friars at Dunstable a few years afterwards. Melchbourne had a preceptory of the Knights Templars (later Knights Hospitallers) founded as a result of the Crusades.

Apart from the great Norman interiors of Elstow and Dunstable, the period is represented by various features in different parts of the county, for example, the twelfth-century tower arch at Blunham, with alternate voussoirs of oolite and the local ironstone. Notable details exist, like the crossing tower and arch at St Mary's, Bedford, and the charming south door at Little Barford with its zigzag arch and scalloped capitals. A good idea of what the complete small village church may have looked like is St Thomas's chapel at Chapel Farm, Meppershall, three-quarters of a mile from the village on the north-east side. It consists simply of a nave and chancel but has a handsome Norman door and window. It was a chapel of St Thomas the Martyr and was attached to Chicksands Priory from the 1170s.

One of the most intriguing aspects of this medieval scene is the number of holy men and holy women who inhabited the countryside at different times, called to be solitaries and mystics and to teach by practice and precept. Some of them were the indirect founders of religious houses; most of the others lived lives of saintly contemplation and are only known to us as names or simply from the names of the fields where they dwelt. They were well loved for the advice they gave to ordinary folk, they taught others and sometimes had disciples of their own. Cardington had its own recluse, named Isabel, in the twelfth century and Wilden had one in 1145. In the thirteenth century there was a hermit at Renhold, Simon of Welbury, who put his followers in the charge of the prior of Newnham. There were hermits at various times at Milton Ernest, Eaton Socon, Bletsoe, Luton and Barton. At Clophill, the baron, Henry d'Albini, granted a hermitage to a man known as Ralf, which later became a small Benedictine cell for four or five monks at St Albans, then called Beaulieu. Bushmead had also started as a group of unrecognised disciples of a hermit who were later enfolded by the Augustinians.

The most interesting figure to emerge from a tradition which seems to us today more eastern than western, is Saint Christina of Markyate. Her story is so extraordinary and yet so typical of this strange twilight period that it is worth telling in detail. Christina was born at Huntingdon into an Anglo-Saxon family of some status before the Conquest. Her father was a merchant, and when Christina was fourteen years old he took her to St Albans Abbey where she walked up to the high altar with a penny. Standing there she repeated: 'O Lord God, to thee as a surrender of myself I offer this penny.' From that moment she dedicated herself secretly to the religious life and to celibacy. Some time later a young man came into her life named Buhred. He wished to marry Christina but to the fury of her parents she refused him. She would not conform by drinking wine at guild feasts, taking water instead. After some time she was pushed into a betrothal by her parents, believing that the marriage need never be consummated. Finding this impossible, she escaped from her husband on horseback, disguised as a man, and took refuge with the hermit of Flamstead.

Between Flamstead and Dunstable there lived another hermit called Roger, and it was he who finally took responsibility for this beautiful young woman. In order to determine her seriousness, he had her walled up in a cell where she could hardly move and was only released once a day for a walk. This affected her health, because she could only answer the demands of nature in the evening. After four years Roger was convinced of her spirituality and called her his Sunday daughter – 'myn sunendaige dohter'. He released her from her trials and she eventually inherited his hermitage. By this time she had become a well known mystic and was consulted by Abbot Geoffrey of St Albans. She was offered a community of nuns in York, but declined, finally settling for a nunnery closer to her home. She became first prioress of the Benedictine nuns of Markyate (partly in Bedfordshire) in 1145. She was known as 'Christina of the wood', she received recognition from the king and she personally embroidered mitres for the English Pope, Adrian IV.

Apart from the discipline and structure imposed by the church, there was a growing system of local government under the Normans. The sheriff of the county was enormously important until the twelfth century. He was responsible for the king's lands and manors, the calling out of men to fight and the imposition of fines in the courts. These consisted of the old hundred courts, which met monthly in their area, and the sheriff's court which was more centralised. The hundreds courts dealt with minor offences of brawling and bad behaviour, the sheriff's court with offences against the king. From about 1166, twelve men from the hundred court had to report cases at the sheriff's court and this became the origin of the jury system. In the courts of the barons, procedures were still rather primitive, feuds often being settled there and then with a fist fight organised between the disputants! From the close of the twelfth century, things became more formalised when itinerant judges were sent out on circuit by the king.

As there were no police, law and order rested very largely on the public spirit of the populace. Seizure of a criminal could be undertaken by any citizen once the hue and cry had been raised, and the felon might seek sanctuary in a church for up to forty days after which he could be expelled from the kingdom. There was a good deal of violence, most of it connected with subsistence theft in a poor community. Some examples give details of clothing and life. One evening in June 1272, John of Chellington was visiting Simon Pattishall's house at Cainhoe, near Clophill, when he was set upon by Robert Atewater of Gravenhurst. The robber took his hood of perse (blue-grey), his red belt with metal bars, his purse of white sheepskin, his gloves, his cowskin shoes, knife and trencher knife.

The ordinary person lived in a house of stud and plaster, with wooden shutters to the windows, and little in the way of separate rooms for privacy. His diet was bread, ale and bacon, most of it the produce of his own piece of tillage. It is small wonder that the solidity of the great Norman churches of Elstow, Dunstable and Warden and the life that went on within them was impressive to people from such a background. Their lives were controlled by the lord of the manor (another Norman designation) who might be the local baron, or the local abbot in a number of Bedfordshire cases. A few villagers were free tenants and there were between four and nine of these in the villages of Barton, Cranfield and Shillington, which came under the ownership of the abbey at Ramsey. They each held a few acres and had only one obligation: to attend the shire and hundred courts. Villeins owed labour service to the lord and held about one virgate a piece (about 30 acres) from him (virgate, meaning slender and straight); and the cottagers, another class, were in specialised trades and held small pightles near their homes. Although the villeins who were obliged to do labour service had year long obligations, particularly at harvest time, they frequently worked only till noon and were able to spend the rest of the day on their own plots. Harvest was always a time of celebration, feasts and games, such as catching the sheep in the hay field at Barton and claiming as much hay as you could carry at Shillington!

Dunstable continued to be a place of great importance and the monastery continued to produce men of a high calibre who served in national affairs. The most distinguished prior was Richard de Morin, who began to keep the Dunstable Chronicle, a survey of the happenings of the priory and its estate and also of national and international events. Prior Richard, who had studied at the University of Paris, advised the king and attended the Lateran Council in 1215. He was also instructed to preach the Sixth Crusade in Bedfordshire.

The pattern of life among the upper classes was very similar in the early fourteenth century to what it had been a hundred years earlier. The four important castles in the county were still in the ownership of the original Norman families: the Beauchamps at

Bedford, the Albinis at Cainhoe, the de Wahulls at Odell and the de Traillys at Yielden. But the centre of power was shifting throughout the country from the strong king to the stronger barons. The high-handedness of King John brought these tensions to a head in 1215 and the younger members of the aristocracy, including William de Beauchamp of Bedford and William de Cantilupe of Eaton Bray, forced the king to sign Magna Carta at Runnymede. As a result of his opposition, William de Beauchamp lost his castle at Bedford and it was at this point that a rather less attractive figure comes on to the stage.

This was Fawkes de Breauté, a French professional soldier of fortune, who allied himself to King John in a truly opportunistic spirit. Fawkes attacked the Beauchamp stronghold at Bedford and it was surrendered to him in December 1216. Fawkes was given his prize by the king and proceeded to rebuild the motte and bailey castle, using stone commandeered from St Paul's church and other places. He became immensely powerful in the area, was in command of all the castles from Oxford to Cambridge and constructed another stronghold for himself at Luton. Fawkes was a plunderer and a bully, but he helped the king, and after John died, supported the young heir, Henry III. Once this new king was established, Fawkes's role was ended, but this terrible thug continued to harass and molest. While he was at Bedford there was no peace; before 1224 he had murdered a monk from Warden Abbey and put other monks in prison at the castle. When the judge at Dunstable charged him with these offences, he had him apprehended and brought to Bedford in chains.

This was the signal for Henry III to act over the misdeeds of his father's loyal servant. The King came to Bedford in person and summoned the sheriffs for men, tools and weapons to batter down Bedford Castle and capture Fawkes and his followers inside it. Six mangonels (huge stone-throwing catapults) were drawn up before the keep while miners were called in to remove the foundations from under it. Two large wooden towers were erected from where the Kings' archers shot volleys of arrows into the interior. When the fortified entrance was stormed, the Dunstable contingent set fire to the outer buildings while the miners were again employed to undermine the inner wall. The garrison surrendered on 14 August 1224, and Fawkes's brother was taken prisoner and eighty of the defenders were hanged. Fawkes himself surrendered to the king and laid down his armour. This included a shirt of mail, back and breast plate, iron hose, iron cap and helmet, a linen tunic underneath and a skull-cap. [Godber, *ibid*. p. 75] Bedford Castle was mostly demolished, although William de Beauchanp was allowed to build a dwelling house on the site of it, provided that it was not crenellated.

Beauchamp became an important person in the court and a baron of the exchequer, but the removal of the castle had severely clipped the wings of the Bedfordshire barons. Nevertheless, some handsome houses were being built. The chronicler Matthew Paris mentions the house of Paulinus Peyvre at Toddington, a huge mansion which he acquired after 1230. 'He was a most insatiable purchaser of lands, and an incomparable builder: his home at Toddington is stated to have been like a palace, with chambers and a chapel and other houses of stone, and surrounded with orchards and parks, which filled with astonishment all beholders.' [Blundell, *Toddington*, p. 21] This was on the north-east side of the parish in the area which is known as Old Park.

When the barons again rose under Simon de Montfort in 1264–5, three Bedfordshire knights were captured by the king; Simon de Pateshull of Bletsoe, Ralf Pirot of Harlington and Hugh Gobion of Higham Gobion. At the Battle of Evesham, Simon de Montfort was slain and so was the young John de Beauchamp of Bedford, the last of that line at Bedford Castle. A more positive development was the calling of a Parliament in 1265 and the beginning of some parliamentary representation with knights of the shire, gentlemen at arms with some experience who could answer questions. The first recognisable figure to represent the county was one Robert de Crevecoeur of Great Barford in 1275. Bedford was still an important administrative centre and well placed geographically for meetings. It had established a mayoralty in the late thirteenth century. Prince Edward held a tournament there in 1268 which was attended by the king, who slept at Elstow. This was a social occasion as well as a display of skill and from its practice evolved the first use of heraldry on the shields of the participating knights. The sheriff had to see that all men of a certain status in the county procured arms and put themselves forward for knighthood. At a tournament, a roll of arms was called out with the symbols of the knights, and in Dunstable, in 1308 and 1334, the names reflect the locality from which they came. Among the contestants were Sir John de Morteyn (Marston Morteyn), Sir David de Flitwick, Sir Ralf de Goldington and another Sir Ralf Pirot of Harlington. [*ibid.*, p. 78] From about the middle of the thirteenth century, families appear that were to exist in Bedfordshire until our own time, notably the Greys of Wrest who were beginning to acquire the older estates.

King Edward III channelled opposition and discontent into war abroad. The Hundred Years War was the great period of chivalry, it saw the battles of Crécy, Calais and Poitiers. One heroic figure emerges from this time of strife: Sir Nigel Loring, a landowner from the Bedfordshire heartland at Chalgrave. Loring was a professional soldier who served under Edward, the Black Prince, and saw many important victories in France. He was present at the naval victory of Sluys when the French were defeated as much by archers as by sailors and he was knighted for his bravery. He took part in the Battle of Crécy in 1346 and the Battle of Poitiers in 1356, while he was chamberlain to the Black Prince. Sir Nigel was created a Knight of the Garter at the institution of the Order on 23 April 1349. He is believed to have attended the banquet at Windsor Castle a few months earlier when twenty-six knights were entertained by Edward III, like the Round Table knights of King Arthur. His stall in St George's Chapel, Windsor was the tenth on the Black Prince's side. The Lorings held a large estate at Chalgrave and a substantial hall house, with a cellar below, was situated in a compound defended by mud walls and with a gatehouse. His offices included two larders, a pantry, a buttery, bakehouse, brewhouse, malthouse, kilnhouse and wellhouse, and the manor had its own chapel and garden.

The manor has long since vanished except for a mound, but the nearby parish church has much in it to mark the long association with the Lorings, where they established a chantry priest to say prayers for their souls. All Saints, Chalgrave, is the parish church for what were the hamlets of Wingfield and Tebworth, but now has no village of its own. Set by the Toddington to Houghton Regis road in a square of trees, time seems to have stood still here, although the marching suburbs of Toddington may very soon give it a village again! Quiet, remote and rural, the interior is untouched by the restorer and gently evocative. Until comparatively recently there was no lighting here other than that from oil lamps and candles, so that a service of evensong had a strange beauty of its own. The pale light from the lamps had a way of catching the flat facets of pillar and pew, investing them with a kind of mystery, while the waving flames of the candles sent moving shadows round the church. In the south aisle they illuminated the recumbent figure of Sir Nigel Loring with a lion at his feet, and in the north aisle, another knight with quatrefoil decoration. All around, half obscured by the dusky light, were the great forms of mural paintings starting out of the walls, mostly early fourteenth-century, a lovely Annunciation and a masculine St Christopher. These are memories which the harsh light of electricity can never replace.

Despite the period of the Barons War and the beginnings of the long wars in France, the years of transition from the thirteenth century to the early fourteenth century were ones of rich artistic activity. The outstanding monument to thirteenth-century design in the Early English style is the west front of Felmersham church, a web of delicate detail, the main doorway consisting of slim shafts, a blind arcade of seven arches above it and a tripartite composition of pointed arches above that to crown the achievement. The whole cruciform building dates from the years 1220 to 1240 and is that rare thing, a complete entity. The interior with its lancet windows, central tower and crossing with grouped shafts is like a miniature cathedral and even its later features, like the fifteenth-century screen, fit perfectly into the whole. It is probably the most beautiful single parish church in Bedfordshire, greatly helped, one must say, by its splendid position above the Ouse crossing, the arcaded west end looking out on the old stone bridge and beyond it to water meadows and willows that can hardly have altered for four or five hundred years.

The capitals to the pillars at Felmersham are all in moulded decoration but not in the celebrated stiff leaf of early English architecture. For that, one has to go further south in the county to the churches of Chalgrave, already described, Studham and Eaton Bray. The carved capitals at Studham, 1220, are lively and inventive but nothing compared to the virtuoso performance on the capitals at Eaton Bray: intricate brackets on the south arcade of 1220 and eight shafted piers of great richness on the north arcade of 1235–50. Perhaps there was a greater tradition in the south for decoration. We know that Thomas of Leighton was a master smith who made ironwork round Queen Eleanor's monument in Westminster Abbey in 1293. It is assumed that he made the wonderful iron scrolls on the door of Eaton Bray church, and the equally magnificent examples at Turvey and Leighton Buzzard may have come from his workshop.

In passing, one should mention that it was not only Leighton that was connected with Queen Eleanor. In 1290, when her funeral cortege was moving south, it halted at Woburn and Dunstable, where Eleanor crosses were erected in her memory. Both crosses were the work of John de Bello and the figures were enriched by the goldsmith William Torel. Not a trace of either of these monuments exists today.

For a good picture of a small religious house in the thirteenth century, one could not do better than travel north to Bushmead Priory on the Cambridgeshire border, where one range of the building survives. This is the refectory of 1250, built of small stones with ashlar quoins, and limestone buttresses from Barnack. The south façade had lovely doors and windows which originally looked on to the cloister, the church standing on the south side, an unusual position but giving easier access to the river and fishponds. The terrain of flat and wooded countryside is idyllic and the seclusion gives a clear idea of the contemplative nature of their lives. The real excitement however is provided by the timber roof, a complete construction of 1250, which has survived miraculously down the centuries. The form is really transitional between Early English types and the graceful crown-posts of the fourteenth century; Bushmead combined crown-posts and collar purlins with double braces and parallel rafters. To stand on the uneven cobbled floor and stare right up into this 'forest' of wood is an awe-inspiring experience, particularly when you notice the blackening of the timbers by the monks' central hearth seven hundred years ago! As a property of English Heritage, it is beautifully maintained and regularly open to visitors. Another fine survival of the thirteenth century is the Chapter House at Elstow, originally the outer parlour of the nunnery. It is a square chamber with a central Purbeck marble pillar giving it the Chapter House look. The most remarkable thing about it is its rib vaulted ceiling with a complicated pattern of vaulting springing from brackets, that is decorative and satisfying. Like so many of the best parts of Bedfordshire churches (Toddington and Dunstable to name but two) it is now a vestry, and not readily accessible.

Living standards were reasonable in the thirteenth century and an agricultural boom kept pace with a growing population. The yield from medieval farming was not very good and it was usual to work on a two field system, one field cropped and one fallow each year. In order to get more food, arable land was extended and took in more of the waste ground where ordinary people could graze livestock. People with common rights could either graze this common land or graze the arable land after cropping. The downs in the south of the county were used for sheep, but the flocks were not big, the largest at Barton being about forty sheep. Crops grown in North Bedfordshire included wheat, barley, oats, dredge (mixed barley and oats), peas and beans. Milling facilities now included windmills as well as watermills and one windmill was set up by the religious house at Leighton as early as 1200.

The first half of the fourteenth century was a period of architectural grace and beauty which saw the gradual perfecting of a flowing and ornamented style that has come to be known as Decorated. It is best seen in Bedfordshire in complete churches such as Wymington, St Laurence, rebuilt by the wealthy John Curteys, Mayor of the Staple of Calais, before 1391. At Our Lady of Lower Gravenhurst, a wealthy knight, Sir Robert de Bilhemore 'fiet faire cette eglise de nouele' before 1360. This little building is untouched because it is situated in a rural area and has the larger parish church of Upper Gravenhurst close by. It is only necessary to peep through the open door to see the delights that await within, including the lovely original bench-ends and an original Jacobean pulpit. The huge town church of St Mary's, Luton, boasts one of the great masterpieces of this period: the octagonal baptistery with its eight richly crocketed gables in limestone and interior rib vaulting. Dating from 1330–40, it is the Decorated at its peak and one can imagine the colours and gilding which originally embellished it. Beneath the canopy is the earlier marble font. It was the glory and the invention of such things that came abruptly to an end in the next generation.

Good times were very quickly followed by hard times in the early fourteenth century and, in 1349, by that worst of all scourges, the Black Death. This was the bubonic plague carried across Europe by black rats which reached London in November 1348, and Bedfordshire in the following March to August. Bedford was ravaged by the plague, but so too were the towns of Luton, Leighton and Biggleswade. Although records are few and far between, it is known that fifty-four priests died out of the incumbents of one hundred and twenty-three benefices. Among them were several chantry priests, Richard of Staughton, prior of Bushmead (who was planning a grammar school), and a number of prioresses at Markyate. At Cainhoe, the village by the side of the castle was devastated by the disease, the lord of the manor died and the village was deserted, being replaced by modern Clophill. The effect on agriculture was profound, fields were uncultivated, watermills stopped production and those staples of medieval life, the dovecotes, were let to fall into ruin. The countryside wore an aspect of neglect and dereliction. Bedford was badly affected by loss of trade, but the wool merchants were starting to thrive there, the vanguard of a less labour intensive industry. [Godber, *ibid*. p. 118].

The early fifteenth century saw one family pre-eminent in the county; the Greys of Wrest, who had risen from being minor knights to great landowners. Roger, Lord Grey of Ruthin who succeeded to the estates at Wrest, Thurleigh and Brogborough in 1323, married the heiress Elizabeth Hastings, and their grandson inherited the vast properties of the Hastings in East Anglia. Reynold, Lord Grey (*d*.1440) was a close friend of King Henry IV and involved in the war against Owen Glendower, whose prisoner he was on one occasion. But in the Bedfordshire of the 1430s Lord Grey was too old to hold down the baronial discontent that was shortly to break out between the Houses of York and Lancaster.

Already other war lords were looming on the horizon in the centre and south of the county, notably the powerful Wenlocks at Luton and the partly royal family of Lord Fanhope at Ampthill. Sir Thomas Wenlock's family were established at Luton in the late fourteenth century when William Wenlock of Shropshire acquired land there and another Wenlock became master of the Farley Hospital (founded by Henry II in 1156). Sir Thomas Wenlock was a soldier in the French wars and on his death was succeeded by his more powerful brother, John Wenlock. This John Wenlock (d.1471) was M.P. for the County in six Lancastrian parliaments between 1433 and 1455–6, when he was Speaker of the Commons. He had steadily risen in the king's service, mostly due to his early connection with Sir John Cornwall, Lord Fanhope of Ampthill.

Sir John Cornwall (d.1443) was an illegitimate descendant of the royal line through the younger son of King John. He was however a self-made man who had won his position through his chivalry and ability while fighting in France. His skill at a tournament at York in 1400 had won him the hand of the Princess Elizabeth, sister of the Lancastrian King Henry IV. He was a Constable of Sheppey Castle and a knight of the shire for his native Salop, but he acquired the manor of Ampthill through purchase and made it his official residence. Created a Knight of the Garter in 1409, his arms can still be seen on his stall at St George's Chapel, Windsor.

After the death of Henry IV and the succession of Cornwall's nephew, the young King Henry V, Cornwall served with distinction in the French wars and fought bravely at the Battle of Agincourt in 1415. He collected high ransoms from French prisoners like the Count of Vendôme, besieged Rouen and was temporarily in charge of the army during Henry V's absence. Sadly, his only son, John, was killed in the French wars in 1421 at the age of seventeen and the Princess Elizabeth died in 1426. Cornwall was created Lord Fanhope of Fawnhop in Hereford-shire in 1433 and Baron Millbrook of Millbrook, Bedfordshire in 1442. He is commemorated in Milbrook church by his arms and the garter high up in the north clerestory. There are also portraits of him and his wife in stained glass at Ampthill, reproduced from old drawings by a modern artist.

Fanhope built a very extensive castle at Ampthill with 'four or five faire Towers of stone in the Inner Warde, beside the Basse Court'. There were two large gatehouse towers in front and nine other towers on the curtain walls at irregular intervals. Although

Fanhope used this as his residence it was also a place of defence and imprisonment. From 1429 to 1432 it held Charles, Duke of Orleans, who had been entrusted to the Baron after the Battle of Agincourt.

As a man of action with royal connections, Fanhope expected to rule and be obeyed in his own territory. Unfortunately, Ampthill Castle was only four miles away from the home of the more established Grey family at Wrest. In 1437, a meeting of specially appointed justices was called at Silsoe church, the most suitable central point in the county. Lord Grey was incensed that his church was being used in this way and appeared on the scene with fifty or sixty retainers. Lord Fanhope then arrived, claiming that the choice of Silsoe was a move by Lord Grey to obstruct him! Further reinforcements on both sides came and a skirmish seemed to be the inevitable outcome before Sir Thomas Wauton, former Speaker of the Commons, persuaded the opposing forces to withdraw. At the Epiphany Sessions in the Moot Hall at Bedford in 1439, a dispute arose between Fanhope and John FitzGeffrey of Thurleigh, Fanhope's troops in doublets, swords and bucklers proving menacing. Sir Thomas Wauton threatened to report the matter to the king. Fanhope shouted: 'Complain as you will – I defy thy menacing and all thine evil will.' A mêlée ensued and eighteen people were crushed to death when Fanhope's men tried to rush the staircase.

Fanhope died in the winter of 1443, leaving bequests to his two illegitimate sons and asking to be buried at the Friary of Ludgate which he had founded. His will was read out in the great parlour of the castle in the presence of the Archbishop of Canterbury and the Bishop of Lincoln. Ironically, the whole estate was sold to Fanhope's enemies, the Greys, eleven years later. Fanhope's great achievements in the county were the creation of the deer parks at Ampthill and the rebuilding of the parish church of St Andrew; in his time the edifice was widened and heightened, its fine roof carved and its tower built.

One of Fanhope's henchmen at the Bedford disruption had been the young John Wenlock of Luton. He was appointed Fanhope's executor and he became the strong man of the next generation. Wenlock was ambitious, clever and ruthless in an age when might was definitely right. After rising to prominence with

Fanhope, he became M.P. for the County of Bedford and Speaker of the Commons. He had consolidated his position by two important marriages, one with a Bedfordshire heiress. In 1441 he married Elizabeth, daughter of Sir John Drayton of Kempston, bringing that manor into his hands and later acquiring the manor of Aspley and lands at Stondon, Gravenhurst and Barton. His second wife, Agnes Danvers, whom he married after 1461, was the widow of Sir John Fray and came from an influential legal family.

Wenlock was a diplomat who undertook numerous foreign missions for the king and negotiated a treaty with France in 1442. He joined the royal household and by 1448 was chamberlain to Queen Margaret of Anjou and laid the foundation stone of Queens' College, Cambridge on her behalf. But Wenlock was a remarkably opportunistic man and as the Lancastrian court got into increasing difficulties, both political and financial, Wenlock, who had been knighted in 1448, began to side with the Yorkists.

As Speaker of the Commons which was largely Yorkist, a lender of money to the beleaguered king and a holder of state appointments, Wenlock was in a powerful position when the Wars of the Roses broke out. He fought on the side of King Henry VI at the first Battle of St Albans on 23 June 1455, where he was severely wounded, and returned to Luton 'in a cart sore hurt'. In 1458 Wenlock was still a member of the King's Council and was trusted sufficiently to travel to France to negotiate marriages between the Lancastrian princes and the daughters of the French royal dukes. He was also acting for the Yorkists.

Playing his cards very close to his chest, Wenlock did not directly side with the Yorkists till the outbreak of civil war in 1459, when he was attainted for high treason after the Yorkist defeat of Ludford. He returned with the invading army from Calais and was with the Yorkist forces at such important victories as Mortimer's Cross in 1460. He was made a Knight of the Garter in 1461 and was with Edward of York at London in February 1461 when he declared himself king. His cunning way of siding with the winning side led to further honours being showered on him; he was made Chief Butler of England by the new King Edward IV and raised to the peerage as Lord Wenlock on 26 July 1461.

By the later 1460s this mercurial character hed become strongly influenced by the Earl of Warwick, 'The King Maker', and disenchanted with the Yorkist king. When Warwick landed in England in 1470 with the express purpose of restoring Henry VI, the duplicitous Lord Wenlock was hard on his heels. In the spring of 1471, he crossed from Honfleur to England with his former royal mistress, Margaret of Anjou, and the young Prince Edward. Gathering forces in the West of England, they marched to Glastonbury (where Wenlock left his treasure with the abbot) and then to Gloucester which they failed to take. Reaching Tewkesbury the following day, they found themselves facing the army of Edward IV. Wenlock was in charge of the Lancastrian centre at the battle, but it developed into a heavy defeat for Queen Margaret and Wenlock was killed. For this reason, he was buried at Tewkesbury Abbey and not at Luton as he must have intended.

Whereas Fanhope has little to remember him by except Ampthill church and the plateau of his castle, there is much to recall Lord Wenlock's stormy career. At St Mary's, Luton he created the Wenlock chapel in about 1461, between the north transept and the original vestry, opening it up to the chancel with a magnificent double arch in the Perpendicular style with panels to the insides of the arch and a carved Garter badge above it. It is rather like a luscious jewel casket with no jewel inside, for though there is the tomb of William Wenlock and probably Sir Thomas, there is nothing to Wenlock and his two wives. This delightful chapel became the burial place of their successors, the Rotherhams. Its east window originally had a representation of Wenlock in the Yorkist livery of suns and roses as founder of the chapel dedicated to the Virgin. In 1466 he had petitioned the Pope that all parishioners of St Mary's might be allowed to eat milk-foods in Lent and at other fast days and that they should pray for his body in this life and his soul in the next life. [B.H.R.S., Vol. 38, p. 47]

Fragments of his castle still stand at Someries, about a mile and a half south-east of Luton, the only medieval castle to survive in Bedfordshire. The ruins consist of the gatehouse, vestibule and chapel of the castle, forming about three-quarters of the north range. It is all of exquisite fifteenth-century brickwork, the earliest in a county to be so associated with brick. The handsome four-centred arch of the gateway has an arcade of moulded bricks above it, and elsewhere there are a spiral staircase and doorways. Even in its ruinous state one gets an impression of the grandeur of the place and its impressive craftsmanship and solidity. Queen Elizabeth was to stay here, but later the old walls were plundered for the buildings and cottages of the nearby farm.

The great Perpendicular churches that arose at this period tend to be near the centres of population or in the vicinity of some great family. The most prominent of these are the spired masterpieces of St Paul's, Bedford and All Saints, Leighton Buzzard, although the former hall church is very much a nineteenth-century rebuild, and the spire of the latter is earlier. The siting and silhouette of St Paul's are magnificent and the south side with its medieval porch is specially fine. All Saints, Leighton Buzzard, has a superb soaring spire that can be viewed for miles. It was an important ecclesiastical centre in the Middle Ages and the focal point of a series of chapelries in the neighbouring hamlets of Billington, Eggington, Heath & Reach and Stanbridge. These all became separate parishes in the nineteenth century. The mother church is grand and collegiate, particularly the chancel with its fine original stalls from St Albans Abbey, benches with poppyheads, and misericords with carved heads and foliage. The church is also notable for its mason's graffiti on the walls, a fine drawing of a four-light east window with geometrical tracery and an amusing drawing of 'Simon and Nellie' baking a cake! Leighton's importance as a trading centre at this time is denoted by the Market Cross at the top of the High Street, a marvellous fifteenth-century monument in the shape of a pentagon with a vaulted and enclosed lower stage, and a buttressed and recessed upper stage tapering to a pinnacle. The upper part contains some fine statuary. This Market Cross must be the most painted and photographed memorial in Bedfordshire. Crosses were focal points in many medieval villages but few have survived. The one at Stevington is perhaps the finest village cross to be seen today; the preaching cross in the churchyard at Knotting is also late medieval but much restored. Other dignified Perpendicular churches are Flitton, built for the powerful Greys of Wrest in 1440–89, and Willington, created for the influential Gostwicks, mentioned in a later chapter.

In the early fifteenth century, Dunstable was the birthplace of John Dunstable (*d.*1453) a mathematician and composer who was described in contemporary literature as England's chief musician. His works were entirely liturgical and he is held to have been one of the fathers of musical composition. Well known in Spain, he is best remembered today for his setting of 'O rosa bella'. It is not always possible today to appreciate from surviving buildings and fragments the richness of worship and dress in the fifteenth century. Some indication of this splendour, however, can be seen in that tiny masterpiece, the Dunstable Swan Jewel, discovered on the site of the Dominican friary in 1965. A golden jewel with a white enamel swan on it, it dates from 1400 and may be of Burgundian workmanship. It was probably lost by a wealthy but religious visitor and is now in the British Museum.

In many ways this must have been the period of Luton's medieval glory; it was certainly the period of one of its most prestigious foundations, the Guild of the Holy Trinity. The Rotherhams who succeeded Wenlock at Someries were an important dynasty. Thomas Rotherham (1423–1500) was successively Bishop of Lincoln (1471), Chancellor of England (1474) and Archbishop of York (1480). But he did not forget the town where his family had settled, and with his brother, Sir John Rotherham (1432–92), he founded the Guild at Luton in 1474. This was the age of the guilds, and when the Rotherhams set up their fraternity it was only one of a number in Bedfordshire. The others were the fraternity of Dunstable, Corpus Christi of Eaton Socon, Holy Trinity of Bedford and minor guilds at Blunham, Cranfield and Shillington. It is noticeable that all these places are celebrated for their fine late-Gothic churches. The fraternities were corporate bodies which, when they had received a royal charter could purchase land, erect chapels and altars, support chaplains in a church and hold processions and meetings.

Luton's was by far the wealthiest of the fraternities and its register still exists in Luton Museum, beautifully illuminated and recording the names of the members. They include Edmund, Earl of Kent, his countess and his son, the prior of Dunstable, the abbot of St Albans and a large number of gentry. The charter was written in English and Latin and kept in a great coffer in the Brotherhood House on Market Hill, not far from the parish church. The Guild possessed a silver cope and silk banners for its ceremonies in St Mary's, and feasts were celebrated in the Brotherhood House when a parcel-gilt silver salt was placed on the table with eleven dozen spoons and a knife for every guest. Such a profusion of cutlery was very unusual at the time. The brethren ate off wooden platters but occasionally pewter plates were hired from St Albans. In 1521 they used 61 geese, 47 pigs, 61 capons, 74 chickens, 7 dozen rabbits, 20 lambs, 600 eggs, 27 gallons of milk besides beef, mutton, cloves, citron, cinnamon, ginger, almonds, dates, saffron and comfits! Cooks and spit turners were taken on for the four-day feasts and minstrels and Morris men engaged to entertain the guests; a group of three musicians from London cost ten shillings but they also used Thomas Thredour the local harper. Much of their money appears to have been used for beautifying the churches and singing 'dirges' for the dead.

III

A World of Change, 1470–1550

Bletsoe village is situated just off the main route from Bedford to Rushden, a quiet loop of lane that includes the ancient parish church and the remains of a castle. With the Ouse meandering through the North Bedfordshire villages to the west and the ridge of Milton Ernest to the south, Bletsoe's exposed position makes it an unlikely place for a major building. Bletsoe Castle now consists of the two remaining storeys of one range of a Tudor court, but when Thomas Fisher drew it for his *Collections* in about 1814, there appear to have been three storeys remaining with four fine gables at parapet level. This was the seat of the St John family in Bedfordshire from the fifteenth century and in many ways it is where a recognisable history of the region began.

The St Johns were of Norman origin and originally had estates in Glamorganshire. In about 1425, Sir Oliver St John married the sole heiress of the Beauchamps of Bletsoe, Margaret Beauchamp. She owned both Bletsoe and Lydiard Tregoze in Wiltshire and Sir Oliver came to live with her on her Bedfordshire estates. Sir Oliver St John died at Roan in Normandy in 1437, leaving his young widow to succeed to these important properties as well as a family of two sons and three daughters. Margaret Beauchamp seems to have been a very personable woman as well as a wealthy one, for she subsequently married twice, first to John Beaufort, Duke of Somerset and then to Lionel, Lord Welles. The result of her marriage to the Duke was the birth of an only child, Lady Margaret Beaufort, at Bletsoe Castle on 31 May, 1443. Her father died the following year (after being disgraced) and so the young child became heir to vast estates as well as to the dubious privilege of being one of the leading women of the land in very uncertain times.

The Duchess lived in considerable state at her castle with a large retinue of servants, and her own Cofferer and Keeper of the

Wardrobe, one Ralph Lannoy. This information comes from a tomb inscription in the delightful thirteenth-century church hard by. The young heiress was brought up in the castle with her St John and Welles half-brothers and sisters, a link which was to have important implications for later St Johns. Lady Margaret was considered well educated for her day and had an astonishing breadth of wit and understanding. She was a brilliant embroideress (her work is still preserved in the Victoria & Albert Museum), a skilled herbalist in the use of medicines and a great friend of the new learning, which was beginning to seep into this country from the Continent. She was probably educated with the St John brothers, accounting for the fact that she understood Latin as well as speaking French fluently, a rarity for women of her day. The celebrated Beaufort Book of Hours was certainly kept at Bletsoe at this time and contains several entries on members of the St John family. It is now in the British Library.

Soon after the end of her schooling, Margaret Beaufort was removed to Court, where she received addresses from John de la Pole, but finally married in 1455 Edmund Tudor, Earl of Richmond, a half-brother of King Henry VI. On the death of Henry VI Margaret's only son, Henry Tudor, became head of the House of Lancaster and ultimately King Henry VII. On the outbreak of the Wars of the Roses, the Countess of Richmond moved to Pembroke, where she was confined by the Yorkists in 1461. After this terrible and bloody period came to an end with the Battle of Bosworth and the victory of the House of Lancaster, the Countess became a very significant figure, the mother and grandmother of sovereigns and a great patron of learning. It seems likely that she occasionally visited Bletsoe on her way to Northamptonshire. The family connection was kept up in the next generation, for Sir John St John of Bletsoe was her chamberlain from 1504 and her executor, while Sir John St John of Lydiard Tregoze was part of her household. The inscription already mentioned in Bletsoe church states that the grandson of Sir John St John was educated with Prince Henry (Henry VIII) at Court. This St John became guardian of the Princesses Mary and Elizabeth in the next reign and a chamberlain to Queen Elizabeth in the following reign.

In many ways Margaret Beaufort is the first modern

Bedfordshire woman. Her concerns – for education, for the dissemination of knowledge through books, for civilised pursuits and values – are very much our concern today. Out of the barbarity of the wars at the close of the fifteenth century steps this sensible and far-sighted female. She married her son to Elizabeth of York, thereby uniting the warring factions of York and Lancaster and bringing a much needed peace. As a scholar, she translated *Imitatio Christi* and other works from the French and supported the work of William Caxton and Wynkyn de Worde in introducing printing into this country. Both of these men undertook printings at her express command and de Worde called himself in 1509 'Printer unto the most excellent princess my lady the King's grandame'. In her will, she left Sir John St John a copy of the *Canterbury Tales* which may have been one of Caxton's printings. She was the foundress of two great colleges, Christ's College, Cambridge (1505) and St John's College, Cambridge (1508), both of which still honour her as their patroness. As a lover of learning, she reserved rooms in the college for her own use and left 1,632 ozs. of plate to the foundations. She did not die until 1509, and therefore lived to see her grandson married to Catherine of Aragon.

The period of calm under Henry Tudor, following the wars, enabled some of the great families to increase their influence and also aided lesser folk to move up the social scale. Bedfordshire needed a powerful leader to promote the county's cause at a national level. There had been nobody since the days of Lord Fanhope and Lord Wenlock to fulfil this role however indifferently and the 1490s provided this opportunity. At Wrest, near Silsoe, in the centre of the county, the Greys had been settled since the thirteenth century. Edmund Grey, 1st Earl of Kent (1420–89) had been a supporter of Henry VI before joining the Yorkist party and becoming Lord High Treasurer. His son, George Grey, 2nd Earl of Kent (*d.*1503) was married to a sister of Queen Elizabeth Woodville, wife of Edward IV and was therefore an uncle by marriage of the Princes in the Tower. He attached himself to the new monarch, Henry VII, and greatly increased his wealth and lands. He appeared at court in the richest costumes and rode a sorel horse decorated with Venetian gold harness. Lord Kent also began to develop sheep-farming on his land. This was a comparatively new innovation; Bedfordshire had not been a sheep county, there were no great churches built from the wool trade as in Suffolk or the West Country and no great fortunes were made in this line of business. However, Richard Fermor of Luton Hoo was a wool merchant and at this time there was a statue of St Blaise (the patron saint of wool-workers) in Luton church.

Some families began to enclose parish land for sheep and others amalgamated smallholdings to make them more efficient economic pasturage. It was a very good time for able and ambitious freeholders who held their land in fee simple to a lord to make their own way. The villeins were no longer bound to hold this land by bond-service and became copyholders, their tenure based on a copy of the manorial court roll. A copyholder who saw his way to becoming more independent often became a bailiff or steward of a larger property, enabling him to learn management as he worked. A few of these families seized the opportunity in the early 1500s to fence their land and eventually to attain yeoman or gentry status.

For all his careful stewardship, Lord Kent was succeeded by a useless and vain son, Richard, 4th Earl of Kent (d.1524) and the Wrest property was incumbered by debt within a few years. It took a hundred years for the Greys to restore themselves finally! The brass of this wastrel's nephew Henry Grey, 1545, is to be seen in Flitton church where they were all interred; he and his father were so poverty-stricken that they did not even use their titles!

London was still remote and was likely to remain a two or three day journey away until the eighteenth century, but there were the first stirrings of some merchant links. Sir William Stocker of Eaton Socon was a member of the Drapers' Company and Lord Mayor of London in 1484 although he only survived a few days. George Monoux of Wootton, Master of the Drapers' Company, was Lord Mayor in 1514 and William Boteler of Biddenham, a Grocer, was Lord Mayor in 1515–16, probably the only occasion when Bedfordshire Lord Mayors succeeded one another. Some of this city wealth may have filtered down into the Bedfordshire estates, most likely into the beautification of the churches with richly coloured fittings, painted niches, statues of the saints and mural decorations. The Perpendicular style was graceful, structural but unembellished, and the soaring shafts and great windows demonstrated the power of the builders to construct the thinnest of mullions and the most attenuated of traceries, defying natural laws. The richness of the interiors was no longer contained in carved ornament or fussy detail but in the colours and textures of painted saints, great areas of glass, embroidered copes and altar cloths and the clash of gold and silver vessels in the light.

One wonders where the first dawn of a classical revival was to be seen in this inland county. Classical architecture followed classical literature into the seats of learning and any scholar who travelled must have been aware of what was taking place in Italy. There is certainly no classicality to be found in the handsome alabaster figure and tomb chest in Clifton church, the monument of a recumbent knight of about 1510. This is pure late Perpendicular, a row of facing angels holding shields, running along the front under delicate arcading, neat and well preserved but traditional. Nor is it to be found in the superb corbels of Totternhoe church, carved with such delicacy and imagination a few years earlier. Probably the first vestiges of the Renaissance were seen here in a psalter or a Paris printed book brought to Bletsoe by the Countess of Richmond or to Ampthill by that classically minded prince, Henry VIII; certainly nothing permanent seems to have survived.

As we have seen, the early years of the Tudors were ones of great social mobility in Bedfordshire; while the ancient families continued to run their estates, the new royal house and its servants gave opportunities for other names to emerge and become prominent in the county. A notable example of these were the Gostwicks of Willington. The Gostwicks were settled in eastern Bedfordshire from the end of the thirteenth century and by the close of the fifteenth century were prominent yeomen and landowners in Willington parish, acting as deputies for the absentee landlords. Some members of the family became influential clergy.

The most remarkable member of the family, and the one to raise it to wealth and influence, was John Gostwick (c.1480/90–1545), the elder son of John Gostwick of Willington, who was born in the family house there and educated at Potton. As a comparatively young man, John Gostwick received a recommendation (perhaps from his kinsman Sir William Gascoyne of Cardington) to Henry VIII's almoner Thomas Wolsey. Wolsey, an equally self-made man, took Gostwick into his household and the young man prospered, gaining increasing influence as his master became Archbishop of York and Cardinal-Legate. Gostwick had ceremonial duties to perform in the cardinal's vast retinue: he was involved with the revels and pageants that were a Tudor pastime, but also gained some of the profitable sinecures without which no man could succeed. Astute businessman that he was, Gostwick obtained a licence for importing 'caps and hats of all colours from Milan, France and Flanders'. [B.H.R.S., Vol. 36, p. 58] He became a member of the Mercers' Company in 1515 and a surviving helmet and tabard in Willington church are believed to have been his ceremonial armour at the Field of the Cloth of Gold where he attended Cardinal Wolsey. In 1522 he was appointed auditor of the king's castles in Yorkshire and in 1529 he was able to consolidate his wealth by purchasing from the Duke and Duchess of Norfolk the manor of Willington for £1300.

With characteristic good luck, Gostwick had arranged all this with the help of his friend Cardinal Wolsey, just before the Cardinal himself was disgraced at Michaelmas 1529. Another friend of Gostwick's was now in the ascendant, Thomas Cromwell, who had acted with him on delicate matters for the cardinal and was well aware of the Bedfordshire man's tact and ability. Gostwick lost little time in despatching letters to Cromwell from Willington: 'I send you by the bearer, a calf and two dozen pigeons, the best novelties I can send you at this time.' [ibid.] Such flattering gifts were not lost upon Thomas Cromwell, who had Gostwick in mind for a newly created post.

The King had broken with the Papacy (dealt with later) creating some interesting fiscal difficulties where the 'first fruits' of a diocese had traditionally gone to Rome after the appointment of a new bishop. As there was now no Pope in control, the money of the 'first fruits' was to be vested in the Crown, but with a sting in the tail. With Tudor logic, the payment of 'first fruits' was to be extended to include the first year after *any* vacancy, whether see, monasteries or religious establishments, and these institutions were disappearing at an increasing rate. Gostwick was made Treasurer and Receiver General of the First Fruits and tenths (or tithes) at a salary of one hundred pounds a year with powers to enforce the recovery of these debts.

Such an appointment brought Gostwick unequalled opportunities for acquiring former monastic possessions. On the dissolution of Warden Abbey, he obtained reversions on land at Renhold, Cople, Goldington and Ravensden on purchase from the crown. Gostwick's attitude was not as a plunderer of monastic lands. He was an upholder, like the king, of the old religion, but was prepared to pay the market price for land that became available. He was present at the trial of the abbot of Woburn in May 1538 and was involved in the ending of the Grey Friars at Bedford in October of the same year. Commenting on this, Gostwick wrote that 'The king will have a great benefit here in lead and other things'. It was later stated that the lead was used for the building of the Gostwick family chapel in Willington church. Gostwick later gained from the dissolution of the Elstow convent, enabling him to buy the nearby manor of Goldington.

Lord Cromwell was still a staunch friend and stayed for three or four days at Willington Manor with the Gostwicks while Henry VIII's court was at Ampthill Castle in September 1539. Cromwell's accounts mention a gratuity for 'minstrels at Mr Gostwick's'. In 1540, Cromwell, (now the Earl of Essex) was attainted and disgraced, Gostwick skilfully distancing himself from the fallen minister, who had become the most hated man in England. Gostwick's position was also unpopular, but by collecting assiduously for the King and revealing monies that Cromwell did not know about, he was duly rewarded with the honour of knighthood. On 21 October 1541 the Privy Council, returning from York, held a meeting at Willington Manor and it seems likely that Henry VIII himself was the guest of the Treasurer of the Court of First Fruits. Gostwick refers in his will to the King's Chamber at Willington and elsewhere to that where 'King Henry VIII, of famous memory, of late lay therin'. [*ibid.*]

An interesting sidelight on Gostwick's beliefs is provided by an incident at the end of his life, in January 1545. Like many of the Bedfordshire gentry he remained a conservative in religion and objected to Archbishop Cranmer's preaching against the Real Presence in the Eucharist. He raised this at the Westminster Parliament early that session and brought down a heap of invective upon his old head. Henry VIII was furious to have his primate criticised and despatched a chamberlain with a peremptory message: 'Tell that varlet Gostwick, that if he do not acknowledge his fault unto my lord of Canterbury, and so reconcile himself towards him that he may become his good lord, I will soon both make him a poor Gostwick and otherwise punish him to the example of others.' Gostwick personally called on Cranmer to make his peace, but within a few months he was dead and was buried in the chancel chapel of his church at Willington in April 1545 beneath the plain altar tomb that still remains.

Gostwick's heir died shortly after his father and although his daughter-in-law married again, to the Earl of Bedford, and the family was to make influential marriages in the next twenty years, his successors were never to distinguish themselves as had the first Sir John. William Gostwick was created a baronet on 25 November 1611 and the title belonged to the family for a further one hundred and eighty years. Their manor house, which must have been a substantial stone building if not grandiose, was demolished in the eighteenth century. Today it is a handsome grouping of stables and dovecote (owned by the National Trust) which reminds us of the Gostwicks' long connection with the county. The great gabled dovecote, with its honeycomb of nesting spaces for 900 pigeons is a testimony to the scale of their living and the presents sent to Thomas Cromwell. The view from the upper floor of the stables towards the church is magnificent, as the tall late Perpendicular windows of the Gostwick chapel are in the line of sight. The land is flat here and one can well imagine Sir John sweeping the horizon with his eye and congratulating himself on how much of it was his own.

The Gostwicks were on the edge of that national drama, the divorce of King Henry VIII, in which several scenes were played out in Bedfordshire. The settings for the King's troubled married life, turbulent relations with Rome and a trial that gained European attention, were the Castle of Ampthill and the town of Dunstable. Catherine of Aragon (1485–1536) was long married to the king without producing a male heir. The unsuccessful

marriage and the king's boredom with the Queen became a
constitutional and religious issue when her royal relations
forbade the Pope to release Henry from his wife. Henry was
unable to obtain an annulment of the marriage, although
Catherine was the widow of his deceased brother, sufficient
grounds for this under canon law. Catherine therefore became a
convenient excuse for the King to break with Rome and to
acquire the unbelievable wealth of the medieval Church in
England.

Early in 1533, Catherine had been removed with her household on her husband's orders from London to Ampthill Castle.
This was still the old building of Lord Fanhope, with its central
living quarters and chain of outer towers, but it had been
refurbished for royal use. Catherine would have remembered it
from the royal hunting expeditions here in earlier days when the
King showed his prowess at stag hunting and hawking. The
terrain was ideal for the sport as the castle was elevated on the
ridge and gave good views of the royal park sweeping down to the
plain on the north side and the oak filled woods to the south. The
deer were bred in Little Park to the south and then let loose in
Great Park and Dame Ellensbury Park on the ridge. The hunt
began early in the morning when the scents were good and the
deer were driven by mounted hunters in the direction of the king
and his lords. There was a construction called the stand set up in
the park so that the ladies and the older gentlemen who did not
ride could fire at the deer with their crossbows. Visiting
dignitaries like the Bishop of Bayonne attended on the stand, and
after a good drive, gifts of venison were sent to the Lord Mayor of
London 'to make merrie with his bretheren the Aldermen'.
[Underwood, *A Goodly Heritage*, p. 17]

In the eyes of the King, Ampthill was an ideal place for his
unwanted wife, sufficiently remote from London and the
tumult of popular mobs, but close enough for speedy contact.
Catherine was virtually a prisoner in the old castle in the
custody of her chamberlain Lord Mountjoy, and was likely to
remain so until she voluntarily renounced her title. It was a sad
irony that Lord Mountjoy, the only really scholarly servant of
the Queen, was given this unenviable duty. The widely read
Catherine had enjoyed his company and found him one of the

few courtiers she could converse with easily. A deputation headed by the Dukes of Norfolk and Suffolk met her there, but Catherine refused to co-operate.

Lord Mountjoy stated that she could no longer use the title of Queen and her servants would have to refer to her as 'Princess Dowager', her allowances were also to be reduced. She only asked to be allowed to keep her confessor, her physician and two maids to care for her chamber; she would be content to beg for alms. At this point the Duke of Norfolk delivered a piece of unwelcome news: the King was already married to Anne Boleyn. The Spanish Ambassador, who was Catherine's champion in this affair, wrote to the Emperor Charles V on 10 April 1533: '. . . you can hardly avoid making war now upon this King and Kingdom'. If the Emperor could have been persuaded, there would certainly have been a war, but Catherine, immured in her Bedfordshire castle, was set against any bloodshed. She considered that if she was to cause a fight she would be 'damned eternally'.

The legality of the Queen's marriage had to be tried openly and on 8 May 1533, Archbishop Cranmer opened his court in the market town of Dunstable in the nave of the Priory Church. Cranmer summoned the Queen to his court, but was far from anxious that she should attend, a popular clamour being quite likely even in this country district. Catherine ignored the Dunstable court, having signed two protests prepared by the Spanish Ambassador. On 10 May, the Archbishop pronounced her 'contumacious' and on the 23rd, her marriage to Henry was declared null and void. Anne Boleyn was crowned Queen of England on 1 June 1533.

Things were not perfect, however, as long as Catherine remained obstinate. In July, another deputation was sent to Ampthill with Lord Mountjoy to try and browbeat the former Queen into submission. They found Catherine troubled with a cough and lying down on a pallet because she had pricked her foot with a pin and could not stand. She ordered all her servants into her chamber to hear what the lords had to say to her. She objected at once to the title of 'Princess Dowager' and finished with a noble speech; '. . . The King may do in his realm by his royal power what he will, but those who decided against me, did so against their consciences . . . My matter dependeth not on the universities nor on the realm, but in the court of Rome, before the Pope, whom I account God's vicar and judge on earth as I have answered heretofore.' [Mattingley, *Katherine of Aragon*, 1942, p. 263]

The deputation made vague threats to her daughter, Princess Mary, and to her servants, but she would not be moved by these or the bribe of a rich estate if she agreed. The next day they brought a written version of their requests and she struck out the offending title wherever it occurred in bold pen strokes. She referred to Cranmer as a man of the King's own making. She added that 'I think the devils themselves do tremble to see the truth so oppressed!' Lord Mountjoy soon found his task disagreeable and realised that he could not argue with this injured woman.

The divorce, which was discussed by everybody, became part of wisdom prophesied by the Holy Maid of Kent, an obscure nun who claimed to make divine utterances about the future. Lord Cromwell tried to entrap Catherine and her circle into treasonable statements about the nun's foreseeing the death of the King when he remarried. Catherine was too clever, however, to fall for such subterfuge. By July 1533, Ampthill was regarded as being too public for the Queen's residence and she was removed to Buckden on the edge of the Fens. Shortly afterwards, she went to Kimbolton in Huntingdonshire, where she died on 7 January 1536.

There are few contemporary relics in the county today of this unfortunate woman and her place in history, but there is one that should not be missed by anybody with a deeper curiosity. In Dunstable Priory there is a remarkable screen of carved balusters separating the north side of the chancel from the vestry. They are Renaissance work of high quality and are believed to have come from a Lady Chapel dismantled at the Dissolution. Carved on these columns are fine symbols of the Catholic Church and of the marriage of Henry and Catherine, including the fleur de lys of King Henry, the pomegranate of Queen Catherine, a castle for Castile and a feather for the Prince of Wales. There are also ewers and shields of the Passion, vine leaves, bunches of grapes and acorns and other pieces of decoration referring to the Mass. How these things survived the plunder of the sixteenth and seventeenth centuries it is hard to tell. [T. W. Bagshawe, *Apollo*, Vol. 29, 1939, pp. 179–81]

Catherine's downfall was the prelude to the overthrow of the influence of Rome and the end of the monastic orders as touched on in the history of Gostwick. Most of the Bedfordshire religious houses had been the centres of small thriving communities, but monasteries were not always popular and found it difficult to defend themselves against allegations from the King's henchmen. The earlier visitations of the Bishop of Lincoln had not found all to be well in the Bedfordshire houses. At one time the canons of Caldwell were forbidden to ride on horseback, eat and drink in the town of Bedford or keep hounds for hunting. Immorality was always the great threat, so they were strictly forbidden to see the nuns of Elstow.

Elstow Abbey, two miles from Bedford, with its glorious church and cloisters on fertile land, was a refuge for upper class ladies and always a problem for its worldliness. The nuns lived a comfortable existence here, had their own rooms and servants and enjoyed eating away from the refectory, where they were not bound by the rules of their order. There were many complaints about the nuns' slackness in attending services and of their gaudy clothing. They were found to be wearing silver pins, silk gowns and rings, and they dressed their heads in the latest fashion with 'covered crests . . . showing their foreheads moore like lay people than religious'. They were ordered to keep their veils over their eyes and stop wearing decorated shoes, low necked gowns and red stomachers! At Harrold Priory, where there were four or five nuns and a prioress, Dr Layton found in 1530 that one of the nuns had 'two faire chyldren and another one and no mo'. [Steward, *A Bedfordshire Village*, 1898, p. 77]

The Dissolution not only changed the pattern of life in the county with the disappearance of great buildings, the absence of monastic libraries, medical care, good husbandry and learning in the religious houses, it greatly enriched some existing families and more significantly gave impetus to new blood. The spoils from this disbandment in Bedfordshire included nine abbeys, two friaries and a preceptory, but the wealth included manors and farms elsewhere as well as land owned by the religious houses of Berkshire, Buckingham shire, Huntingdonshire, Leicestershire and Northamptonshire. It is only necessary to look at the accounts of the Court of Augmentation, set up in 1536 to dispose of the monasteries, to appreciate how very wealthy some of them were. The first stage of the procedure dealt with the smaller institutions, the heads were offered pensions, the nuns could move to the larger houses and those who had entered orders under age could forsake their vows. Under these statutes Markyate Priory, Caldwell Priory, Bushmead Priory and Harrold Priory were abolished by Michaelmas 1536–7. The larger fish were surrendered the following year: Warden Abbey in December 1537, Woburn Abbey in 1538, Elstow Abbey in August 1539, Newnham Priory in January 1540 and Dunstable Priory the same month.

Newnham Priory had a large number of farms throughout the county as well as a surprising number of properties concentrated within the parishes of Bedford itself. The county town was still very much a small settlement and citizens combined a livelihood of town trade from the river with their own tenanted farms. The Abbey of Elstow had property in its own neighbourhood, but also in the villages of Wilstead, Kempston, Yelden, Mulsoe (over the border), Harrowden and Houghton Conquest, not to mention Maulden and Flitton further south. Dunstable owned large swathes in the centre of the county from Toddington to Westoning and Flitwick. Warden Abbey had lands in Bedford as well as at Potsgrove, Tebworth, Hockliffe, Wingfield and Battlesden, as well as much more outside the county boundaries.

The rights were not surrendered without a struggle, albeit a struggle for conscience rather than for worldly wealth. The most unhappy episode took place at Woburn Abbey in about 1537 where the Abbot, Robert Hobbes, took the oath to Henry VIII as head of the Church of England and then had second thoughts about it. He and two other monks were reported by an assistant priest at the Woburn chapel, a strong supporter of the new ideas, who gave evidence against them. They were tried for treason and hanged on an oak tree within sight of the Abbey and only two hundred yards from the west front of the present house. Tradition has marked this site out as a particularly unhappy place. The high-born ladies of the Elstow nunnery had a happier fate, they were allowed to leave with the Mother Abbess, Dame Elizabeth Boyville, and to set up house together in St Mary's parish,

Bedford. There had been twenty-three nuns at Elstow and six of these are recorded as dying in the parish of St Mary's, Dame Elizabeth herself dying in 1550 and leaving her altar ornaments to the rector. [Bell, *Belief in Bedfordshire*, 1986, p. 35]

One of the chief beneficiaries of these events was the family of Russell. John, Lord Russell of Chenies (*d*.1554/5) was a Dorset man who had risen high in the service of the King. He had acted as envoy for Henry VIII to Pope Clement VII in Rome in 1527 and was actually in Italy when Rome was sacked. Henry was anxious that this trusty servant should be given lands worth one hundred pounds a year and in 1547 he received the reversion of the Abbey of Woburn, at that time an inconsiderable part of his growing estate. He was created Earl of Bedford in 1550 and it is unlikely that he had much to do with the county from which he took his name. He lived mostly at Chenies in Buckinghamshire, although it is possible that he had attended his master on hunting parties to Ampthill in earlier years, and it was to be more than fifty years before the family began to enjoy the benefits of their acquisition.

Less spectacularly, Edward Staunton of Woburn, who had been steward of the Abbey lands, was able to set himself up as squire of Birchmoor with a handsome small estate on the south-east of the town. This was the beginning of a dynasty lasting well into the eighteenth century, when they were ousted by Russell influence. Their alabaster memorial survives in the old parish church building at Woburn. The new rich of the early Tudor years were quick to seize opportunities, especially the merchant families from London. Ralph Farrar, a city grocer, acquired the Priory of Harrold; the up and coming Osborn family of grocers bought the former Gilbertine house of Chicksands in 1578. The Boteler family gained the Biddenham properties of the local priories in 1540 and the Crawleys of Luton acquired the former lands of St Albans Abbey. It was natural that the greater magnates, the St Johns and Kents, should eventually square off their estates, and newcomers like the Gostwicks did the same thing in competition with the St Johns. One of the Gostwicks, Robert Gostwick (*d*.1561), had been steward of Warden Abbey. From 1546 he was able to occupy the site of this enormous church and build a very handsome mansion there. His family did not succeed him, which may account for the gradual decay of such an important house. The fragment that survives today with its crisp Tudor brickwork, elegant stone dressings, twisted chimney and crenellations, shows with what sophistication domestic architecture was conceived in the last years of Henry VIII. In 1912, this charming little building was a dovecote, [V.C.H.] but is now let as a cottage by the Landmark Trust.

Strangely enough, the monks of Old Warden were not best remembered for their four hundred years of tenure, their sanctity or even the artefacts that have recently been excavated on the site – but for their pies! The monastery was well known for a particular variety of pear which grew in their orchards and which lent its fame to the arms of the Abbey – a crozier between three pears. Warden pie was celebrated enough to be mentioned in Shakespeare's *The Winter's Tale* where the clown says: 'I must have saffron to colour the Warden pie.' Warden pie was served at mayoral banquets at Bedford in the nineteenth century and the pears were hawked through its streets with the cry of 'Hot-baked Wardens!' Perhaps it is due for a revival.

Whatever the defects of these places, their presence had attracted the arts, learning and trade to their areas. It must have been because of the scholarly atmosphere of Dunstable Priory that the distinguished scholar George Cavendish (1500–61) resided in the town. Cavendish was married to a niece of Sir Thomas More and was gentleman usher to Cardinal Wolsey. Unlike the more opportunist Gostwick, Cavendish remained with Wolsey till his death at Leicester Abbey. Cavendish then spent his declining years after 1557 writing up the life of Wolsey and the changed world in which he found himself. He was a zealous upholder of the old religion until the last.

The Burgoyne family who had settled at Sutton in the east of the county in about 1500 gained former monastic lands and the Gerys of Cambridgeshire took over Bushmead Priory in 1562, which has one of the best remaining monastic buildings. Elstow Abbey went to the Radcliffe family and then to Thomas Hillersdon who adapted the living quarters as a mansion in much the same way as the Osborns were to do at Chicksands and the Russells were to do at Woburn. Where a family was in residence, the buildings were often saved, and in the case of Dunstable

Priory and Elstow Abbey the much reduced edifices were retained as parish churches.

IV
The Elizabethan Age

After the traumatic upheavals of the early sixteenth century and the suspicion and accusation engendered by the persecutions of Queen Mary Tudor in the middle years, the county settled down to a period of relative calm under Queen Elizabeth. The brief reign of Elizabeth's brother, Edward VI, had brought in another wave of reformation into the English church, this time the removal of ornaments from the altars and candlesticks and censers from the chancels. One of the chief instigators of this was Thomas Norton, a right-hand man of the Duke of Somerset and of Sharpenhoe ancestry. As well as being a firm Protestant, Norton was also a translator of the works of Calvin into English, another sign that the Reformed faith went hand in hand with printing and literacy. Parishes had been ordered to have a translation of the Bible in their churches in 1539 and Cranmer's *Prayer Book* was adopted nationally by the Act of Uniformity of 1552. In the brief reversal to Roman Catholicism in 1553–8 under Queen Mary, some of the Bedfordshire priests who had married were deprived of their livings and some old families refurbished the ornaments in their churches. Dame Joan Conquest at Houghton Conquest ordered a silver chalice for the sanctuary, a cope of white damask with spread eagles of gold, worth £10 and two great standing candlesticks; perhaps these were swept away again within a few years! [Godber *History of Bedfordshire*, 1969, p. 188]

Cranmer's great works, his *Prayer Book* and his *Reformatio Legum Ecclesiasticarum* (1550), laid down the model for a national church which must have been very welcome. From the accounts of some contemporaries it appears that many people were confused and uncertain what path to take in their faith and, in consequence, what part to play in their county. One parson, John Rogers, vicar of Potton, had started life as a Roman

Catholic vicar choral at Westminster, had then been a chantry priest and had finally ended up as a married parish priest in the new Protestant church! His library included many pre-Reformation volumes and the Latin Bible to which he clearly clung, along with the old ways of the medieval church. [*ibid.*]

This period also saw the beginning of a formalised education system in some towns, partly as a result of the new learning, partly as a result of the disbanding of the monasteries, but also, surely, from the growth of a greater civic awareness. Bedford was no exception, and in 1552 the Harpur Endowment began its long and interesting life in the town with the refounding of the old town grammar school by Sir William Harpur.

The Harpur family was settled in north-east Bedfordshire in the later Middle Ages and gradually moved into the county town by about 1500. William Harpur, the brightest and most ambitious of the family, was educated at the old town grammar school in School Lane, Bedford and sent to London as a youth to be apprenticed to a city merchant. It seems likely that it was to a tailor, as Harpur's later connections were all within the Merchant Taylors' Company, an organisation for members of that trade though not exclusively. Harpur was admitted to the Company in 1533, ascended through the various levels of office and was elected Master in 1553. He was an alderman of London, a sheriff in 1556-7 and a treasurer of St Bartholomew's Hospital. Among his circle were liverymen who were interested in education such as Sir Thomas White who founded St John's College, Oxford, and Sir Stephen Jenyns who endowed a school at Wolverhampton. Harpur possibly recognised that with the monasteries dissolved and centres of learning like Newnham Priory which ran the old grammar school abandoned, there was a threat to the continuity of teaching in his beloved county. In 1548 Harpur's friend John Williams obtained a grant of former monastic land in Bedford and in that year a scholar from New College, Oxford, came to teach in the town. Harpur probably paid for this, but made no further moves because of the political uncertainty brought about by Edward VI's ill health and Mary Tudor's fierce Roman Catholicism.

During the mayoralty of John Williams in 1551, and the

following year, the corporation were granted letters patent to endow a grammar school for instruction in grammar, literature and good manners. Harpur is supposed to have admired Winchester College and so the master and usher of the new foundation were to be appointed by the Warden and Fellows of New College, Oxford, which had the same foundation as Winchester. No further developments took place in the turbulent reign of Queen Mary, but in 1561, William Harpur, the Bedford boy, became Lord Mayor of London.

All too little is known about Harpur's period as Lord Mayor; he chose 'harpers in history and legend' as the theme of his Lord Mayor's show in 1561, a pun on his own name. With this in mind, his barge procession was met by a pageant of children representing King David, Orpheus and other characters famous for their musical talents. He held the traditional Christmas revels with a great feast and a lord of misrule, followed by well chronicled processions round the City. Harpur began to arrange his endowments for the new school at Bedford. In September 1564 he purchased thirteen acres of land in Holborn, formerly belonging to the Charterhouse, but near enough to the expanding City to grow in value. This land was conveyed by Harpur and his wife Dame Alice to Bedford corporation in 1566. Three years later Dame Alice died and in 1570 Harpur married his second wife Margaret Lethers. Although in his seventies, he was still active in the City and was a subscriber to the purchase of the Exchange by Sir Thomas Gresham. When he finally died on 27 February 1574 at the age of seventy-seven, he was buried at St Paul's Church, Bedford, where his wife joined him after her death in 1596. Strangely enough there are no Elizabethan monuments to them.

Harpur's imaginative endowment was run by the corporation of Bedford and by New College, the Holborn rents being collected by the corporation and the school administered by the College. It was an important step for a modest market town of not more than two thousand people; neither the town fathers nor Harpur himself can possibly have envisaged how it would grow. The early facts about the school are sketchy, but in the late sixteenth and early seventeenth centuries it had some distinguished masters, among them William Smyth (1573–7) who became a lawyer and Francis White who became Bishop of Norwich. In 1629 the salary of the master was £20 per annum and that of the usher £10 per annum. Some of the masters held other posts such as the livings of neighbouring parishes or, in one case, the town-clerkship of Bedford! Latin and Greek had to be taught, but as these languages went further and further out of favour except with the Anglican clergy, a smaller number of Bedford boys required this type of education. From an early date, the school took in boarders who lived with the usher over the school. Boys from further afield were expected to pay, only the Bedford children had free places – free, that is, except for an entry fee and a quarterly payment of a few pence. The Harpur Charity was also involved in providing almshouses for derelict house-holders, marriage portions and apprenticeships for Bedford people. It was the phenomenal rise in income produced by the Holborn estate in the eighteenth century that resulted in the astonishing expansion of the Harpur Charity as a great educational institution to the present day.

A similar foundation to the Harpur Charity was that formed more than fifty years later at Houghton Conquest. This was a small grammar school funded by Sir Francis Clerke of Houghton in 1632 and attached to his almshouses. The schoolmaster was to be a graduate and appointed by Sidney Sussex College, Cambridge, but unlike the imaginative Harpur, the income was a fixed sum charged on land in the parish which became less and less. The school eventually ebbed away, but the building remained in the main street of the village until 1967; the infamy of the County Council in allowing this gem to be demolished leaves one lost for words! At one swoop they destroyed an important link in the history of Houghton Conquest as well as its principal visual asset; this was the only Jacobean school to have survived in the county in anything like its original condition.

One would certainly have expected other comparable schools to have emerged in the other towns, but the Dissolution left an unaccountable vacuum. The most likely place would have been Dunstable, a strategic market town with a very long and distinguished tradition of ecclesiastical patronage. The nearest that it came to it was a proposal to create a new bishopric of Dunstable out of the huge existing diocese of Lincoln. With its fine priory buildings and excellent communications in the south of the old diocese, it would have been ideal. There were to have been a dean and six prebendaries, six canons, six singing men, a reader in divinity as well as two students each at Oxford and Cambridge. Most significantly, there was to be a schoolmaster and a grammar school for twenty scholars where Latin was to be taught. The endowment was to be £800 but Henry VIII thought this too much and so the scheme was abandoned. Although Dunstable's magnificent church survived, its position as an ecclesiastical centre was reduced and the status of the town sharply declined. Unlike her predecessors, Queen Elizabeth did not stay there, and there were no influential patrons to found schools and charities at this time, although a hospital did continue till 1606. Dunstable remained a town of inns; there were twelve major hostelries along the main street in 1540 and many of the proprietors were very prosperous. Because the town had the major north-south artery running through it, it was always beset by travelling vagrants, the sturdy poor, walking down to London to find work. These nomads frequently brought the plague with them: Dunstable had five outbreaks between 1573 and 1603 and numerous strangers collapsed and died on this stretch of road, being buried in paupers' graves.

The only other town to entertain the possibility of a grammar school appears to have been Luton. There, John Norris of the town, who died in 1537, left provision in his will for a Latin grammar school to be situated near the parish church of St Mary's, but his family disliked the provision and nothing came of it. At Woburn, the Free School was founded in 1582 by Francis, Earl of Bedford. This little building still survives, nestling against the graveyard of the old parish church, but it is much restored despite the survival of Tudor windows and old ironstone walls. In most of these small towns teaching operated on a haphazard basis: some local man of education might decide to take in pupils at a fee, but for anyone other than the sons of local landowners and prosperous tradesmen, such a step was impossible.

Dunstable and Bedford were probably the towns most immediately affected by the Dissolution. The thirteen canons of Dunstable were cast out, but ten of them secured benefices in the Anglican church and three of them remained in Bedfordshire. In

Bedford the churches of St Peter Dunstable and All Hallows were suppressed and destroyed, although in an interesting example of respect or economy, the Norman door of St Peter Dunstable was transferred to St Peter Merton where it still is.

The reforms of Edward VI had probably affected a wider range of parishes than anything before. This not only included the imposition of the *Prayer Book* and the removal of ornaments but the termination of small charities. These included beadrolls for the prayers of the departed and, at Biddenham, the very important provision for the upkeep of the bridge over the River Ouse. Chantries had sometimes included small schools as at Houghton Regis, or a chapel-of-ease, as at Wroxhill in the parish of Marston. Some small chapels had been neglected, and that at Silsoe had not had a priest for thirty years. Although the village priests were not very learned and the endowments small, their continuation had at least offered a presence of succour and charity in these villages.

In 1556, at the end of Queen Mary's reign, there were still seventy pensioners of former Bedfordshire religious houses receiving money, some of them deprived of their livings under Queen Mary, others hoping for the return of the old order. Her reign had revealed those Roman Catholics who were lying low, notably the Mordaunts of Turvey and the Conquests already mentioned. In the early years of Queen Elizabeth the infant church became more structuralised, and national features were implemented to bring Bedfordshire into line with other counties. Two books, Bishop John Jewel's *Apology* (1562) and *Foxe's Book of Martyrs* (1563), were purchased by many churches to be read alongside the *Prayer Book*. The new Bishop of Lincoln, Nicholas Bullingham, successfully stamped out the pagan festivities of May Day and Midsummer Day; Morris dancing and May men's feasts disappear from the records after about 1575, although they may have continued surreptitiously.

With the transfer of so much church land and the destruction or pillaging of ancient edifices, it is hardly surprising that most of the building work of the later sixteenth century was confined to secular projects. But the county is able to boast one rare and beautiful Elizabethan church, constructed when the skills of the masons were at their height, even though ecclesiastical architecture was then at a standstill. St Nicholas, Hulcote is a jewel of a church, set in a matchless position and yet unknown and unvisited.

The Chernocke family of Lancashire moved here in 1541 to occupy the manor house that lay on the north-east of the church. The church is actually approached down a fine and ancient avenue of limes, and these originally led to the mansion which, with its church and outbuildings, must have made a fine group in such a sequestered spot. It was Richard Chernocke (d.1615), who probably spent most of his life at Hulcote, who made all the changes. According to his monument in the church he 'reedified his parish Churche at his own proper charge, newe built his Mansion House, thrice bare office of High Shrife in this Shiree: and Lastelye Having attayned the age of 84 years peaceablye and piouslye Deceased the 14th Day of August Anno Domini 1615'.

The mansion had a long façade with a central gable and gabled ends, a sundial over a pedimented doorway and a small bell turret above; a good squire's house, sturdy and simple. It was the residence of about seven generations of Chernockes who were created baronets in 1661 and served the county well. The second baronet, Sir Boteler Chernocke, represented Bedford Borough from 1740 to 1747. The house was demolished in the early nineteenth century.

St Nicholas gives us a unique insight into the new Elizabethan Church, struggling to find its way architecturally and liturgically in an era of Reformed Christianity. In feeling it is late medieval, consisting of an undivided nave and chancel and a tower at the west end; an essentially Gothic structure which has none of the fittings of a Gothic church, screen, piscina, sedilia! In fact, it has a closer kinship with the college chapels of Oxford and Cambridge, or with the kind of small places of worship for one family or one community such as Little Gidding. Inside, there is a superb austerity: the gallery, communion rails and communion table are all part of a piece, and the only splash of colour is provided by the Chernocke monument. There, the kneeling figures are framed by columns and their own heraldic achievement. The church was being built during the 1590s and the date on the bells of 1593 suggests that it was completed in that year. Here and there are slight hints of Classicism and the windows are particularly Elizabethan in form. It is odd to think of this going on only a decade before Italian styles were to arrive a few miles away at Houghton.

As can be seen by the Chernocke monument, the landed gentry were very often desirous of recording their lives in memorials, even if they were not so forward as the Chernockes in rebuilding their churches. The emerging Renaissance style was having its greatest advance in the tombs set up by these distinguished families in the Elizabethan period. The most elaborate and eye-catching are those at Turvey to Sir John Mordaunt and his wife (1506), and the handsome monument by T. Kirby to the 1st Lord Mordaunt (1560), which is very chaste and classical for its time. The effigies are in alabaster and the superstructure consists of Roman Doric columns and an arch decorated with chains and circles, pedimented above. Even more spectacular is that to the 2nd Lord Mordaunt (1571) and his two wives; eight Tuscan columns supporting a grand cornice and coffered ceiling. The 3rd Lord (1601) has a tomb chest with a black shroud of stone hanging like a pall with a white inscription on it, rich and sombre. The Mordaunts' house was on the north-west side of Turvey and must have been very magnificent; its site is marked by a farmhouse. Elsewhere there are tombs to John Thompson of Husborne Crawley (1597) at Crawley church and to Sir Humphrey Radcliffe of Elstow (1566), curiously placed above the altar at Elstow Abbey. One at Bletsoe to Sir John St John (1559) is in alabaster and in superb condition. It has the traditional form of St John and his sons kneeling on cushions to the east side, and Lady St John and the daughters kneeling on cushions on the west. The monument was moved from the St John chapel into the nave of the church many years ago.

With such grand funerary objects as these, one expects grand houses. Bedfordshire is not noted for any great Elizabethan houses today, but in its time it had a number of remarkable country seats. These have tended to be obscured behind later rebuildings as at Hawnes Park, where the Elizabethan gatehouse survived into the eighteenth century, or at Melchbourne, where the plan of rooms and long gallery are hidden behind the façade of 1741. Houghton House and Hillersdon Hall, Elstow are both ruins which can be visited; Old Warden is a fragment, and the outbuildings of Willington have been mentioned earlier.

There is ample evidence how unsuitable the old monastic houses could be, from a letter written at this time by the Earl of Bedford. Having neither improved nor rebuilt his property at Woburn, he was much put out to receive a request from Queen Elizabeth for accommodation in the old buildings in 1572. The Earl wrote

> I am now going to prepare for her Mat^{ies} coming to Woborne, which shall be done in the best and most hastiest manner that I can. I trust yor L^p will have in remembrance to provide helpe that her Mat^s tarrieng be not above two nights and a daye, for, for so long tyme do I prepare. I pray God, the Rowmes and Lodgings there may be to her Mat^s contentacion for the tyme. If I could make them better upon suche a sodeyn, then would I, be assured, they should be better than they be. [Parry, *History of Woburn*, 1831, pp. 11–12]

Probably the most palatial and ambitious house to be built in the county during the reign of Elizabeth was Toddington Manor, created *c*.1562–80 for Sir Henry Cheyne, afterwards Lord Cheyne or Cheyney of Toddington (1539–87). He was the son of Sir Thomas Cheyne, a Kentish landowner who as Lord Warden of the Cinque Ports was created a Knight of the Garter. Sir Thomas was a trusted servant of Henry VIII, and by his second marriage to Ann, daughter of Sir John Broughton of Toddington, acquired considerable estates in Bedfordshire. There is no evidence that Sir Thomas lived in the county, but long before his death in 1588, his son Henry had begun to build in a most splendid fashion. He appears to have pulled down the old manor house of the Broughtons between Toddington and Harlington in order to erect a palace in a hollow by the Toddington to Woburn road and half a mile from the church. This house must have been well under way when Queen Elizabeth visited him there in 1563 and conferred a knighthood upon him in his own hall. On a second royal progress in 1576, she again stayed in the house and conferred a peerage on this loyal and hospitable subject.

It was evidently on this occasion that his wife made a handsome gift to the Queen: 'a border containing vii butons or broches of gold, in every of them iv mere perle . . .' This was recorded in 1576–7 as being given 'by the Lady Cheyney in Progresse-tyme'. [Nichols, *Queen Elizabeth*, Vol. 2, p. 2] Other gifts by the Cheynes included sumptuous clothing, 'a fore part and a pair of boddys of a french kyrtill of bleue cloth of silver, embraudered al over with Venice golde, with a small garde of black vellat, embrowdered with Venice golde and silver, an lyned with black sarceonet'. The very words seem to conjure up this rich and luxurious style of living in which colour and textile played such a part. In return the Cheynes received New Year gifts from the Queen in 1577–8 of 'guilt plate'. There are no records of any masques being performed at these Bedfordshire houses, but the Bedfordshire poet and courtier George Gascoigne (1525–77) did have his Masque performed before the Queen at Kenilworth in July 1575.

Lord Cheyne served as a justice of the peace for the county and must have pleased the Queen by assisting at the trial of Mary, Queen of Scots in 1587. He was a reckless and extravagant man, much given to bragging and gambling as one surviving anecdote shows. Once, while playing at dice with Henry II, King of France, he won a priceless diamond. On being asked by the King what would have happened had he lost, Cheyne replied 'I have enough sheeps' tails in Kent with their wool to buy me a better diamond than this.' [Blundell, *Toddington*, p. 49] He was flamboyant and imaginative as his building projects show. Toddington Manor has been described as a 'Bedfordshire Nonesuch' and it was only a little less striking than that famous example in point of size and elaboration. Surviving drawings and a bird's eye view on a map show it to have been built round a great inner courtyard, three storeys in height, marked at the corners by turrets with cupolas rising to four storeys in height. The entrance to the court was gained through a central towered gateway and subsidiary courts lay in front and behind the main block. John Thorpe, the seventeenth-century surveyor, was interested enough to sketch the elevations of the mansion and showed some remarkable features, the most extraordinary being a bay window on the garden side running the full height of the building and tapering outwards to a point like the prow of a ship. As the façade included other windows of tall and elegant proportions, the appearance of this south front could have been little short of the grandeur of

Hardwick Hall. A later inventory gives some indication of Lord and Lady Cheyne's sumptuous living conditions: besides a great hall and a great parlour, they had two dining-rooms, four galleries, a chapel, a nursery and a fencing room. One room is described as 'the Queen's Chamber' to remind the family of the royal visitor and another 'Leicester's Chamber' to record that her favourite, Lord Leicester, was with her. The mansion was also furnished with shovel boards and billiard tables as well as with the comfortable leather chairs and tapestries of the period.

Lord Cheyne's house was decorated in the fashionable humanist style of the later Elizabethan age, the walls carved with inscriptions in Latin referring to stories in history and mythology. There was a great deal of heraldry, finely painted on the doors and in the glass of the windows and some bas-relief sculptures that are now in the Victoria & Albert Museum. It was also Cheyne who was responsible for ordering the magnificent 1581 map of Toddington, the most detailed of any in the county. It is by the master map-maker, Radulph Agas, Surveyor, who gathered his information 'by the Oath and Information' of 'free and copie holders'. The map shows all the houses of Toddington town as they then existed, the Cheyne estate and even accurate renderings of the church, the market cross and the maypole set up on the green.

Lady Cheyne's entourage must have been considerable even in widowhood. A sad footnote to life at Toddington Manor is provided by a small alabaster wall tablet in Toddington church. It states 'Gyles Bruse Esq Youngest Sone to Sr Iohn Bruse of Wenham In Suff Knyght who cominge to Toddyngton to Visyte His Sister Alice Bruse Then Attending On Ye Right Hoy^e Ladye Cheyne There Dyed Ye 13 of March 1595 And Was By His Sayde Syster Here Intombed Ye 14 of March Regus Reginae Elizabeth 38 Aetatis Suae 33'. The Cheyne chapel in the south transept of Toddington church is disappointing, the great tomb chests are battered and disfigured from nineteenth-century neglect and there is no attempt today to present them attractively; a few historical labels would help!

There is no doubt that Lady Cheyne was at the centre of an important circle of metaphysical poets and musicians at Toddington in the late years of the sixteenth century. Christopher Brooke (*d.*1627/8), the minor poet, was part of her household and dedicated one of his most lovely verses to her. It is entitled 'Upon The Right Vertuous And Honourable Lady, The Lady Cheney; And Her Court-Like House At Tuddington.'

> Unto that vale-built Place, of lowely height;
> Where Joy, Peace, Love, make an harmonious chime;
> Where civill sports, Musique and Court delight,
> Doe runne division in the houres of Time . . .

Brooke goes on to refer to her 'fame' that makes her 'turrets shine'. Brooke was a close friend of John Donne and left the poetic Dean something in his will. This charming poem was set to music by Lady Cheyne's resident master of music, Henry Lichfild. Little enough is known of Lichfild, but it is thought that he may have been a steward at Toddington and therefore an amateur musician. This is certainly suggested in the preface to his one published work. There he writes: 'I bestowing the day in your Ladyshipss more necessarie businesses, borrowed some howres of the night to bestow upon these my Compositions, so that whatsoever dulnesse and unpleasingnesse is in them may well be imparted to the dull and sullen time wherein they took their being . . .' His *The First Set of Madrigals* was published in London in 1614 by M.L. I.B. and T.S. They include settings of the Brooke poem and his most famous song, 'I always loved to call My Lady Rose'. Lady Cheyne left him £20 in her will. The poet Brooke also wrote a poem in honour of Elizabeth Croft, a relative of Lady Cheyne's.

Although the childless Lady Cheyne (her only daughter predeceased her) continued to live in the house until 1614, her great-nephew, Thomas, Lord Wentworth resided with her. The family had made a few marriages with the local gentry although all the honour was clearly bestowed by the Wentworths. Lord Wentworth had married as his first wife, Anna daughter of Sir John Crofts of Saxham in Suffolk and, for a short time, of Chalgrave, Bedfordshire. Anna Crofts' sister, Arabella, married Sir William Briers of Pulloxhill. Sir John Crofts resided at the now vanished manor of Chalgrave and Sir William Briers at the manor of Upbury, Pulloxhill, now little more than a moated lump in the ground. Both of these gentlemen must have formed part of the court of Lady Cheyne and her nephew at Toddington; certainly the flamboyant monument to Briers in Pulloxhill church shows the influence of this circle. Despite all of this, the fortunes of the mansion continued to decline. The estate was sequestrated in the Civil War and became the home of the tragic Lady Henrietta Maria Wentworth who appears in a later chapter.

The flavour of these times can be judged from one very remarkable room that still survives – though not, unhappily, with its original house. This is the so called Haynes Grange Room, which was discovered at that house in the early part of this century and is now in the Victoria & Albert Museum. Peter Osborn M.P. (1521–92) purchased the abandoned priory at Chicksands in 1576. He was a man of parts, a scholar and a lawyer who had served Edward VI as keeper of the privy purse. He was also a relative of the Greek scholar Sir John Cheke (1514–57) and, like him, a strong reformer. It is highly likely that Osborn would have begun improving Chicksands shortly after his purchase and new scholarship suggests that this magnificent room of 1580 is connected with him. It is panelled in pine, a very rare wood at the time, and carved with austere but accurate classical details and an inscription based on Virgil over the chimney-piece. Such sophisticated work could have been gleaned from Italian pattern books in currency with Osborn and his friends. The ceiling is decorated with plaster pigeons and it is this that gives a clue to its origin. At Chicksands there is a space known as the Pigeon Gallery, which seems to have been altered and reduced in height, but which may have housed this handsome room. If so, it was probably dismantled during the alterations by Ware or Wyatt between 1749 and 1815

An important arrival in these Elizabethan years was the family of Dyve, who bought the Bromham estate four miles north of Bedford in 1565. Sir Lewis Dyve came from Northamptonshire and he was followed by his son, John Dyve, at Bromham Hall in 1592. It is probably his house that we see today, a complicated pattern of jutting gables, steep roofs and many chimneys, concealing a rabbit warren of small panelled rooms and a fine oak staircase. The position at the bottom of an open park on the banks of the Ouse is a fine one; even today it seems fragrant with antiquity, disturbed by little more than the rustle of trees and the flow of the river. In the upper part of the park and closer to the village is the church of St Owen where the Dyves are buried.

John Dyve married as his second wife Beatrice daughter of Charles Walcot of Walcot in Shropshire in January 1599, and their first child, Lewis Dyve, was born at Bromham on 3 November 1599. His arrival was to be important for Bedfordshire and his unusual upbringing and talents were to mark him out. John Dyve was knighted in 1603 but died in 1608 to be buried in Bromham church 'with great solemnity'. Lady Dyve shortly afterwards married Sir John Digby (later 1st Earl of Bristol) and a son, George Digby (later 2nd Earl), was born to them in 1612. In this way Lewis Dyve was brought up by the powerful and influential Digby family and was increasingly the confidant and adviser of his half-brother. Sir John Digby (who was lord of the manor of Bromham in right of his wife) was a trusted diplomat of James I and ambassador to Spain from 1611 to 1624. Although the young Lewis Dyve was at Oxford in 1613–14, it is supposed that he spent his formative years in Madrid; it is recorded that he was a fluent Spanish speaker and a cosmopolitan by background and inclination.

Lewis Dyve was certainly in Madrid in 1622, the year his stepfather was created Earl of Bristol and the year the family received Prince Charles on his ill-fated journey to win the hand of the Infanta. Dyve was only twenty-three but was already having his head turned by the Spanish women. Sir Kenelm Digby records that Dyve was much attracted by a young lady playing the lute on a balcony and was challenged by her Spanish admirer. A fight ensued where Dyve shouted out his innocence and protested that a foreigner should be so treated. 'Villain, thou liest,' came the reply, 'thou hast done me wrong which cannot be satisfied with less than thy life.' [Life & Letters of Sir Lewis Dyve, B.H.R.S. Vol. 27, 1947, p. 6] Such exploits must have been repeated in Bedfordshire where Dyve had an increasing reputation for daring exploits and a fiery temper.

Bedfordshire at this period, the transition from the sixteenth to the seventeenth century, must have been a shire of small towns and small villages, numerous hamlets and scores of manors and homesteads with their satellite farms. So many of these small domains have vanished that it is difficult to get a complete picture, but the moated houses of the gentry were everywhere, from the far south at Tilsworth to the lands at Sharpenhoe and Eaton Bray. They are usually situated in the clay areas, easy for construction and drainage, the centre of productive arable lands. Sir William Briers' house at Pulloxhill had an elaborate moat system, utilising a nearby stream, and must have been of a substantial sandstone construction. More survives at Tilsworth, where a handsome fifteenth-century gatehouse borders a moat and walls, once the home of the Chester family. A good indication of the type of robust manor that must have been common to Elizabethan Bedfordshire is Newberry Farm, Silsoe, built by Edward and Stephen Daniell (great-grandchildren of the Exchequer Baron Denny) in about 1600. Its three gables and a central doorway give it great dignity; one side of the moat survives although the building is now foolishly hemmed in by modern housing. It is small wonder that the inhabitants of such places were out to protect their rights against an absolutist monarch within fifty years.

The succession to Elizabeth was a question that occupied the minds of many people. Her increasing frailty represented that frail thread that hung between the certainty of a Protestant succession and a return of the Roman Catholic party. There had been plots and counter-plots, and in 1603, as the Queen's life drew to a close, one Bedfordshire family became deeply involved. One of the chief contestants for the throne was Lady Arbella Stuart, the first cousin of King James of Scotland and the granddaughter of Bess of Hardwick. There was always speculation that Arbella might have turned Catholic, so the safest place for her was in exile. The party that had control of this young woman would have a formidable voice in the future of the monarchy. In March 1603, Bess of Hardwick had her granddaughter under lock and key in Hardwick Hall, not wishing her to fall into the clutches of the Cavendishes. Lady Arbella (never written Arabella), however, escaped with the help of her uncle and was brought to Wrest House near Silsoe.

Lady Grey of Wrest, married to the heir of the Earl of Kent, was her cousin and it was considered that she should stay in Bedfordshire while the momentous events of the succession were unravelling themselves at court. She remained at Wrest for about three months, restrained, but not without some freedoms to enjoy the place and the company of her much loved cousin.

The death of the great Queen Elizabeth in 1603 ushered in a new age although many of the actors were the same. It was by then some years since the Queen had visited Bedfordshire, but her successor was to make numerous visits. James the sixth of Scotland (and First of England) made a slow royal progress through his new kingdom in April and May 1603 but skirted Bedfordshire, travelling through Huntingdonshire and Cambridgeshire to Theobalds. The scramble to welcome and receive the new king was intense and the same was true when the new Queen, Anne of Denmark, journeyed south in June. The Countess of Bedford went to Scotland to attend her, along with other ladies-in-waiting, but Lady Anne Clifford gives an amusing account of herself and the Countess of Warwick and Cumberland trying to meet her in Leicestershire.

> About this tyme my aunt of Warwick went to meet the Queene, haveing Mrs Bridges with her, and my [cousin] Anne Vavisor; my mother and I should have gone with them, but that hir horses, wch she borrowed of Mr Elwes and old Mr Hinckley, weare not ready; yet I went the same night and overtooke my aunt at Tittenhanger, my Lady Blunt's house, where my mother came the next day to me about noone, my aunt being gone before. Then my mother and I went on or iourney to overtake hir, and kild three horses that day with extreamitie of heate, and came to Wrest, my Lord of Kent's house where we found the dores shutt, an none in the house but one servant, who only had the keyes of the hall, so that we weare forced to lie in the hall all night, till towards morninge, at wch tyme came a man and lett us into the higher roomes, where we slept three or four houres. [Nichols, *Progresses of James I*, 1828, Vol. 1, pp. 173–4]

It is interesting to note that Lady Arbella Stuart had already left Wrest, summoned to meet the new king. James was highly suspicious of his relation and had suggested she should remain at Wrest, but his advisers had suggested leniency at the start of a new reign. The new Queen also skirted Bedfordshire, meeting the King at Grafton, but John Dyve, Sheriff of Bedfordshire was knighted at Salden, Buckinghamshire on 28 June.

The royal couple did come to the county for a royal progress two years later. They began in South Bedfordshire on 26 July 1605 when the King stayed at Mr Sandys' at Dunstable and the

Queen stayed with Sir John Rotherham at Farleigh, near Luton. On the following day, they left for Ampthill, the King lodging with Sir Richard Conquest of Houghton Conquest at Conquest Bury and the Queen with Sir Roger Newdigate at Hawnes; the two ancient houses were only a mile and a half apart through the country lanes. On the 28th, as it was a feast day at Houghton, the King and most of his retainers attended the service at the parish church and on the 30th they paid a visit to the Queen at Hawnes, attending divine service in the parish church and listening to Dr Thomas Archer of Houghton Conquest (1554–1630) preaching on a text from the Song of Solomon: 'Take us the foxes, the little foxes which destroy the grapes, for our vines have small grapes.' It was a singularly appropriate sermon for the royal party who spent their five days at Ampthill in hunting and sport. The King appreciated the sermon and Archer was immediately sworn in as one of the Chaplains in Ordinary to the King. His hosts at Hawnes, the Newdigates, had intermarried with the ancient family of Conquest, but were newcomers to Bedfordshire. In the 1580s, Newdigate claimed that the servants of the Greys of Wrest had attacked him on the high road and set the St John faction against him. The county was still very territorial.

On 1 August, the King removed to Thurleigh, the seat of Sir William Hervey, while the Queen was entertained at Bletsoe Castle by the 3rd Lord St John. This visit lasted two nights before the court moved to Northamptonshire to be entertained by another Bedfordshire magnate, Lord Mordaunt. It is interesting to note that at this juncture the county could not boast a single house (with the exception of Toddington) capable of holding both courts. Ampthill Castle was no longer in a fit state to accommodate anyone.

King James was to continue the practice of the Tudors of coming to Bedfordshire for the hunting in the royal parks of Ampthill and Houghton. It is very significant that immediately after the 1605 progress, indeed in August of that very year, the Earl of Dorset wrote to the Officers of the Works about a new house at Ampthill:

I have received signification of his Majesty's express pleasure for the building of a convenient house upon the ruins of Ampthill in which he may be lodged, though not in state, yet sufficient to serve for the enjoying of his pleasures of hunting and hawking, by the attendance of all such necessary officers and no more as are requisite for his royal person to have. [*The Country Seat*, cd. by H. Colven and J. Harris 1970, p. 31]

A plan, possibly drawn up by Simon Basil, is among the most elaborate known for a Jacobean hunting lodge, containing separate apartments for the King and Queen round a court, the corners formed of canted towers of cruciform shape. The scheme was not carried forward and it was not until 1608 that John Thorpe was asked to prepare a more economical scheme, utilising the old castle walls. This included a great columned loggia on the edge of the scarp slope of the ridge, facing north, where the royal family would have had a view of twenty miles. Wells were sunk and some building work begun, but the project came to nothing. It was the last attempt for a royal palace in the county, but certainly not the final episode of the royal parks!

The whole court was fitted into Toddington Manor in late July 1608 as guests of Lady Cheyne and Lord Wentworth. On this occasion the king had a 'slight distemper' caused 'by the heat of the weather' as mentioned in a letter of Prince Henry. [Nichols, Vol. 2, p. 201] On 5 August that year the King stayed at Bletsoe and wrote an amusing letter to his Lord Treasurer, Robert Cecil, beginning 'My Littill Beagill'. This most pedantic of kings could not resist a pun on his host Lord St John's name. He wrote: 'And hair hath beene this daye Kept the Feaste of King James deliverie at *Saint jonstoune* in *Saint Jon's* house'. [Nichols, p. 204]

Another semi-royal visitor came in 1609. Lady Arbella Stuart, now in favour with the King, was allowed to make a progress through the county once again. She was entertained by Lady Cheyne at Toddington, distributing 4s 11d to the poor on the road from St Albans to Toddington. At the Manor she was attended by grooms, bakers, butlers, cooks, yeomen, porters, 'boyes in the kitchen, Clerke of the kitchen, and a woman wayted on the chamber' at a cost of £7. Her clothes were washed at a cost of 10s. After travelling north, she returned to dine with Sir Edmund Conquest at Conquest Bury and then was led by a man to Wrest House for another stay with the Greys. She was travelling both by coach and litter, for on this journey the coachman broke his leg and 'the lytter men in reward for their paines' received £3 besides 13s 2d for the charge of lying two nights in the inn at Wrest. [Hardy, *Arbella Stuart*, 1913, p. 223]

The court was again in Bedfordshire in 1614, but the visit was interrupted. 'On the 22nd [July], the King pursued his Progress to Hawnes, where it had been intended that he should stay three nights, but which he left in the evening of the 23rd, having received, about 8 o'clock in the morning, certaine intelligence of his Brother the King of Denmark's private and unexpected arrival at London.' Returning to London that evening, the King had a hazardous journey: 'By the way he was encountered with a very fierce storme of haile and raine, the violence whereof was such, that as they were coming downe a hill, it forced the King's coach-horse and the rest of the horse in their company to turne their heads from the storme.' [Nichols, Vol. 3, p. 14] The King was again at Hawnes and Bletsoe in July 1619 when 'he was most nobly entertain'd at the Lord St John's, which he took in so good part that he will not forget so honourable usage'. [*ibid*., p. 565]

Although enthusiasm for the Bedfordshire hunting grounds waned, this was largely due to the lack of accommodation in the ranger's house or Great Lodge at Ampthill. But about this time a figure of equal interest emerged to live on the hilltop there. This was Mary, Countess of Pembroke (1561–1621), the forceful and blue-stocking widow of the 2nd Earl of Pembroke and the sister of Sir Philip Sidney. Twenty-five years younger than her husband, the Countess consoled herself in a difficult marriage by surrounding herself with books, learned men and writers at Wilton House, which John Aubrey described as a 'College'. She appears to have been on tolerable terms with the Queen, for the masque 'A Dialogue between two shepherds' was performed before Elizabeth at Lady Pembroke's London house in 1600. On the Earl's death in 1601, the Countess was not well provided for, and lived first as a pensioner of her son at Wilton and then at Crosby Hall, Bishopsgate Street, from 1609 to 1615. She was obviously close to the new court and kissed hands with King James and Queen Anne at Windsor in 1603. Perhaps this explains why, in 1615, she was granted the royal manor of Dame Ellensbury or Houghton Conquest for life by the King. It was held in the names of her trustees Matthew Lister and Leonard Welstead who had it under the Crown. The late seventeenth-century squire of

Houghton Conquest, Edmund Wyld, claimed that Lister built the house for her, acting as manager of her estate and her surveyor. [Young, *Countess of Pembroke*, 1912, p. 116] A further reason for her coming, suggested by an early nineteenth-century writer, is Ampthill's proximity to Cambridge, where this bookish woman loved to be. [*Gent's Magazine*, 1845] Houghton House is one of the great surprises of Jacobean Bedfordshire. It is a comparatively small and compact mansion of delicious, small, seventeenth-century bricks, crisp with stone dressings, but quite modern by virtue of its lack of a great hall or a court. Although it is now ruinous (and run by English Heritage), it remained very complete until the late nineteenth century and surviving photographs show the sophistication of its corner towers with balustrading in a kind of Jacobean strapwork, fluted chimneys and turrets. Its position on the greensand ridge above Ampthill, slightly in a hollow on the northern side of the hill, and with views across the countryside to Bedford is spectacular. One feels it is the summer retreat of an intellectual lady of great personality, who even at the age of fifty could exert her powers of attraction over gentlemen and was active enough in mind to lure her own 'court' into the wilds of Bedfordshire. Surely nobody but a scholar like Mary Sidney could have ordered the two great stone frontispieces at Houghton which are among the most advanced examples of classical architecture of their time in England. The work is pure Palladio only twenty years after the death of Andrea Palladio, and the name of Inigo Jones has been associated with this work, particularly through his conjectural work at Wilton, the home of the Countess's son.

John Aubrey, the chronicler of seventeenth-century life, almost certainly visited Edmund Wyld at Houghton Conquest and so his gossip about the house and its occupants, recorded only fifty years later, is worthy of note. Aubrey claims that Sir Matthew Lister (1571–1656) was Lady Pembroke's lover and perhaps her secret husband, which is corroborated by at least one other source. Lister was an eminent physician, trained at Oxford and Basle, and doctor to Anne of Denmark and Charles I. Considerably younger than the Countess, this well read, well travelled man would probably have appealed to her learning. If he was also knowledgeable in design and architecture, as many physicians were in that polymath age, his ascendancy in the Countess's affections may have been crucial at Houghton. Of the house Aubrey writes:

> The architects were sent for from Italie. It is built according to the description of Basilius's house in the first booke of the *Arcadia* (which is dedicated to her). It is most pleasantly situated and hath fower vistos, each prospect 25 or 30 miles. This was sold to the earle of Elgin. The house did cost 10,000 li the building [Aubrey, *Brief Lives*, Vol. 1, p. 312]

If the Countess of Pembroke was so badly off, it is a puzzle where she obtained so much money to fit up a palace, but a scion of the Sidney and Herbert families was probably never without resources and the crests of both these noble houses appear on the frieze of the loggia here. If the house was begun in about 1615, the Countess and Sir Matthew would both have been taking the waters at the time, at Spa on the Continent where the Countess had been since 1612. She returned to this country in October 1616 but could scarcely have moved into her new lodge before the spring of 1617. If this is the case, her fitting up of the house and her life there must have been confined to the following five years when she was probably resident in the summer. The zenith for her must have been on 21 July 1621 when King James I stayed at the new mansion on one of the royal progresses. Just over two months later, the Countess died at her home in London, a victim of smallpox. Lister was left a considerable sum of money by Lady Pembroke but was said to be 'well worne in her service, for they say he lookes old'. [Young, *Countess of Pembroke*, 1912, p. 117] Lister strengthened his Bedfordshire credentials however, by taking as his wife Jane, Lady Gostwick, widow of Sir William Gostwick of Willington. The marriage took place at St Dunstan's in the East on 2 June 1625.

At the same time as the Countess of Pembroke's residence at Houghton, another formidable lady was residing at Wrest. This was Elizabeth, Countess of Kent (1581–1651) whom we have already met as the Lady Grey who befriended Arbella Stuart. Her husband had succeeded as Henry, 8th Earl in 1623. She was actually nearly related to the Pembrokes, for Mary Pembroke's son was married to her younger sister. Lady Elizabeth Talbot was the daughter of the 7th Earl of Shrewsbury and granddaughter of

Bess of Hardwick. She had married Lord Kent (then Lord Grey) in 1601 and resided at Wrest. In 1603, when Arbella Stuart was at Wrest, Elizabeth Grey was named among the six ladies to whom John Florio dedicated his first translation of Montaigne's *Essayes*, already denoting the young lady's literary bent.

Her father-in-law, the old earl, had played an unpleasant part in the trial of the King's mother, Mary, Queen of Scots, and would have expected to be out of favour but for a happy windfall. In March 1605/6 a terrible rumour was spread abroad in London and the south of England that the King had been assassinated. The rumours were rife in Bedfordshire and the Earl of Kent wrote from Wrest to the Earl of Shrewsbury to notify him of the situation.

> I received yesterday your honourable and friendly lines by John Sibley, wherby it pleased your Lordship to advertize me of the untruthe of those reportes and bruits spread abroad of so horrible a treason against his Majestie's precious life. These false bruits, as your Lo doth well note, came very speedily, not onely to your Honors of the Privie Councell at the Corte, and so to London, but also into these parts, and, not onlike, into a great parte of the Kingdome. All the other daye, being Sondaye, we here knew nothinge certenly to the contrary but that the worst might be feared by that which wee heard; . . . Shortly after the receipt of your Lo' letters I received also his Majesties Proclomation, publishing the same joyfull newes; which I thought fitt to send forthwith to Bedford to be there presently proclaymed, if before it were not. [Nichols, *James I*, Vol. 2, pp. 41–2]

The support of this letter and their extreme Protestantism seems to have put the Greys very much into royal favour. Six years later, on 21 July 1612, the King and his retinue arrived at Wrest to spend three days with the now aged Lord Kent. Interestingly enough, early portraits of King James, Queen Anne and their son Prince Henry were at Wrest till the nineteenth century and may well have been presentation pieces on this visit. [*ibid.* p. 452]

When the 8th Earl succeeded to the title and estates in 1623, Wrest became the centre of an intelligent humanist circle which gathered round the childless couple. Learned, hospitable and altruistic, the Kents employed John Selden (1584–1654), the scholar and jurist, as their steward and adviser at Wrest. Seclusion kept him out of political controversy and it was possibly during this time that he helped to compile the *Marmora Arundelliana*, 1628, a list of the statuary collection of Lady Kent's other brother-in-law, Lord Arundel. Selden employed as his secretary a 'strong sett, high coloured, sorrel haired' young man named Samuel Butler (1612–80) who had entered Lady Kent's service as a page. Butler was to move onwards to be clerk to Sir Samuel Luke of Woodend, Cople, the man who was to be the model for Butler's famous satire *Hudibras*. Another assistant to Selden was Richard Milward (1609–80), born at Flitton, who completed Selden's *Table Talk* after his death.

Among this distinguished galaxy of visitors was the cavalier poet Thomas Carew (1595–1639/40). Carew was the intimate of Ben Jonson and John Donne and became the elegiast of Wrest, extolling its beauties and its hospitality at this time. Carew expounds on the simple, heartfelt attitude of the Greys: 'No Dorique, nor Corinthian Pillars grace/ With Imagery this structures naked face/ The Lord and Lady of this place delight/ Rather to be in art, than seeme in sight:/ Instead of Statues to adorne their wall/ They throng with living men, their merry Hall'.

Why should Carew have been in Bedfordshire at all? This has never been explained, but here is an inspired guess. Relationships and friendships were immensely important in the seventeenth century, especially in the small world of the court and the smaller world of a county. The link would seem to be once again the ubiquitous family of Crofts, sometime of Chalgrave and married into the Wentworths of Toddington. One has only to step across the boundary at Wrest Park to be in the manor of Upbury where Sir William Briers and his wife Arabella Crofts lived. Their brother, John Crofts, was Thomas Carew's closest friend and travelling companion in France. Carew was a frequent guest to the Crofts' seat at Saxham, Suffolk and he composed an address for John Crofts to speak to King James there while his sisters performed a masque.

It is not surprising therefore that John Crofts wanted his friend to compose a poem on the death of his niece at Toddington. She was Lady Maria Wentworth, second daughter of Thomas Wentworth, Earl of Cleveland, who died in 1632 aged only eighteen. She is remembered today by the extraordinary monument to her in the north transept of Toddington church, which reputedly cost £2000. It shows the young girl almost life size, seated in a chair with her sewing basket at her feet and her needle on the ground beside her. Above her head is a carved stone canopy like that to a throne and angels with bells. Carew's lines are inscribed on the plinth:

> And here the precious dust is laid,
> Whose purely – temper'd clay was made
> So fine, that it the guest betray'd.
> Else, the soul grew so fast within
> It broke the outward shell of sin,
> And so was hatch'd a Cherubim.

This splendid memorial is unfortunately in a very inaccessible place behind the vestry.

The young Wentworth girls at Toddington must have been very alluring to the cavaliers, for Carew wrote another poem 'Upon My Lord Chief Justice. His Election of My Lady A.W.' in 1636. This was to Lady Anne Wentworth, the Earl's third daughter. It comes as a bit of a shock to learn that Lord Chief Justice Finch was fifty-two years old and his mistress 'a wench of thirteen'.

Carew's other Bedfordshire connection was one of blood. He was a cousin of the Countess of Bristol, Sir Lewis Dyve's mother and second cousin of Lewis himself. Lady Bristol mentions that Carew was one of the attendants of Prince Charles on his Spanish trip in 1622. Twelve years later, Dyve was involved in a duel between his brother and William Crofts, the nephew of Carew's friend. Young Crofts, the Queen's Cup Bearer, insulted Lord Digby in the Spring Garden, Whitehall. They drew their swords but were parted. The report continues: 'Will Crofts steps to Dives and tells him that, if his Brother had any care of his Honour, he should presently meet him at a Place near Paddington, with his Sword in his Hand. Dives replied, he should attend him there. There they met and fought long enough to have killed each other, then were parted, no Hurt done.' Both parties were reprimanded by the King for drawing swords in Whitehall. [*B.H.R.S.*, Vol. 27, p. 11] All this shows what an interesting circle of cavaliers frequented South Bedfordshire at this time, of whom we know too little.

Wrest Park was probably known to Dr John Donne (1573–1631). He was presented to the living of Blunham by the Grey family in 1621 and was rector for ten years. He was occasionally resident and was probably entertained by his high-minded patrons. He gave a fine silver chalice to the church in 1626.

The Earl of Kent died in 1639 and the title passed to distant cousins. Of the intellectual countess, it was said she so 'laments the death of her husband that Mr Selden cannot comfort her'. But Aubrey reported that the elderly couple were lovers and lived in the same relationship as the Countess of Pembroke and Lister. The chief and lasting fame of the Countess lies in the charming book she compiled and which was printed after her death. *A Choice Manuall Or Rare and Select Secrets in Physick And Chyrgery: Collected, and practised by the Right Honourable the Countess of Kent* was published in 1658 and went into nineteen editions by the early eighteenth century. The remedies are typical of those collected by the diligent country house wife of the time, ranging from strange physicks to traditional ways of treating a sore throat and even some from Sir Walter Ralegh. The second part was entitled *A True Gentlewoman's Delight, wherein is contained all manner of Cookery.*

James I's reputation as 'the wisest fool in Christendom' may have been justified by his judgement of people but not, certainly, by his grasp of ideas. His decision to convene the Hampton Court Conference in 1604 resulted in the formation of a working party to undertake a new translation of the Bible. The fact that this was carried out at the moment of the greatest flowering of English language was a happy coincidence. Most of the clerics chosen for the task were great theologians, but well rounded in classics and poetry. Two Bedfordshire clerics were involved in this task which resulted in the King James Version in 1611. They were Francis Dillingham (*d.*1624/5), rector of Wilden, and Andrew Byng (1574–1651), vicar of Everton. Dillingham was to be the first of a dynasty of scholars: Theophilus Dillingham became master of Clare College, Cambridge, and William Dillingham was a Latin poet and rector of Odell. The fledgling national church was already producing its scholars and eccentrics. Dr Thomas Archer of Houghton Conquest, already mentioned, was both. At Houghton he compiled a commonplace book where he noted down obituaries, tree plantings and proverbs. At nearby Haynes, the vicar, Thomas Brightman (1562–1607), wrote his Bible commentaries, including a book on the Apocalypse which he believed was the result of divine inspiration.

The easy availability of the scriptures after 1611 and the high proportion of the gentry attending universities created an articulate, deep-thinking and forthright community in the county. Careful reading and interpretation meant that controversy that had lain dormant suddenly flared up. The passionate beliefs of the early seventeenth century, well tailored to the tract and broadsheet, only needed a matching political controversy to set them alight. This happened in the next generation, but was already revealing itself in the 1620s.

Odell, in the north of the county, has not altered a great deal since the days when the Bulkeleys, father and son, were parsons here. The crenellated church tower and the mound of the castle keep on the other side of the road seem a thousand miles from the hectic life of South Bedfordshire. Edward Bulkeley was rector of Odell for many years, a good Protestant priest of the Elizabethan Settlement at a time when church affairs were remarkably peaceful. His son Peter Bulkeley (1582/3–1658/9), born at Odell, was a very different figure. Educated at St John's College, Cambridge, he represented the new generation which believed and acted with vehemence. He first served as his father's curate, succeeding to the rectory in 1620. Bulkeley married well and had a numerous family, but his convictions as a member of the reformed religion were coming increasingly at odds with the new direction of the Anglican Church. The Catholic measures introduced by Archbishop William Laud became more and more unacceptable to this convinced Puritan. Bulkeley objected to the use of the surplice and the sign of the cross in baptism regarding them as 'ceremonies, superstitious and dissentaneous to the holy word of God'. [Godber, *The History of Bedfordshire*.]

After the death of his first wife and his marriage with a second wife, Peter Bulkeley left in May 1635 with her and his three children on the ship 'Susan and Ellen' for a new life in America. A victim of conscience, Bulkeley became the founder and first minister of Concord, Massachusetts and died there in 1659. Bulkeley endowed the college library at Harvard and his son

became the first graduate there. A great-grandson was Ralph
Waldo Emerson.

V

The Turbulent Years, 1630–60

From the 1620s, the political, religious and social divide in the county began to be more overtly defined. The hidden tensions which had only occasionally become public were exacerbated by the Stuarts' determination to raise taxes, and most of them by unparliamentary means. The extraordinary culture of Charles I's civilised court, enjoyed by a privileged few, was little compensation to the people who had to pay for it in the shires.

The first years of Charles I saw one or two arrivals in Bedfordshire, which though they did nothing to popularise the Stuarts, did give the county a slight taste of the splendour of Whitehall. The first was the appearance of the Russell family at Woburn in about 1625–6. In July 1625 the plague had struck the village of Chiswick where Francis, Lord Russell of Thornhaugh was living with his wife and ten children. Aware that to remain there would be fatal, he begged his cousin, Edward, Earl of Bedford to lend him the unused Woburn Abbey for the duration of the outbreak. Francis was the Earl of Bedford's heir and had actually petitioned the King at one point to save Woburn from being sold for debt, so he was clearly interested in the place. The family removed to Woburn for the whole of that summer and perhaps grew attached to the rolling hills and well wooded villages of that part of the county that gave their family its name. When Francis Russell succeeded as 4th Earl of Bedford in 1627, he announced that Woburn Abbey was to be his chief residence.

The 4th Earl was young enough and vigorous enough to enjoy the challenge of rebuilding the Abbey. He was already planning to build over another part of his inheritance, Covent Garden, and was consulting Inigo Jones on the creation of a piazza there and a new church dedicated to St Paul. At the Abbey, he created a partly new house on the site of the old monastic buildings, grouping the state rooms and the private living accommodation around a central courtyard. The family rooms were all on the north side facing on to what had been the monks' burial ground.

At the centre of this façade was a three-arched loggia containing an elaborately embellished grotto. This still survives and is the most tangible link with the sophisticated and fantastic court style of Charles I. It is almost certainly the work of Isaac de Caus (*c.*1577–1626) who worked for Queen Henrietta Maria and who was a tenant on the Bedford family's London estate. [Colvin] The fact that de Caus died before the 4th Earl succeeded is a puzzle. Is it possible that this delicious mannerist conceit was planned for Lucy Harington, Countess of Bedford, the spendthrift wife of the 3rd Earl and an intimate of Inigo Jones? Her portrait, in a dress designed by the great architect, still hangs in the house. The grotto could have been begun for her (if she occasionally visited Woburn) and finished by the 4th Earl whose arms it bears.

The house was ready to receive King Charles and Queen Henrietta Maria for an official visit in July 1636. There are no records of the visit, but it is believed the King presented the Earl with a portrait bust of himself by Hubert Le Sueur, a magnificent bronze which is still in the collection. At the same time he left, by accident or design, a handsome ebony walking cane that can still be seen below the portrait. That year the 4th Earl was painted by Anthony van Dyck, the full length showing a firm and unsmiling Puritan gentleman in the sober dress of that party, a small King Charles spaniel pawing playfully at his knee. A moderate supporter of Parliament, he died before the great actions of the Civil War began, leaving it to his country-loving son to fight on that side.

The second arrival was at Houghton House which had been granted between 1623 and 1627 to the Scottish family of Bruce. They were great favourites of King James I, and the founder of their fortunes, Lord Bruce of Kinloss, had helped him secure the English throne. In 1633, Thomas Bruce was created Earl of Elgin shortly after he had been awarded the Seneschal of the Royal Manor of Ampthill. Lord Elgin lived a very retiring life at Houghton in the 1640s. A timid man, he had been persuaded by his wife not to join the king at Oxford at the outbreak of hostilities; it was a decision that the family had to live down in the next generation.

The St John family, now Earls of Bolingbroke, owned huge estates in the north of the county and were leading figures in opposing the religious changes of Archbishop Laud. Lord Bolingbroke joined Lord Bedford for the Council of Peers at York in 1640 which preceded the Long Parliament. At Toddington Manor, the Wentworths, Earls of Cleveland, declared for the King. The 10th Earl of Kent, who had succeeded to Wrest in that crucial year 1639, was a commissioner of the great seal under Parliament. The Earl of Peterborough of Turvey, on the contrary, remained a staunch royalist. The ranks of the aristocracy may have been divided equally, but in general the county tended towards Puritanism. The strength of Parliament was now paramount and that strength was vested in an articulate and well educated gentry rather than in the great families.

The Parliamentarians of 1640 included many newcomers of the professional and merchant class who had prospered with the Tudors and had been made baronets by the Stuarts, among them Sir William Boteler of Biddenham, Sir Thomas Alston of Odell, Sir John Burgoyne of Sutton and the Duncombes and Vaux of Battlesden and Whipsnade. The Parliamentary committee was to raise trained bands of pikemen, musketeers and dragoons to defend the freedom of Parliament. Most of these Bedfordshire volunteers saw service elsewhere in the kingdom, the fighting in this county being principally raids and skirmishes.

Bedfordshire, at least its western border, was an important defence between the predominantly Parliamentarian East Anglia and the Royalist strongholds of Oxford and the West Country. The key position was Newport Pagnell, which Sir Lewis Dyve of Bromham Hall (1599–1669) held for the Royalists in 1643 before being overturned by Sir Samuel Luke (d.1670) of Cople in 1644–5. In this way, families that had grown up only a few miles apart became sworn enemies almost within the confines of their own county. The animosity between these two must have been considerable, Dyve, with a party of horse, having ransacked Luke's home at Cople Wood End in October 1641.

Dyve, as we have already noted, was a flamboyant figure whose loyalty to the King was almost unparalleled in the county. Returning from court to his mother's home at Bromham, he became the focus for royalist feeling in a predominantly Puritan county. In July 1642 he had 500 bullets cast at Bedford and on entering the town declared: 'Now you Roundheads, I have provided for you.' [*B.H.R.S.*, Vol. 27, 1948, p. 23] In the following month, Sir Samuel Luke tried to apprehend him at Bromham Hall but was met with stiff resistance and pistols thrust into the faces of his followers. While Luke was away getting reinforcements, Dyve escaped, some said by swimming the River Ouse nearby. A rather fanciful pamphlet was printed of this event as *A Terrible Combate fought in Bedfordshire Between Two Knights, The one sent in Commission of Array by the King, the other for the Militia by the Parliament. Wherein is declared the mighty overthrow of the King's Commissioner, who with great losse was fain to fly for his life.* Dyve's swashbuckling style is peculiarly attractive but most of it was performed outside his home county. Nevertheless, as an important character in our story it needs to be included.

After the fall of Newport Pagnell, Dyve was made governor of Abingdon and was engaged in battles in the West Country where his wife came from and where his brother owned estates. He was involved in the brave attack on Weymouth in February 1645, before he and his wife defended Sherborne Castle for the King in March of that year. The castle, belonging to Lord Digby, was besieged by Lord Fairfax and only fell when mines and earthworks were used to breach the walls. Dyve was brought by sea to London and imprisoned in the Tower. He did not live badly there and the House of Commons resolved in March 1646 'That Sir Lewis Dive, a Prisoner in the Tower, shall have allowed unto him out of his own Estate in Bedfordshire for the Maintenance of himself and Children Four Pounds per Week; And that the Committee of Bedfordshire do pay him out of his own Estate the said Four Pounds per Week accordingly.' [*B.H.R.S. ibid.*] Lady Dyve died the previous month without being given access to the prisoner.

Dyve spent his time in the Tower carrying on a secret correspondence in cypher with the King and another leading royalist, John Ashburnham. The facts that he gleaned from a fellow prisoner, the Leveller, John Lilburne, were immensely helpful to the King's cause. Dyve also fed Lilburne with disinformation, knowing that it would go straight to the Cromwellians. These fascinating letters were only discovered about forty years ago. Dyve was eventually moved to the King's Bench Prison from which he escaped in January 1648 and fled to Scotland. This was his second daring escape and Dyve was to become celebrated for many such escapades in the future. Dyve wrote an account of it and it was published as a pamphlet. The gist of it was as follows: hearing in the King's Bench that he was to be removed to a secure gaol, Dyve had asked a number of friends to dinner and then escaped while the guards were distracted by the serving of the dinner. In Scotland, Dyve joined the Duke of Hamilton who was preparing to invade England for the King, but was again captured at the Battle of Preston. This time he was taken to Whitehall but escaped yet again on the very day that Charles I was executed. In robust, seventeenth-century language, the newsletter 'The Moderate' records his flight:

> The last night Sir Lewis Dives desired to go up to the house of office; two Souldiers guarding him thither staid at the door for his coming out; but casting himself down the Jakes shewed them a shitten trick for his escape. Some say he is swallowed up into the depth of Hell, there to visit his brother; others; that Hell hath vomitted him up again on the dry Land; but for my part I conceive Dives is yet in Hell. [B.H.R.S. ibid. p. 92]

This was probably Dyve's most famous exploit, one that became legendary. He is the only Bedfordshire man to be mentioned by both the diarists Samuel Pepys and John Evelyn. Pepys recorded on 6 December 1667: 'This day, in coming home, Sir J. Minnes told me a pretty story of Sir Lewes Dives, whom I saw this morning speaking with him, that having escaped once out of prison through a house of office, and another time in woman's apparel, and leaping over a broad canal, a soldier swore, says he, this is a strange jade.'

Dyve was to serve the royalists in the Isle of Man, Ireland and France before returning to this country to an honourable retirement at the Restoration. He lived his last years with his daughter in Somerset.

Chicksands and Campton were royalist strongholds under the families of Osborn (they later added an 'e') and Ventris. There can be few places in the county that retain the atmosphere of that time as well as Campton Manor, the home of the Ventris family. I remember visiting it thirty years ago when it had been in the occupation of one lady for nearly half a century. It stands in the centre of the village, close to the church, one of the finest surviving timber-framed manors in the district. I remember approaching it through the mysterious wooded drive and entering the stone flagged hall with its magnificent crested screen at one end. There was a film of white dust everywhere, almost as if it was the last exit of the Ventris family that had created it. I remember that in the great parlour on the garden side of the house there was a piece of lead shot buried in the panelling. An inscription alongside recorded that Sir Charles Ventris was 'in the night time by Oliver's party, shot at, as he was walking in this room, but happily missed him'. This brought home as nothing else could the domestic and internecine nature of the struggle. Ventris was the son of Sir Francis Ventris of Campton and fought for the King throughout the Civil War. He was knighted in 1645 and died before 1651 when his estate was sequestrated. The lead shot was removed in recent years by Sir Danvers Osborne.

A very accurate picture of the period can be gained from the letter-books of Sir Samuel Luke, whom we have already mentioned. These five volumes, dating from his command of Newport Pagnell, give a fascinating insight into the life of this active man. They show how much he relied on the reports of spies, the acquisition of intercepted letters and the interviews with witnesses to gauge the progress of war. Luke wrote almost every day to his father Sir Oliver Luke, Member of Parliament for the County, in London. Sir Oliver was a strict Presbyterian and an intimate friend and supporter of John Hampden. These were exciting months, when despite the Parliamentary defeat at Lostwithiel, the indecisive Battle of Newbury and the King's sacking of Leicester, the Royalists were soundly defeated at Naseby. On the Bedfordshire borders, Sir Samuel Luke was aware of all these events and got his clerks to copy all documents that seemed to have relevance to the campaign. Luke was always concerned about his own neighbourhood and wrote to his father in March 1645: 'Put them [the Commons] in mind of Bedford, for if that should be lost now it will be a great prejudice to us and not easily redeemed. If I have any command concerning it I shall do my utmost for the securing it.' [B.H.R.S., Vol. 42, 1963, p. 185] Luke was continually looking for manpower and horses to stock his hard-pressed garrison, under threat from royalists at Great

Brickhill and elsewhere. He makes frequent appeals to the Bedfordshire Committee, which was not part of Cromwell's Eastern Association, but strongly allied to it. 'I have summoned in labourers out of every hundred in your county', he writes to them in March 1645, 'to be here on Monday, giving every of them 8d. a day. I have summoned in one cart and team out of every parish in the hundred of Mamsett which are to work here one whole week, and shall have allowed you 4d. a day for each team and quarter for themselves and horses at rates accordingly.' [*ibid.*] One wonders what these labourers thought of the war being prosecuted by their betters for reasons that they were unlikely to comprehend.

The fiercely royalist Earl of Cleveland, of Toddington Manor, had attacked Luke at Newport Pagnell in June 1644 and the garrison was only saved by Luke's having recently laid in artillery pieces, culverins, firing shells of 16–20lbs a piece. The year before, Sir Lewis Dyve had attacked Ampthill with 400 horses as the Bedfordshire Committee were actually meeting in the town, and had then gone on to Bedford to surprise the Parliamentary commander in an ale house. In the summer of 1644 Dunstable was raided and the landlord of the Red Lion shot because he would not supply the royalist horse with fodder. The following summer there was a skirmish on Bedford bridge when the King's army passed through Great Barford. One of the worst incidents took place in November 1645 when royalist horse from the west fired the town of Woburn and burnt down about a score of houses in its centre 'whereby many families are left harbourless and utterly ruinated'.

Luke's despatches from Newport Pagnell have the ring of almost any war about them, except that they are so heavily couched in the voice of scripture. One cannot imagine any other soldiers bringing down the imprecations of the Almighty on their enemies in the language of the Authorised Version and casting them in the role of Sodom and Gomorrah! There are also some extraordinary acts of courtliness as when Prince Charles's master falconer is captured by Luke's men. Sir Samuel writes to the Prince on 9 March 1645: 'By command from the Earl of Essex I return herewith your hawk and falconer.' Elsewhere there are doubts cast by both the Lukes, strict Presbyterians, on the growing influence of the sectaries and the Independents within Cromwell's army. Self-made men could rise very easily in its ranks and their fanaticism and liberal views gave them little respect for the established order.

Such a man was Colonel John Okey (1606–62), infamous as one of the regicides, but who played his part in county business for about fifteen years. Okey was born in London, and though the Restoration writers tended to emphasise the obscurity of his origins, he appears to have been a well-considered citizen of London with an abundance of ability and organising power.

Okey was appointed a quarter-master in the Parliamentary army almost as soon as Charles I had set up his standard at Nottingham in 1642. He rose swiftly in the service, seeing some action in the Midlands, possibly in the capture and defence of Lichfield, and commanded a body of 120 horse at the battle for Alresford, Hampshire in October 1644. Okey's opportunity really came in February 1643 when Parliament passed an Act for the establishment of a New Model Army of twelve regiments. This was to counterbalance the ineffectiveness of separate armies under various Parliamentary commanders that had lacked any cohesion as a combined force. The command was given to Sir Thomas Fairfax and the general at once recommended Okey as a suitable colonel to take charge of a regiment of dragoons. The dragoons were really mounted infantry whose job it was to ride to a position and then fight on foot with muskets and swords.

Okey's regiment distinguished itself at the Battle of Naseby, where Fairfax's army was pursuing the King. The two forces drew up near the village of Naseby and Okey's dragoons were positioned between two hedges of a grass trackway, tangentially to General Ireton's horse. Here the dragoons fought on foot, every tenth man holding his own horse and those of his nine companions. Although Ireton's horse were rather dispersed by the royalists, Okey's men fired on the royalist horse as it passed by. Okey then ordered his soldiers to remount and attack the royalist foot who had been cornered by General Cromwell. The royalist retreat became a rout when they were pursued by Cromwell's horse and Okey's dragoons. Colonel Okey wrote a detailed account of this battle to a friend in London: 'Now what remains, but that you and wee should magnifie the name of our

God, that did remember a poore handfull of despised men, whom they had thought to have swallowed up before them.' [*B.H.R.S.* Vol. 35, p. 11]

The colonel was to continue his success in the West Country, being present at the siege of Sherborne Castle (already mentioned) and the siege of Bristol. He saw action at Crediton and Exeter and was instrumental in storming Powderham Castle, before the war ended with the fall of Oxford.

The negotiations between the various parties in 1646 saw fresh conflict. The wish of Parliament (with its Presbyterian majority) to disband the New Model Army was not acceptable to the soldiers and their majority of Independents. Okey was involved with the negotiations, which had totally broken down by May 1647, the army going into open revolt and seizing the King at Holdenby House. It was probably on this occasion that Charles I was moved southwards through Bedfordshire and put under house arrest at the Great Lodge, Ampthill, which he had visited in happier times. On this occasion, the loyal Earl of Peterborough rode over from Turvey to swear allegiance, a fact recorded in Halstead's *Succinct Genealogies*, 1685. The King was under arrest at Woburn Abbey that July, having slept in the house on two previous occasions in June 1644 and August 1645. At this time he was detained by the notorious Colonel Whalley. The following incident there is recorded in Peck's *Desiderata Curiosa*. 'When he came to Woburn, observing my guards, he told me,

'Colonel Whalley, your guards are strong, but do you think you could keep me if I had a mind to go away?' I answered, 'With those commands I had, I could!' 'No,' (said the King,) though you had five times as many more:' – or to that effect. I replied, 'Your majesty's engagement was a greater force upon you than all the guards that I could put up,' – or to the same purpose; his majesty answered, his engagement was, in case he might go to one of his own houses: 'but however, I do now freely and absolutely engage myself to you, that I will not stir from you till I give you warning.' [Parry, *History of Woburn*, p. 18]

It was from about this date that Okey's connection with Bedfordshire began; he was quartered at Bedford that year and again in 1649.

The illegal trial of the King and his execution in Whitehall on 30 January 1649 were turning points. Many of the Bedfordshire

Presbyterian gentry such as Sir Oliver St John, the Chief Justice, Samuel Browne of Arlesey and Sir Oliver and Sir Samuel Luke could not subscribe to such a thing. Okey however signed the death warrant after the signatures of Bradshaw, Lord Grey of Groby, Oliver Cromwell, Colonel Whalley (who had held the King at Woburn) and Sir Michael Liversey. Okey's position under the republic might have been more powerful but for an unfortunate association. He was in communication with dis-affected members of the administration who were critical of the constitutional basis of Cromwell's fledgling government. Some officers, and possibly Okey himself, met at various taverns and drew up a document: *The humble Petition of several Colonels of the Army.* This was considered to be seditious by the Lord Protector and consequently Okey and his friends were arrested and court-martialled. It was the end of Okey's first military career and so he left the army and retired to the Bedfordshire estate he had purchased four years earlier.

In that short space of time between the victory of the Cromwellians and the death of the King, the land ownership in Bedfordshire had greatly changed. An act of 1593 against Popish Recusants had been used to sequester the land and property of royalist supporters. The list was exhibited on 9 December 1648 and included the names of Margaret, Lady Mordaunt of Turvey, Sir William Boteler of Sharnbrook, Lord Brudenell, Sir Lewis Dyve, Sir William Palmer of Old Warden and Lord Cleveland of Toddington. Their possessions were itemised in inventories, giving some idea of the comfortable style of living of some of these well to do families, although it is likely that precious things had been previously removed. It seems highly unlikely that all these people were Roman Catholics although all were royalists and sympathisers. William Gery of Bushmead, Captain of the King's Horse in Huntingdonshire, had been captured in 1642 and not released until his family had paid a large ransom. At the time of the assessments, Gery was fined £740, a sixth of his estate in the north of the county. The Gerys claimed that the Civil War had ruined the family, but their finances were already precarious before it broke out. The Gostwicks of Willington survived the Civil War without difficulty: the Gostwick baronet of the day was both deaf and dumb, an extremely useful disability in these times!

Okey was one of a number of Parliamentary officers who had benefited from the sale of Crown lands. In 1650, Okey's regiment was tendering for the Honour and Manor of Ampthill and the Manor of Millbrook. The Brogborough Park estate nearby was part of this regimental purchase, although Okey himself was by far the largest shareholder. It appears that at a later date Okey bought out the other officers thus becoming the sole proprietor of this handsome hilltop property. The Round House at Brogborough is still a feature of the mid-Bedfordshire landscape, a tall, square house with a central chimney commanding views for miles around. Its simple classical proportions, mid-seventeenth-century details and stone fireplaces suggest that it was indeed built by Okey in the 1650s. Its rooms are interconnecting on the ground floor plan, hence the term 'round' house, and its position and garden lay-out suggest a semi-fortified purpose. Austere and serviceable like Okey himself, the Round House now sits in a lunar landscape of old brickfields and earthworks and post industrial lakes. It is a pity that this rare survival of Commonwealth architecture is not more cherished by Bedfordshire as an integral part of its history. From this 'commandery' Okey exercised power and influence as justice of the peace and registrar throughout the Commonwealth years.

Okey continued to live the life of a country gentleman, attending as registrar of marriages at Ampthill and elsewhere. In 1657 he was one of the signatories to 'The Humble and Serious Testimony' of Bedfordshire landowners appealing to Westminster against the suggestion that Cromwell should become king rather than Lord Protector. Several people were arrested but Okey was not among them. Okey was, however, temporarily placed in the Tower that year after the scare of a plot by the Fifth Monarchy men, who were fanatical Puritans. On the accession of Richard Cromwell as Protector in 1658, Okey was summoned to Parliament in January 1659 as member for the County of Bedford. He returned to the army as colonel of his regiment of horse and was made commissioner for the Bedfordshire militia. Okey was once again despatched to put down unrest in the West Country, but there was growing discontent in Bedfordshire itself. Close to the colonel's own doorstep at Houghton Conquest, a family named Denton, suspected of being royalists, had been discovered purchasing pistols. Lord Bruce, the son of Lord Elgin of Houghton House, was also implicated by association.

Unbeknown to Okey and others, Houghton House had become a hotbed of royalist intrigue. Lord Elgin was too weak to take sides, but his formidable sister, Christian, Countess of Devonshire, had been residing there for much of the 1650s. Christian Devonshire (*d*.1675) had been married to the earl at the age of twelve, when she was described as 'a pretty red-headed wench'. [Thomas Lodge, *Works*, Vol. III, p. 351] Her marriage portion was actually made up by King James who approved of the match. Left a widow for many years, she managed the Cavendish estates for her son with skill and was a patron of literature. She became an ardent royalist, an ardour only increased when her son Charles was killed at the Battle of Gainsborough in July 1643. From her homes, including Houghton, she carried on a clandestine correspondence with royalists at home and abroad. 'To this end', wrote her biographer, Thomas Pomfret, 'many Letters passed between her and Duke Hamilton, the Earls of Holland and Norwich . . . and many others of eminent conduct; which Letters were both written and received in Characters, in the writing and opening of which she instructed none but her Nephew, the Lord Bruce . . . and her Chaplain, Mr Gale.' [Cardigan, *The Life and Loyalties of Thomas Bruce*, 1951, p. 11]

The kind of tensions that the Civil War brought with it are best expressed in the love letters of another Bedfordshire heroine, Dorothy Osborne of Chicksands Priory. It is true that her correspondence all dates from the 1650s, but the divide between her father, a staunch royalist, and her prospective father-in-law, a parliamentarian, must have been the dilemma of too many families. Dorothy Osborne was the daughter of Sir Peter Osborne, the prominent royalist and Governor of Guernsey, who had had his Chicksands estate forfeited in the Civil War but returned to him in 1649. On their way to France, where her mother was living, Dorothy and her brother had fallen in with young William Temple at an inn on the Isle of Wight. In an act of bravado, Osborne had inscribed on the window his opinion of the parliamentarians, resulting in Temple, himself and Dorothy being arrested. Dorothy valiantly took the blame upon herself and, as she was a very beautiful and intelligent young woman, they were immediately released. Temple's admiration for her grew into love and although they seldom met, the affection grew through letters, Dorothy writing them at Chicksands and Temple receiving them on his travels.

Neither of the young people had money, Temple was a struggling career diplomat and Dorothy a spinster daughter whom her brother wished to see well married. The mutual antipathy of the older generation was no help (Dorothy had lost two brothers in the royalist cause) but her letters are neither impatient nor bitter, in fact they are full of humour about her other suitors and her rural life. Chicksands Priory, the converted monastic house with its vaulted rooms and cell-like windows, still stands today and it can never have been very comfortable. It is not surprising that Dorothy, nursing her sick father there and seldom able to leave, was a constant victim of colds.

But it does come as a surprise how tranquil and sedate country house life could still be under the Commonwealth. Dorothy played cards for small stakes, enjoyed a game of battledore and shuttlecock with her friend Lady Di Rich, and tried to form a collection of engraved seals. In Temple's absence she imagines him in this rural scene.

> You are admitted to all my entertainments; and 'twould be a pleasing surprise to me to see you amongst my shepherdesses. I meet some there sometimes that look very like gentlemen (for 'tis a road), and when they are in good humour they give us a compliment as they go by; but you would be so courteous as to stay, I hope, if we entreated you ... 'Tis our Hyde Park, and every fine evening, anybody that wanted a mistress might be sure to find one there. [Parry, Ed., *Letters of Dorothy Osborne*, 1888, p. 104]

Dorothy was courted by the Lord Protector's son, Henry Cromwell, who promised to supply her with dogs. Temple is asked a similar commission to procure an Irish greyhound. 'Whomsoever it is that you employ, he will need no other instructions but to get the biggest he can meet with; 'tis all the beauty of those dogs, or any kind, I think.' [*ibid.*, p. 105] She reads the latest French novels and occasionally one of the newsbooks which kept the gentry informed of what was taking place politically.

But Dorothy is ever interested in love and marriage and sets down her recipe of the perfect husband for Temple and for us in a most beguiling way.

> ... he must not be so much a country gentleman as to understand nothing but hawks and dogs, and be fonder of either than his wife; nor of the next sort of them whose aim reaches no further than to be Justice of the Peace, and once in his life High Sheriff, who reads no book but statutes, and studies nothing but how to make a good speech interlarded with Latin that may amaze his disagreeing poor neighbours, and fright them rather than persuade them into quietness. He must not be a thing that began the world in a free school, was sent from thence to the university, and is at his furthest when he reaches the Inns of Court, has no acquaintance but those of his form in these places, speaks the French he has picked out of old laws, and admires nothing but the stories he has heard of the revels that were kept there before his time. He must not be a town gallant neither, that lives in a tavern and an ordinary, that cannot imagine how an hour should be spent without company unless it be in sleeping, that makes court to all the women he sees, thinks they believe him, and laughs and is laughed at equally. (*ibid.*, pp. 171–2]

Dorothy's letters are pointedly unpolitical in such difficult times, but one gets hints of attempts by the Bedfordshire gentry to be reconciled. The Puritan, Sir Samuel Luke, can hardly have been a very welcome guest at Chicksands, but he was making overtures to the Osbornes in the 1650s. '. . . I know not how, Sir Sam has grown so kind as to send me for some things he desired out of this garden,' she wrote to Temple, 'and withal made the offer of what was in his, which I had reason to take for a high favour, for he is a nice florist.' [*ibid.*, p. 84) She later goes to hear a sermon preached by the divine Stephen Marshall (1594–1655) and is aghast at his levelling and democratic sentiments. '. . . what do you think he told us? Why, that if there were no kings, no queens, no lords, no ladies, nor gentlemen, nor gentlewomen, in the world, 'twould be no loss to God Almighty at all.' [*ibid.*, p. 190]

A considerable rupture in Dorothy's relations with Temple occurred at Christmas 1653 and it took some months and several letters to heal. Finally, she was able to write to him towards the spring of 1654: 'Here, then, I declare that you have still the same power in my heart that I gave you at our last parting; that I will never marry any other; and that if ever our fortunes will allow us to marry, you shall dispose of me as you please.' [*ibid.*, p. 218] Temple visited her at Chicksands in March 1654 but the engagement was still a secret from the Osborne family. Lady Grey of Wrest appears to have been a confidante and at the same time Dorothy was in contact with the Countess of Devonshire. When Temple goes to Ireland, Dorothy hopes to meet him or send a letter to Brickhill on the Watling Street, but is fearful of servants who are 'too talkative'. Sir Peter Osborne died in the middle of March and Dorothy prepared to quit Chicksands in the middle of April. She afterwards lived with her aunt and her brother-in-law until she was married to Temple on 31 January 1655. Her later life was lived abroad, as ambassadress at Brussels and The Hague, but she still corresponded with her nephew at Chicksands until her death in 1695.

A man who lived his life out during these difficult times was Dr John Symcotts (1592?–1662), a physician with a practice in both Bedfordshire and Huntingdonshire and brother of the vicar of Sandy. Symcotts was educated at Queens' College, Cambridge and based at Huntingdon, where his sympathies were naturally with the Parliamentary cause and his fellow townsman, Oliver Cromwell. Symcotts attended Cromwell and noted that the Protector had taken mithridate to avoid the plague, which had actually done his pimples some good! His Bedfordshire patients included Mrs Baldwin of Great Staughton, Cromwell's first cousin, Lady Alston, Lady Luke and Lady St John as well as leading Parliamentary officers such as Lord St John who died of wounds.

It is not surprising that the freedom (more apparent than real) produced by the end of the Civil War and the coming of the Protectorate, should have given rise to many new ideas both religious and political. All the accepted practices of church and state had broken down, the judiciary and corporations were in tumult and the gentry were no longer in a position to give an undivided lead. Since the introduction of the Authorised Version in 1611, humbler people had read the scriptures and had begun to hear God speaking to them in their own language at the plough or in the weaving shed. The response to the Christian message was more personal and the Anglican Church had seen the estab-lishment of communities like Little Gidding just as the extreme Puritans had formed sectaries. Some of these dedicated men, who had expected much of Cromwell's victory, had been disillusioned by life under the Commonwealth. They turned instead to the inner voice of the Spirit: the pursuit of Truth and Peace and the acknowledgement that all men were equal before God.

William Dewsbury (1621–88), the travelling preacher, was the first to bring this doctrine of the Friends into Bedfordshire in 1654. His simple message and pious demeanour greatly affected one Bedfordshire man, John Crook J.P. (1617–99), who became the father of the Quaker movement in this county. Crook was a substantial figure: he had served as an officer in Cromwell's army and had in 1649 (like Okey) retained the purchase of the Crown Lands of Beckerings Park in the parish of Ridgmont. As an officiating justice for the new civil marriage registers set up by Cromwell and a Commissioner for the Ordinance for ejecting 'Scandalous, Ignorant & Insufficient Ministers', he was a powerful man in the neighbourhood. His 'convincement' at the close of 1654 from the preaching of Dewsbury was a very significant acquisition for the Quakers, most of whom were of working-class origin. Crook was described by his contemporaries as 'famous for all manner of learning, an eloquent, neat and accurate Man, both in his Discourses and Writings'. [Croese, *History*, 1696, Vol. 1, p. 61] He was a very able pamphleteer at a time when the printed tract was of paramount importance and he was to pen a score of books. He certainly suffered for his faith; the Protectorate proved a less tolerant period than it claimed to be and Crook lost all his public offices.

George Fox (1624–91), the Quaker leader, made his first visit to Beckerings Park in March 1655. 'I was moved of the Lord to go into Bedfordshire to John Crook's, where there was a great meeting (18 March), and people generally convinced of the Lord's truth.' The following day, several gentlemen of the county came to dine with the preacher. Fox reported that the movement in Bedfordshire was gaining ground and could no longer be ignored. 'The Judges', he wrote, 'were in a great rage in Bedfordshire, and many of the magistrates.'

Strangely enough the Independents did not welcome the arrival of this new unstructured and meditative Christianity. The young John Bunyan, who was a good deal more doctrinaire in those days, felt that the Quakers' dismissal of the pastoral ministry and their subjective approach to scripture was a dangerous development. He set out his feelings in the tract *Some Gospel Truths Opened* and was answered by Fox's associate Edward Burroughs. Bunyan then replied to this with *A Vindication of Some Gospel Truths Opened*, 1657.

It was in 1657 that the greatest event in the history of Beckerings Park occurred, the first national gathering of Friends, held there probably on 31 May. Crook's house was considered to be central enough for this meeting which was to embrace members of the Society from both the north and south of England. Fox recorded of this gathering: 'After some time we came to John Crook's house, where a General Yearly Meeting for the whole nation was appointed to be held. This meeting lasted three days, and many Friends from most parts of the nation came to it, so that the inns and towns around were filled.' There were probably well over a thousand people. Crook's large mansion could not contain the numbers and the meetings were held in the orchard where 'the Lord's power came over all'. (J. Godber, *Friends in Bedfordshire & West Hertfordshire*, 1975, p. 15]

Crook was taken into custody at the Restoration, but he was back at Beckerings in August 1661 and in Aylesbury gaol by 1662. Following his release, he was gaoled once more at Newgate for attending a meeting in May of that year. At his trial at the Old Bailey, for refusing to take the oath of allegiance to the King, Crook brilliantly defended himself and his speech was printed and circulated. He was in prison once again at Ipswich in 1664, but always able to speak out through his great gifts as a pamphleteer. He appears to have been in exile from 1672 to 1676 in Holland, where his works were published in Dutch and French. He returned to Bedfordshire by 1678 and was living at Luton in his later years, although he died at Hertford at a ripe old age in 1699. He was laid to rest in the Quaker burial ground at Sewell, near Dunstable. Crook's influence in this part of the world, supported by the Rushes of Kempston, the Samms of Houghton Conquest, the Richardsons of Turvey and the Gambles of Pulloxhill, kept the meetings alive during a period of persecution and laid down deep roots for the future.

Crook's neighbour, Colonel John Okey, was to meet a very different end from that of the gentle Quaker. In the months leading up to the Restoration, Okey was one of the last to defend the dying Protectorate. He marched with his force to Bristol, where there was a royalist revolt, and subdued it, but on his return to London in March 1660 he was relieved of all his Bedfordshire offices in favour of Lord Bedford. Learning that General Monck was declaring for the King, Okey's blind republicanism made him join his former general, Lambert, in a last ditch stand near Daventry. The republican force was routed by Colonel Ingoldsby, and Okey escaped from the field, flying to the Continent, first to the Low Countries and then to Hesse-Nassau. Okey was finally tricked by a former friend, Sir George Downing, Envoy at The Hague, into coming to Holland where he was arrested. Okey was tried in London and hanged on 19 April 1662. His estate at Beckerings Park was returned to the Crown, but his London house was returned to his widow.

VI

From Restoration to Revolution

After the Commonwealth's period of trial, experiment and uncertainty, most moderate-minded people looked upon the year 1660 and the prospect of the Restoration with undisguised relief. But the next quarter of a century was not to be easy in the county for anyone of a nonconforming spirit, whether religious independents like the anabaptists, Quakers and Roman Catholics or simply the die-hard fanatics of other causes. The days of passionately held beliefs countered by an equally passionately held tolerance had not yet arrived. The Restoration greatly enhanced the position of some Bedfordshire families who became more firmly established in the county than ever before. Others, momentarily honoured, so wholeheartedly identified themselves with the Stuart monarchy that they eventually foundered with it. A few gentry families, like the Gerys, claimed to have been ruined by the Civil War. They had in fact suffered from the extravagant will of Sir Richard Gery in 1638, making a heavy charge of legacies on an already diminished estate at Bushmead. The young William Gery described his predicament as 'plundered to his shirt' and in 1660 he and his sister petitioned Charles II for recompense for the £12,000 they had lost in their loyalty. She said she had inherited 'nothing but sadness' and asked for the position of Dresser to the Queen. He asked to be considered for a companionship. The Gerys were lucky: they returned and are still at Bushmead, but a number never regained their old importance, their estates being gradually surrendered to the aristocracy.

Undoubtedly the most famous life lived in the county at this time was that of John Bunyan. His story is both important and relevant, for he signifies the predicament of those at the bottom of the social scale, as far apart from the Russells and the St Johns as it was possible to be. John Bunyan was born at Elstow, two miles south of Bedford, in 1628, the son of Thomas Bunyan, or

Bonnion, of Elstow, a tinker or brazier and Margaret, his wife. This was only one hundred years after the nuns had vacated the abbey church and the village had ceased to be a place of importance. The presence of this large ecclesiastical building, its dominating tower next to it and the squire's house attached, suggest a place of tradition and conservatism. Fortunately, enough survives in the village street and around the ancient Moot Hall (now a Bunyan Museum) to give us a very good impression of the community that Bunyan knew. Thomas Bunyan's cottage was probably at a remote end of the village bordering on Harrowden and known as Pesselynton Furlong. His grandmother's will demonstrates how poor they were; it contains little more than 'One brasse-pott, one painted table and all the painted cloaths about the house', but she did have a 'joyned stool, a coffer and a trummle bed'. [F. M. Harrison, *John Bunyan*, 1928, pp. 4–5] Coming from such a background, the suggestion that he attended a grammar school at either Bedford or Houghton Conquest seems far fetched. His parents were, however, conscientious enough to have him taught to read and write, although in his *Israel's Hope Encouraged* he says 'they learn till they have learnt the grounds of their grammar, and then go home and forget it all'. Bunyan lost his mother and his sister when he was sixteen years of age and acquired a step-mother within a month; such family disturbances may have accounted for his becoming a rebellious and difficult young man.

In 1644, the Parliamentary army was looking for recruits and John Bunyan, disaffected and wild, took up the soldier's life. Although little is known about this service, it is certain that he joined the troop of Sir Samuel Luke of Cople and was stationed at Newport Pagnell. His troop was disbanded in 1647 and so he was in the army for about three years. Neither his religious nor his political convictions had formed at this time and it seems likely that he was indistinguishable from many in the army, not great idealists but anxious for employment and a little excitement, and excited by the new ideas of the army chaplains.

Bunyan returned to his native village of Elstow and settled down as a brazier and tinker like his father. His anvil, dated 1647, is in the Bunyan Museum. Bunyan's marriage to a local girl, Mary, in 1649 was a turning point. She was a pious and serious young woman, a keen reader of holy books and well versed in the Bible. The birth of a blind daughter to the couple heightened their love for each other and even the wayward Bunyan began to think deeply. The effect was to drive him into the arms of the Anglican Church where he venerated everything in the services and was, as he later wrote, 'overrun with the spirit of super-stition'. Bunyan's first encounter on the Damascus road was after a sermon by the Revd Christopher Hill on the desecration of the sabbath day. The pulpit from which this homily was delivered to the hapless Bunyan is still preserved in the Moot Hall. Bunyan loved to play the traditional village sports, particularly the game of tip-cat, and so rushed out on to the village green in spite of the vicar's admonitions against Sunday sport. But while playing, he was convicted of his sin and slunk home in a state of despondency.

The next few years were to be ones of great spiritual exhilaration for Bunyan, alternating with great periods of acute depression. For someone as passionate and sincere as this young man, the mountain tops were of stupendous height and the valleys of an unbelievable depth. His sensitive spirit was oscillat-ing between the truths that he read in scripture and the hopelessness of his own case. Typical was his concern over ringing the bells in the great campanile tower of the abbey church, where he pulled the rope of Number Four. 'I had taken much delight in ringing, but my conscience beginning to be tender, I thought such practice was but vain ... yet my mind yet hankered.' Bunyan had overheard a group of Independent Christians talking in the streets of Bedford and was fascinated by their conversation. But his greatest encounter was coming into the orbit of John Gifford, a leader of the Bedford Independents, probably in 1653.

Like Bunyan, Gifford had been a soldier, serving on the royalist side in his native county of Kent. In a remarkable way, Gifford was saved from execution in Maidstone prison and after going into hiding, settled at Bedford, working as an apothecary. Gifford remained a fairly reprobate individual until he read the *Foure Last Things . . .* , a book by the Cambridge divine Robert Bolton. The book changed his life and he joined himself to the Bedford Independents who separated themselves from the parish churches and met in each other's houses. As the new order was ruled by the Puritan party, ordained priests were no longer recognised and the ministers of the churches were elected by committees. In 1653, the royalist incumbent of St John's Church, Bedford, was removed and John Gifford, leader of the Independents, as a man of recognised good behaviour and spiritual depth, was appointed in his place. It was in this old church of St John and its neighbouring rectory house that John Bunyan came of age as a believer, listening to the wise counsel and opinions of John Gifford. Church and rectory still stand together on the eastern side of Bedford and the rooms where Bunyan listened so attentively can still be seen.

Gifford died there in 1655 and the job of pastor went to another man, John Burton, who also had a high opinion of Bunyan. In order to be near this community, Bunyan moved with his wife and family at about this time from Elstow to a cottage in St Cuthbert's Street, Bedford, within sight of the tiny church of that name. He was developing as both a writer and preacher (although he may have continued his trade), bringing out four books before 1659 and speaking in the Eastern counties in cottages and barns or wherever he could find hearers. In March 1658 he forced his way into the pulpit of the parish church of Eaton Socon and was admonished for it but not prosecuted. The following year he had an altercation with the Cambridge University Librarian while speaking at Toft. This was mere verbal jousting compared with what was to follow.

The return of King Charles II in May 1660 altered the situation for the nonconformist congregations. The re-established Anglicans were determined to give no quarter to the Puritans who had ousted them for a decade and Lord Chancellor Clarendon's Act of Uniformity saw to it that no defaulter could easily slip through the net. The Act ordered the use of The Book of Common Prayer, recognised only episcopal ordination and accepted that Parliament could change the rules of the Church. The Independents were turned out of the church and rectory of St John's, Bedford, and the original royalist incumbent was re-instated. In 1664, the Conventicle Act was passed and in 1665, the Five Mile Act, so that about two thousand clergy were driven from their livings throughout the country.

With a certain appetite for revenge, the Bedfordshire magistrates in 1660 set about tracking and trapping John Bunyan. His forthright statements were there for everybody to see, for although his congregation might be small, his books reached hundreds. *A Discourse Touching Prayer*, 1663, criticised the Prayer Book's set prayers and static patterns which controlled a man praying with the spirit and understanding. 'For he that advanceth the Book of Common Prayer above the Spirit of prayer, he doth advance a form of men's making above it.'

The Act of Uniformity was not passed when a particularly vindictive magistrate, Francis Wingate of Harlington Manor, issued a warrant for Bunyan's arrest. The magistrate used an old act of Queen Elizabeth's reign against conventicles to validate his warrant. Bunyan had been preaching at an isolated farmhouse at Lower Samsell between Westoning and Harlington on 13 November 1660. He was apprehended by a constable and Wingate's servant and taken back to Harlington Manor House to await Wingate's return the following day.

The interview at Harlington Manor is one of the classic episodes of the Bunyan story, the preaching tinker was browbeaten by his superiors but came out of the ordeal with great credit. Francis Wingate was a well connected and comparatively young man, on the make. His kinsman, Edmund Wingate (1596–1656) was an important Puritan figure and Member of Parliament for the county and perhaps Francis was keen to emphasise his Anglican credentials. Bunyan was not only interrogated by Wingate, but by his lawyer brother-in-law and by the pompous vicar of Harlington, Dr Lindall.

It is recorded that Lindall said to Bunyan: 'I do remember that I have read of one – Alexander, a copper-smith, who did much oppose and disturb the apostles!' Bunyan realising that this was a sarcasm directed at his trade retorted: 'I also have read of very many priests and Pharisees that had their hands in the blood of Our Lord Jesus Christ.' The inquisitors came in and out of the room one at a time as if they were in a stage play, the very setting being like a prologue to *Pilgrim's Progress*.

Bunyan was then marched to Bedford and appeared in front of the Bench of Magistrates at Herne Chapel in January 1660–1. Although he defended himself splendidly and justified his rejection of the Prayer Book and non attendance at church, the magistrates scarcely gave him a fair hearing. The sessions were presided over by Sir John Kelyng (1607–71) who had strong Bedfordshire connections and lived in the county at Gastlings Manor, Southill. He was known to be a bully and an intimidator of juries, facts that did not prevent him becoming a Chief Justice of The King's Bench later in his career. Bunyan's encounter with him is believed to be the origin of the character of Lord Hategood in *Pilgrim's Progress*, the unjust judge who raves at the prisoners. Wingate's uncle was another of the magistrates, so his opinion was hardly impartial!

Bunyan began his long confinement in Bedford Prison where he was frequently visited by his family. Mary Bunyan had died and now he was supported by his strong and resolute second wife, Elizabeth. He also had less welcome visitors such as the wily Clerk of the Peace, Paul Cobb, who tried to persuade him to renounce his vocation. During this period, Elizabeth Bunyan made several impassioned attempts to gain her husband's freedom, delivering petitions to Judge Hale, tossing the document into Judge Twisden's coach and bursting in on the judges' deliberations at the Swan Inn. She was advised to make this surprising entry by Edmund Wylde of Houghton Conquest, the wit and friend of John Aubrey.

Bunyan's twelve years in prison were ones of varying hardship and leniency. One sympathetic gaoler allowed him freedom of passage to ply his trade, visit his religious friends and preach, provided that he was present when the justices came on assize. In the early years he seems to have had a good deal of fellowship. One early visitor recorded: 'When I was there, there was above threescore Dissenters besides himself there, taken but a little before at a religious meeting . . . in the County of Bedford.' His pen was never idle and in 1665 he was responsible for three books, *One Thing Needful, The Holy City,* and *The Resurrection of the Dead*. His spiritual autobiography, *Grace Abounding*, 1666, was the most ambitious of his works up to this time.

The passing of The Declaration of Indulgence in 1672 brought with it religious toleration and a respite for the preacher. Following his release, Bunyan had been elected pastor of the church at Bedford in January 1672 and the following May the community received its licence and purchased an orchard and barn in Mill Lane from Josias Ruffhead for their chapel. This is still the historic site of the present Bunyan Meeting. The repeal of the Declaration brought Bunyan back into custody for a short time in 1675. Works continued to flow from him, but one work had quite a different timbre, more imaginative and more gripping.

Bunyan told a visitor: 'The night I first spent in this dungeon, I had revealed to me, in a wondrous way, my whole life and journey from this world to the one yet to come. It was in a dream; and I cannot withold my thoughts of it; they dwell with me always: they must come out, and I have writ them down . . .' In this way the *Pilgrim's Progress*, the great Christian epic and certainly the most significant book to come out of Bedfordshire, was born.

It was not until 1678, some considerable time after his final release, that the *Pilgrim's Progress* was published by Nathaniel Ponder at the Sign of the Peacock, London. Bunyan was already a popular author; *Grace Abounding*, the autobiography, immediately went into six impressions and his pamphlets were eagerly read. In 1682, he published the *Holy War*, which as an allegory only just misses the sort of acclaim that was given to the *Progress*. In 1684, Bunyan produced the second part of *Pilgrim's Progress* which deals with Christian's wife and children and which had similar success. Within Bunyan's lifetime, the *Progress* was translated into Dutch, French, Welsh and Gaelic. New editions included a portrait of the author, and the fifth edition included 'Thirteen Copper Cuts curiously engraven for such as desire them'. Bunyan died in London on 31 August 1688, and although interred there, his spirit seems very much alive in his home county.

Pilgrim's Progress had defied definition as a book originating from any one literary source. It is a work steeped in the Bible and using the imagery and phraseology of scripture and yet is uniquely itself. Some people have seen a slight analogy to Spenser's *The Faerie Queene* and others are convinced that Bunyan must have read that other great Puritan writer, John Milton. The truth is probably that the seventeenth century was a great age of allegorical writing and that any writer to some extent reflects the period. The language in particular had been greatly standardised by the Authorised Version and there is a sharpness and clarity in the prose of the time which is refreshingly direct.

If *Pilgrim's Progress* is an allegory of the spiritual walk, is it also an allegory of Bedfordshire? As most writers write out of life, one must imagine that Bunyan's personification of injustice, cruelty, ignorance, double standards and fickleness is based on the magistrates, gaolers and officials he met. Lord Hategood is a case in point. Can the same thesis be translated to the Bedfordshire countryside? Since the appearance of the Revd A. J. Foster's book, *The Bunyan Country*, in 1901 it has generally been supposed that certain landmarks were used by Bunyan for his story. With one exception, I think it can only be assumed in the most general terms, the exception being Houghton House which Foster suggested as Bunyan's 'Palace Beautiful'. Houghton was such an unusual building in seventeenth-century Bedfordshire, so astonishingly advanced for its time in stonework and classical detail, that it is quite possible that it caught the eye of the Elstow preacher. One thing is quite certain: the link with Bunyan was the prime reason for this remarkable ruin being saved in the 1920s and for that one is eternally grateful.

The *Pilgrim's Progress* remains a great force in the Bunyan country today with its study centre at Elstow Moot Hall (the fine fifteenth-century timber-framed building which was both meeting place and individual shops) and the Museum at the Bunyan Meeting in Mill Street, Bedford. There one can see not only his books and his chair, but his fiddle, cane and the little anvil already mentioned. When the new museum complex is complete there will be room to display many more relics of himself and his family. Much loved in Protestant Bedfordshire, his book has never been a favourite with the High Church fraternity here, but they have nothing comparable to show.

The euphoria for the restored monarchy in 1660 was short-lived even for some of the landed families. The Stuarts were determined to regain the ground they had lost, perpetuate an absolute monarchy and introduce covertly tolerance for the Roman Catholic faith. The monarchy fed upon published works like Filmer's *Patriarca*, which defended the divine right of kings, and Charles himself was always at odds with his Parliament. The

King's brother and sister-in-law were avowed Roman Catholics and the King's alliances with France were suspected of bringing popery in by the back door. With a Protestant country and a Catholic Court, rumours spread like wildfire, the most famous uproar arising from the allegations of Titus Oates's Popish Plot in August 1678.

Like many aristocrats, the Russells of Woburn felt that salvation lay in the certainty of a Protestant succession. The 5th Earl of Bedford was a sombre and retiring figure who had done little to excite censure during the Commonwealth. He rode in the procession that welcomed Charles II on his entry to London in 1660, received a royal pardon and carried St Edward's sceptre at the King's Coronation. But the Earl preferred a country life at Woburn, organising his vast household, visiting his stables, travelling round his far flung estates in the Fens and the West Country and ordering trees and flowers for his gardens. He employed the well known nurseryman, John Field, to supervise the abbey gardens and to import special varieties of peach, pear and gooseberry.

The Earl was a staunch Protestant and employed as his children's tutor a nonconformist gentleman named the Revd John Thornton. The five sons, while receiving a thorough grounding in Protestant Christianity, also gained a lasting respect and admiration for their teacher. This influence was to have a profound effect on the history of Woburn and one that could have proved fatal. Of the elder sons, Francis, the heir to the estate, was sickly and weak and a great problem to the family. The second son, William, later known as William, Lord Russell, was a more significant person and likely to succeed eventually to the Bedford inheritance.

William, Lord Russell became a Member of Parliament for Tavistock after returning from travels abroad. At first he was dazzled by the Restoration court but soon became disgusted by its shallowness, immorality and flirtation with the papists. His strict upbringing made him critical in a way that soon gained him the enmity of the Duke of York and particularly of his wife, Mary of Modena, who loathed the Russells. Bishop Burnet calls him 'a slow man, and of little discourse, but he had a fine judgement when he considered things at his own leisure'. This mixture of deliberation and conviction was extremely dangerous when allied to Russell's passionate belief in a Protestant succession. James, Duke of York, he reasoned, must be excluded from the throne at all costs, his Protestant son-in-law William of Orange being the only possible successor to the sovereign.

Russell's deeply held views were balanced by the wisdom and courage of his wife Rachel, a daughter of the Earl of Southampton, a great heiress and the widow of Lord Vaughan, whom Russell had married on 31 July 1669. It was she who brought the Bloomsbury estate into the family as well as the country house of Stratton in Hampshire. Both were popular with their country neighbours: Lady Russell comments of him in February 1679, 'Lord Gray says the Bedfordshire gentlemen are ready to break their hearts, that you are gone to Hampshire, and will leave them.' [*Letters of Rachel, Lady Russell*, 1853, Vol. 1, p. 48] She writes to him at Woburn often, requesting him to bring her delicacies including Woburn rabbits. 'My sister Allington desires you to bring her some larks from Dunstable.' [*ibid.*, p. 68] Dunstable was renowned for its larks that went into making lark pie.

It is rather significant that a remark about Woburn's gardens may have triggered off Lord Russell's suspicions. In early 1678, according to the Ailesbury *Memoirs*, Edward Coleman (*d.*1678), Secretary to the Duchess of York, visited Woburn and 'being as lavish as vain he gratified the gardener, (whom I knew to be a pragmatical rascal) far beyond his character, telling him he looked well to his garden, which that rascal falsely interpreted "Pray look well to my garden" which ever after ran in the head of that good but unfortunate Lord Russell . . .' [*ibid.*, p. 27] The gardener can hardly have been the John Field who was so loved by the Russell family. The inference was of course that the Roman Catholic party would restore the abbey to the Church! In 1678, the expected death of the elder brother made William Russell heir to all the Bedford estates. Lord Russell was by this time such a patriot and so concerned for the reformed religion of his country that he was prepared to go to any lengths. By stealth and intrigue, Charles II was trying to infiltrate Tory supporters into civic offices and in 1682–3 he moved against the corporations of England, terminating their charters and rooting out self-government. This is precisely what was going on in Bedford.

As early as 1675, the corporation of Bedford had admitted a number of new names from the aristocracy and gentry to change the political direction of the town. Lord Bruce and Sir William Francklin were avowed supporters of Crown and Church. On 21 September 1683, Paul Cobb, whom we have already met as the irritant in Bunyan's case, was elected mayor, a preliminary for a Tory dominance and an application for a new charter. However, the call for surrender and renewal happened rather rapidly, and the corporation, unprepared for such a speedy outcome, had to pack in fifty-three new burgesses. So in January 1684 the corporation was ready to surrender the charter to the King in return for a new one with all the old privileges and extra ones that His Majesty might consider fit. This new document was approved on 19 July 1684, making great play with the addition of two new fairs to be held in the town and the possibility of county sessions being held there permanently, both events being remarkably good for trade. When the members reconvened in July, the numbers had been reduced from thirteen to eight and by these means most of the nonconformist elements were removed. With Cobb confirmed as mayor, Lord Ailesbury as Recorder and the Anglican William Foster added to the eight members, the Puritan party might well be alarmed.

Russell, at Woburn, must have been well aware of the early stages of these negotiations throughout the country in 1683. He and his friends decided to move. A council of six including in addition Monmouth, Essex, Algernon Sidney and Lord Howard met to plan a general insurrection with a simultaneous rising in Scotland. A day was fixed to assassinate the King and the Duke of York at Rye House, Broxbourne, in April 1683 on their return from Newmarket. But owing to a fire in the town, the royal party returned a week earlier than was expected and the conspiracy was uncovered in June. Lord Howard betrayed his friends and Lord Russell and Algernon Sidney were brought to the bar for high treason. Lord Russell claimed to have been unaware that assassination was the aim of the plot and his defence at Westminster Hall was that he had been misrepresented. Meanwhile, Lady Russell sat close to him to act as his clerk and take notes of his answers. The day the trial opened, Lord Essex cut his throat in the Tower, an event which was said to have greatly influenced the jury. Russell was condemned and imprisoned in Newgate until his execution on Saturday, 21 July 1683. Numerous pamphlets appeared containing Lord Russell's speech on the scaffold, Bishop Burnet's last sermon before him, and his vindications; he was popularly regarded as a Protestant martyr.

When Russell's last testament was said not to be his own, Rachel Russell appealed to the King through the only member of the family who was *persona grata* at court, Colonel John Russell, the friend of Prince Rupert: 'I do therefore humbly beg your Majesty would be so charitable to believe, that he who in all his life was observed to act with the greatest clearness and sincerity, could not at the point of death do so ingenuous and false a thing as to deliver for his own what was not properly and expressly so.' Lady Russell's letters, succinctly expressed and beautifully composed, have gone down into history as classics of their type.

It was indeed a crucial moment for the Russells, the heir beheaded, the Earl elderly and frail, and the family fortunes resting on this woman and her children. It must have seemed that their power and influence built up over a century and a half was to be forfeited. Happily for them, the Catholic party was to go into decline and the Russells were to emerge as the firm favourites after the expulsion of James II in 1688. Lord Russell's attainder was reversed by King William and Queen Mary and the old Earl was created Marquess of Tavistock and Duke of Bedford in 1694, having been Lord Lieutenant of the county from 1689.

The Duke of Monmouth had been a shadowy figure behind the tragic progress of Lord Russell from conspiracy to the scaffold. He was also to play a crucial part in the collapse of another great Bedfordshire family only a few miles away from Woburn Abbey. James Crofts, later Scott, Duke of Monmouth (1649–85) was the illegitimate son of Charles II and Lucy Walters. He had been born in Rotterdam during the King's exile and brought up by Lord Crofts whose name he temporarily took. He was immensely personable and good-looking, as well as wild and reckless, proving to be a great concern to the King while he attended the court. In an effort to quieten him down, the King provided him with a rich wife, Anne, daughter of the Duke of Buccleuch, and he had the young couple, barely fifteen and sixteen years of age, created Duke and Duchess of Monmouth. Monmouth's roving eye soon fastened on various court beauties, notably Eleanor Needham, the daughter of Jane, Lady Needham, widow of Sir Robert Needham of Lambeth, who had been painted by Lely and celebrated in verse by Edmund Waller. In the summer of 1665, Lady Needham left plague-stricken London for Bedfordshire and took refuge at Clophill with Eleanor and her two younger sisters. She died there that autumn and the parentless children returned to London, Eleanor to beguile the erring Monmouth. Monmouth had four children by her and was still associating with her when he was implicated in the Rye House Plot. She was suspected of protecting him when he was at large with £500 on his head, and it is likely that he used her Russell Street property as a safe house on his escape from London. Agile and cunning, he is thought to have made his getaway over the roof of the gatekeeper's lodge at the House of Lords and so to Montague House and Hampstead. His destination was Toddington, and the route to Toddington was found in his pocket in a notebook after the Battle of Sedgemoor.

Monmouth was already turning his attentions to another young lady, this time the Bedfordshire heiress, Lady Henrietta Wentworth of Toddington Manor. Henrietta Wentworth (1657–86) was the only daughter of Thomas, 5th Lord Wentworth who died in 1665 and granddaughter of the Bedfordshire royalist commander, the Earl of Cleveland. The successive deaths of her father and grandfather left the young Henrietta (now Baroness Wentworth) and her mother, Philadelphia, Lady Wentworth, as the sole owners of Toddington Manor.

Monmouth had been raised by his tutor Lord Crofts, whose name he had taken, and this was the same man who had been involved in the duel with Dyves and his brother thirty years before. Lord Crofts was the nephew of the old Lady Cleveland and it is easy to see how his young charge and Lady Henrietta had been forced into each other's company. Old Lady Wentworth apparently encouraged this dangerous liaison, believing that if Monmouth became an acknowledged Protestant pretender, Henrietta might become a royal mistress or, on the death of the Duchess, Queen!

It must have been common knowledge that Monmouth was hiding at Toddington, for Lord Ailesbury, then Lord Bruce, recalled King Charles talking about it at Whitehall. 'I found him in the privy-garden setting his watches at the Sundial. He took me at some distance from his attendants and ordered me to go forthwith into Bedfordshire for to surprise and take into custody by his warrant James, so he called the Duke of Monmouth who was at my Lady Wentworth's at Toddington and that I should take the government of that county by his verbal order until my father's return.' Ailesbury knew full well that King Charles was fond of his scapegrace son and so made various excuses explaining that it would be impossible to capture him. This greatly pleased the King. Ailesbury himself liked Monmouth and describes him as 'ever a noble and good friend' to his family.

At Toddington, concealed in the old Elizabethan house, Monmouth was as reckless as could be. Lord Ailesbury recalls an incident there in the winter of 1683. 'One day a stag

> ran into my Lady Wentworth's park at Toddington which never happened before and what swam the great ponds. I was accidentally thrown out and in a lane beyond the park I saw a tall man in a country habit opening a gate for me. I took no notice but casting my eye perceived it was the Duke of Monmouth who was so indiscreetly being led with the crowd at the death of the stag ... I grew impatient fearing my father might come to know him for he had been obliged to have seized him as being a Privy Councillor and Lord Lieutenant. To prevent which I kept him in continued discourse that he might not look about insomuch that he told me that I had taken a large morning's draft.

On another occasion Ailesbury records: 'Not long after a lady of my acquaintance that lived in a hamlet in the parish of Toddington was invited to dinner by my Lady Wentworth after church service and that lady told me that the mother very inadvisedly carried her into her daughter's chamber who was dressing herself and she saw a gentleman sitting in a great chair by the fireside my Lady's daughter with great warmth reproaching her mother's indiscretion.'

A strange fact of seventeenth-century life was the extent to which educated people were affected by astrological predictions. Monmouth and Henrietta Wentworth were obsessed with charms and the casting up of horoscopes. Their fates were

watched avidly by that superstitious old man, Elias Ashmole
(1617–92), founder of the Ashmolean Museum. He had copies of
their horoscopes in his collection, an interest perhaps aroused by
his visit to Toddington Manor on 28 July 1658 when he copied
down its inscriptions and mottoes.

Monmouth obviously felt it propitious to return from
Bedfordshire to make peace with the King, but by the spring of
1684 he was out of favour again and fled to the Low Countries. In
April, Lady Wentworth and Henrietta travelled there to meet
him. Most contemporaries blamed the mother for allowing the
young woman to appear openly as his mistress under the name of
Madame Vinton. King Charles's death in 1685 removed that
slender protection that had shielded Monmouth's life. His uncle,
James II, immediately requested the Prince of Orange to
apprehend him. While Henrietta waited in Zeeland, Monmouth
attempted a conquest of the West Country in the hopes of
securing the throne. His crushing defeat at Sedgemoor, the last
battle on English soil, ended any hopes of a regal life for his
Bedfordshire mistress. He died unrepentant on the scaffold of
Tower Hill on 15 July 1685 proclaiming Henrietta as his only
wife. Henrietta died nine months later at the age of twenty-nine.
The funeral took place in Toddington church, her guardian
having had the bell ropes cut, so that no offence could be given to
the King by tolling them. Her elaborate memorial faces that of her
aunt in the north transept. The Wentworths' relations were to
own the great house for another hundred years but its life came to
an end with Henrietta's. Only a fragment of it survives today.

Lord Ailesbury, the acute observer of the foregoing tragedy,
was to be the third and final victim of cause and conscience in late
seventeenth-century Bedfordshire. Neither hot-headed like
Monmouth nor easily compromised like Russell, it is difficult to
see why this able head of a famous family should have chosen to
throw in his lot so unequivocally with the Stuarts. Ailesbury was
connected to some of the most famous families in the land; he was
a man of parts, well thought of in Bedfordshire where the Bruces
had been for sixty years, and married to an heiress. But it is only
necessary to go back a short way into history to establish the
bonds and links which made Ailesbury the man he was. His
great-grandfather, Lord Bruce, had been James VI's ambassador

to Queen Elizabeth and so the family was essentially Scottish, even after so long a residence in England. Such ancestry made the young Thomas Bruce a natural supporter of Charles II and James II and this loyalty to the Stuarts went a great deal deeper than it would have done for an English aristocrat. Furthermore, despite being married to Lady Elizabeth Seymour, the daughter of the 4th Duke of Somerset and a great heiress, Ailesbury was never in command of her fortune and always a comparatively poor man. This in its turn made him more beholden to the court and anxious to please the Stuarts in return for their royal patronage.

Added to this, the young Thomas Bruce had grown up at Houghton House immediately after the turmoil of the inter-regnum. The atmosphere had been one of fierce partisanship for the restoration of Charles II, fanned by the intrigues and plottings of his formidable great-aunt, the Countess-Dowager of Devon-shire. It is small wonder that he had come to manhood regarding that lady as a heroine and the place of the Stuart monarchy as divine and sacrosanct. At a very early age, the young Bruce had travelled to France and found friends in a wider and more cosmopolitan circle than that offered by Bedfordshire, or indeed England.

The young man came very early under the spell of Charles II as we have noticed over the incident of Monmouth's stay at Toddington. A curious set of circumstances led the young Bruce into greater confidences with the King in 1679. Although barely twenty-three years of age, he was greatly troubled with a common seventeenth-century complaint, 'the stone' (a calculary of small stones in the bladder) and had attempted various well known cures for it. That summer, he asked leave of the King to travel abroad in search of health at the various Continental spas. This was granted and Charles II put the royal yacht *Mary* at Bruce's disposal to carry him over the Channel to Antwerp. The passage up the Schelde was hazardous, as the Dutch pilot was drunk and the captain a headstrong fool, and Bruce had to take command to prevent disaster.

Although this trip did not cure Lord Bruce's ailment, it brought him into closer contact with the exiled Duke and Duchess of York at Brussels. In this way Bruce became an emissary between the Duke in Flanders and his brother in London, a go-between carrying documents of the greatest secrecy and significance. On a second journey, he travelled in his own time and delivered letters personally to Charles II at Whitehall in the privacy of his bedchamber. The King was surrounded by enemies but referred to Bruce as 'so good and trusty a person'. The King may have suggested to the young courtier a visit to Montpelier, because Bruce visited the spa in 1680 with his wife and baby son, ostensibly for the cure, but also to gain knowledge of Louis XIV's canal building operations for his own monarch.

Bruce and his father continued to be useful at court and attended Parliament (Bruce was Member for Marlborough) when it was convened at Oxford in 1681. Charles's personal rule after he dissolved Parliament there was not very constitutional, but was agreeable to most people. He told Bruce in confidence: 'I will have no more parliaments, unless it be for some necessary acts to be passed . . . for the general good of the nation; for, God be praised, my affairs are in so good a posture that I have no occasion to ask for supplies.'

Lord Bruce had proved himself invaluable to both the King and the Duke but had never had an official position at court. It was only at Christmas 1684 that a suitable post became vacant and not until 18 January 1685 that Bruce was officially confirmed in it. 'Our will and pleasure is that you forthwith cause to be sworne our right trusty and well-beloved Thomas, Lord Bruce, and admit him one of the Gentlemen of our Bedchamber in ordinary in the roome of our right trusty and right well beloved cousin and counsellor Robert Earle of Lindsey.'

It was an astonishing appointment, for the young Bedfordshire landowner was thrust right into the centre of British politics and had an unequalled access to the King's ear. He would also have welcomed the salary of £1000 per annum, a considerable fortune in the seventeenth century. Bruce accompanied the King on his morning drives through St James's Park and out to the village of Chelsea. He also attended the King at supper and was at his going to bed, so that he was with him on the eve of his fatal illness. On that occasion the King was merry and talkative, had eaten goose eggs, and described in detail the plans for his new palace at Winchester. Bruce had slept in the outer room surrounded by the King's twelve dogs and his great collection of clocks. The following morning, 2 February, the King was indisposed and behaving strangely, not able to speak having apparently had a seizure. Later, while the King was being shaved, Bruce prevented him from falling backwards in another fit and ordered that he should be bled. When the King was in bed, he took Bruce's hand and pressed it saying: 'I see you love me dying as well as living.' The King gradually sank in the next few days and Bruce was constantly at his door and only excluded while Father Huddlestone gave him the last rites of the Roman Catholic Church. The young man's post which could have lasted for years had only lasted a few weeks.

The new reign was to be uncertain for the Bruce family at Houghton, although it started with promise when the old Earl of Ailesbury was appointed Lord Chamberlain of the Household in the summer of 1685. The old nobleman was too advanced in years for the burden of office and had to seek rest in Bedfordshire. 'He left the town as I was told (the 16th October) very melancholy,' Bruce later wrote,

> however his Falconers met him on the road, he taking great pleasure at that sport, and passing by the church where is the sepulchre of the family [Maulden], he told his steward, in the coach with him, 'There is my habitation' . . . The Saturday he hunted and hawked in the afternoon, and in the evening returning home he ordered his Master Falconer to prepare all for Monday morning; but God knows I found death in his face. [Memoirs of Thomas, Earl of Ailesbury, 1890, Vol. 1, pp. 123–4]

The death of the old Earl at once placed Thomas Bruce in a position of great authority as 2nd Earl of Ailesbury and 3rd Earl of Elgin. The discharge of his father's will and bequests gives some idea of the great household that went with the mansion of Houghton.

Mr Carleton the steward:
Mr Pomfrett the chaplain:
John Allen the gardener:
Mrs Child, housekeeper:
Robert Huett, under keeper:
Margaret the dairy maid:
Jane the ladies maid:
Joan the laundry maid:
Mary the housemaid:
Robert the butler:

Arthur Witchalse 'my servant'
Thomas Hawe the chief groom
John Chaffin the chief cook
Mrs Launder, 'foster sister'
Mrs Avery, stillhouse woman
Jane the scullery maid
Mary the laundry maid
Margaret housemaid at London
Kitt Hinkley the groom
Peter the French page.

J. Greenwood, under keeper:	Kitt Gray, foot huntsman.
James the footman:	James the kitchen boy.
Edward Basse, caterer:	William Wesley, carpenter.
Thomas the coachman:	Sam Bratland, postilion.
George the footman:	John, gardener at London.
The French cook:	Mr Ruffy, 'my lords gentleman.'
Ann the poultry maid:	Mr Pomfret the page.
Ralph the groom:	Henry the cart boy.

Mr Gaspar, 'gentleman of my horse'
J. Turbatt, 'groom of the chambers.'

Such a household was always a drain on the Ailesbury family and the new Lord Ailesbury remarked ruefully of Lord Bedford: 'He always had lived to himself, and his company in the summers were only his relations from London or else when and sometimes some lords and gentlemen, lovers of bowling and cards, for about a week, but few or none of the country gentlemen ever went thither. He kept a good house for eating amongst themselves but no hospitality, and it had been better for our purses if our family had done the like.' [*ibid.* p. 182]

The new Earl was immediately made Lord Lieutenant of Bedford, Huntingdon and Cambridge and went to Whitehall to kiss hands with James II on his appointment as Gentleman of the Bedchamber. Ailesbury was less secure at the new court: James II surrounded himself with Roman Catholics and Jesuits, and Queen Mary of Modena made stealthy attempts to convert the young earl. His refusal to be moved in this matter left him outside the inner circle of courtiers and therefore less influential, although he was occasionally consulted by the King. During the period 1685 to 1688, Ailesbury had a careful political path to tread, and he chose to be out of town during the infamous trial of the seven bishops who refused to acknowledge the King's authority and at which the population rejoiced at their release. After the birth of a Prince of Wales, the disputed heir who was believed by the opposition to have been introduced to the Queen's bed in a warming-pan, Ailesbury left Ampthill for Windsor to hand in his badge of office. His interview with the King was surprising, for James revealed to him that the Prince of Orange was preparing to invade England. Ailesbury immediately sank to his knees and offered an oath of loyalty: 'he dismissed me with all marks of grace, favour and attention'. This decision was fatal to Ailesbury's life and prospects.

The landing of the Prince of Orange with a 'Protestant wind' in November found the King deserted by his former friends and preparing for flight. Ailesbury tried to persuade the King to stay but no attention was paid to him. He was suspected of being disloyal because of a tendency to gossip with that other Bedfordshire peer, the Roman Catholic convert, the Earl of Peterborough of Turvey. After the King had left, the troops were placed under the command of a Grand Council, but their manoeuvres were interpreted by the mob as being Irish Catholics on the march! A panic followed everywhere, including Ailesbury's home town of Ampthill.

> At Ampthill town near my house, the alarm was the same, and the inhabitants barricaded the five entrances into the town and by overthrowing of carts; and messengers on horseback came crying out from Bedford, Luton, Dunstable and Owborne, that those towns were all set on fire by Irish Papists; and people were so senseless and affrighted that they could not perceive that there was no fire in the air, for the furthest of these towns was but eight miles from Ampthill.' [ibid., p. 200]

Ailesbury could expect no appointments under the new sovereigns, William and Mary, although King William treated him with courtesy. He did not attend the coronation and gave up his Lord Lieutenancy. His position might have been tenable but for the implacable enmity of certain of William's henchmen such as the Dutch Earl of Portland. Ailesbury retired to Houghton and busied himself enclosing the deer park and trying to preserve the woodlands that he loved. He tried conscientiously to avoid any contact with the Jacobite party that was behind King James's unsuccessful uprising in Ireland in 1690, but a warrant was still put out for his arrest. Ailesbury went into hiding in London but was saved by a sympathetic Queen Mary and allowed to surrender on bail.

He was still loyal to that rather rash oath to King James and was convinced that the best case for the country was a restoration of that unfortunate monarch. Although there was now war between Britain and France, Ailesbury undertook a secret visit to James at Saint-Germain in 1693 as 'Mr Allen'. Despite being hurried in a curtained sedan-chair into the exiled King's private apartments, he was identified by courtiers. This was followed by an interview with Louis XIV and a secret return to England. To outward appearances, Ailesbury was still the country landowner at Houghton, managing his estate and disputing with his neighbours about pews and clerical preferments. In 1695, allegations of another popish plot resulted in Ailesbury's arrest at his London house for high treason and confinement in the Tower. Fortunately, the Duke of Bedford was able to arrange for a doctor to attend him, and for his wife to live with him temporarily there. But the tall Earl was regarded as a difficult prisoner; he was kept in two attic rooms and restrained by extra bars put in his chimney. This caused the fire to smoke and Ailesbury's periwig to become 'of the colour of a fox's tail'. The strain of uncertainty resulting from the prosecution of Sir John Fenwick and its effect on the Ailesbury case, greatly weakened Lady Ailesbury. She suffered a seizure on 12 January 1697 and died shortly afterwards, having given birth to a daughter. Ironically, two weeks later, his case for Habeas Corpus came up before the King's Bench and the judges resolved to release him on bail.

There were public demonstrations in London which Ailesbury wished to avoid, and others in Bedfordshire.

> The news of my being bailed on Friday was brought into Bedfordshire on the Saturday by graziers from the Friday Market at Smithfield, and the bells from all parts rang and even until I arrived (Thursday in the afternoon) and illuminations at all the houses in that town, that had never been practised before nor since. In fine they did what they could to express their hearty joy, and the best of the town were most liberal in making the others drink . . . I was met by great numbers on horseback on Luton Downs. The bells of that town rang out, and at all the villages on the right and left, until I came home. Others met me from distance to distance, and at a bridge above one mile from my house there were upwards of three thousand on horses and on foot, cutting down branches from the trees, although without leaves, and strewed rushes and flags with all acclamations and joy. [Memoirs, Vol. 2, pp. 434–5]

The reports of these rejoicings were not music to the ears of King William, and the Earl was advised to return to London and live discreetly, later returning to Houghton. But the Government would not let him rest and in the autumn of 1697 introduced a bill of high treason for all persons visiting France secretly since the Revolution of 1689. Ailesbury consulted Lord Marlborough, who gave it as his opinion that the bill, due to come into force on 1 February 1698, would impale him. The only alternative was flight, and so Ailesbury left the country on the very day the bill became law to set up a new life for himself in Brussels. Ailesbury must have hoped to see Houghton again, but he never did so, resigning the running of affairs to his brothers and his son until his death in 1741. He was the last Bedfordshire Jacobean, who suffered for his conscience and his honour, although whether James II was worthy of that sacrifice of estate, family and country is open to doubt.

VII
Bedfordshire under the Squires

The early Augustan age was a period of extraordinary peace and prosperity in the inland shires of England. Feud and faction were more or less at an end on the national stage: what a man believed was his own concern, how he voted was his master's; Marlborough's wars and the Jacobites seemed a long way away. Country life was typified by that glorious creation of Joseph Addison and Richard Steele in *The Spectator,* Sir Roger de Coverley, the perfect model of the country squire, well loved, just and honest even if his head was packed with strange notions:

> He is now in his fifty-sixth year, chearful, gay and hearty; keeps a good house both in town and country; a great lover of mankind; but there is such a mirthful cast in his behaviour, that he is rather beloved than esteemed. His tenants grow rich, his servants look satisfied, all the young women profess love to him and the young men are glad of his company; when he comes into a house, he calls the servants by their names, and talks all the way upstairs to a visit. I must not omit that Sir Roger is a justice of the Quorum; that he fills the chair at a quarter-session with great abilities, and three months ago gained universal applause, by explaining a passage in the game act.

Such paternalism and patronage have long since ceased to be fashionable, and how many people suffered capital punishment under the game acts that Sir Roger expounded? Nevertheless, many Bedfordshire families flourished at this time, displaying that charming blend of amateurism and pragmatism that makes up the English country gentleman.

Outstanding in this context is the North Bedfordshire family of Orlebar of Hinwick, in many ways epitomising all that was best in the lives of the smaller landed proprietors. The Orlebars were living at Hinwick, Poddington and Harrold in the seventeenth century and became prominent in those years through a number of important marriages. George Orlebar (*d.*1666) married Margaret Child, heiress of the Payne estate at Poddington, and the next Orlebar married Ursula Boteler of the old Harrold family which was about to die out. This Ursula Orlebar known as 'Madam Orlebar' had a son, Richard, who in 1668 married Jane, the daughter of Sir Thomas Hatton, one of the family of Queen Elizabeth's Lord Chancellor. In turn, their son Richard Orlebar married in 1708 Diana Astry, a considerable heiress, daughter of Sir Samuel Astry and step-daughter of Sir Symon Harcourt. The collateral branch of the family, John Orlebar of the Middle Temple, married Elizabeth, daughter of Sir John Kelynge whom we have met before. It was in this way that within a generation or two the Orlebars became one of the leading landowners in North Bedfordshire in that triangle of land that is bordered by other counties.

The long dynasty of the Orlebars and the preservation of their family papers provides us with a unique insight into their lives. There are glimpses of occurrences that have vanished for ever; for instance, the Visitation of Sir Edward Bisshe, Knight Clemenceux King of Arms, who set himself up at the Swan Inn 'at the Bridge foote in the towne of Bedford' to inspect the arms of the gentlemen of the county. The young Orlebar of the day went along to have his crest and grant of arms approved in early 1668, the same year that he married the Hatton heiress at Biddenham. They set up house in the Old House at Harrold, the fine gabled building that one can still see tucked away in a corner of the village. The surviving issue of this marriage were three sons and a daughter, Jane Orlebar herself dying in 1681, when she was buried in 'woollens' to comply with the Act of Parliament to encourage the wool trade! The eldest son, Richard Orlebar, who was born in 1671, is perhaps the most interesting figure of all for it was he who established the family at Poddington and built Hinwick House.

It is probable that Richard Orlebar attended university at Oxford, and although he took no degree, he followed family tradition by being admitted a member of the Middle Temple in 1691. It was after his advantageous marriage to Diana Astry in December 1708 that Richard Orlebar bought back the Hinwick lands from a cousin and was able to begin the building of his house. This progressed from 1708 to 1714 on a new site slightly to the east of an old farmhouse called the Turret, where he and

Diana lived during the construction. Hinwick House is a scaled down version of old Buckingham House, crisp and symmetrical with baroque flourishes here and there, and a faint hint of naivety introduced through the squire's own whims!

The house is of stone, which is unusual for Bedfordshire, though not for this part of the county where it is abundant. In fact the stone is mostly Hinwick stone, dug out of the nearby Stonepit Close, which still survives. The carved features are, however, in Ketton stone including the charming and wayward Diana the huntress in the steep central pediment, a compliment to Diana Orlebar and her husband's love of hunting. The workmen were paid an average of 9d a day and the wages were paid weekly by Mr Orlebar whose signature appears on the bills. The total cost of the wages was £3,647 4s 11d. The name of the architect has not survived, but the names of the workmen have and they are all men associated with Francis Smith of Warwick (1672–1738) On this circumstantial and stylistic evidence, it seems likely that Smith was the architect, closely assisted by Orlebar.

The house is spacious but not too grand within, and has a lovely feel of continuity and family living which is all too rare today. Until very recently it contained all the Orlebar portraits and the early eighteenth-century tapestries, telling the history of Ulysses, which were made for the house. Surviving documents show what the young couple had in their new house. Surely this must have included 'a parigon bed lined with indion Silke and rising tester and bedstead and cornish and foot' which Richard Orlebar bought for £10 10s from Thomas Wollaston on 2 March 1691/2. Diana Astry probably brought with her from Gloucestershire the japanned lacquer cabinet on gilt stand that was always in the house, and Richard certainly had made for him a pair of pedimented looking-glasses in walnut and giltwood emblazoned with the Orlebar arms. They also had a tapering sided coffee pot of 1713 with their arms on it, an early appearance of coffee drinking in the county, as well as high candlesticks dated 1711 and a porringer of 1703.

The completion of the house in 1714 was probably celebrated by an itinerant artist being asked to paint a bird's-eye view of the house and estate, a perspective similar to the engraved books of Kipp and Knyff. The house is shown in a great sweep of countryside, the gardens and walks laid out in formal patterns and the eye drawn to the front of the house by a majestic circle of limes. The only changes in this timeless place appear to be the maturing of the trees, the absence of wrought-iron gates opposite the east front and the greater naturalism of the grounds.

Diana wrote to her sister, Lady Smythe, on 9 May 1710: 'I have a very kind Husban wich do make me improve much upon matrimony as it did you & I belieue by that time I have bin married halfe so long as you have bin, I shall be as fatt as you are, I do find wedlock to be a very happy state and do like it better & better every day, onely do want one such little babe as you have.' Alas, the Orlebars were childless and Diana very delicate, so that Hinwick devolved to their cousin.

One of the most delightful mementoes of Diana Orlebar's time in Bedfordshire is her Recipe Book, dating from 1700 and packed with ideas gleaned from her family and acquaintances. Some of the suggestions are from local celebrities such as 'Lady Torington', 'Mrs Livesay' or 'Cosen Butler'; others were collected from further afield in London, Northamptonshire or Gloucestershire. Christmas at Hinwick must have been delightful with this sort of dish, the forerunner of our own Christmas pudding on the menu:

> To make plumb porridge at Christmas
> Take a legg of beef & break it well, & two marrow bones & put 8 or 10 qtss. water to it, or more as you see fit, & when it boyles up scum it clean. Then crumble in a 2 peny stale white manchet & put into it 1½lb. pruens & ¾lb. reasons of the sun, as much curance, 3 or 4 oz. powder sugar, 2 nutmegs sliced, 2 or 3 blades of mace. Put all these things into your broth & stiue it very close, hang it up that it may boyle it softly 3 or 4 hrs., & when you dish it put a good glase or two of sack into the broth & more sugar if it is not sweet enough. You must put a little clarett in just to culer it. [B.H.R.S., Vol. 37, 1957, p. 118]

A name that occurs in the book is 'H. French', that is Mrs Hannah French, the Orlebars' much loved housekeeper who occupied the Kitchen Parlour at Hinwick and was paid £10 per year. Like all housekeepers, she was called 'Mrs' although she was a spinster, and after her death Richard Orlebar administered her affairs and, like good Sir Roger de Coverley, saw to it that her niece was settled in trade in Bedford.

Besides managing his estate of about 2000 acres, Richard Orlebar was fond of hunting and horse-racing. He raced his horses at Irthlingborough, over the border in Northamptonshire and won some handsome silver mugs with them, one by the Huguenot silversmith, Anthony Nelme. There was no race ground in Bedfordshire until 1730, when one was established in Cow Meadow, south of Bedford, and promoted by the Duke of Bedford and Sir Humphry Monoux; the horses were then raced for a silver plate worth £25. Orlebar's other great interest was fox-hounds and he is believed to have been the first person in the country to have developed a pure bred fox-hound. In 1722 he sold some to the Duke of Grafton who wrote to thank him. 'You have made me the finest present of the best hounds in the world, and I witness how happy you have made me. When parliament meets we shall have another sort of chase, but for the present we are having good sport.'

In many ways this marks the change from stag hunting, the more usual seventeenth-century recreation, to fox and hare hunting in the eighteenth century. There were evidently a number of privately kept packs in the county; the Alstons apparently had one at Odell in the 1730s and Lord Polwarth (son-in-law of Marchioness Grey of Wrest) had kennels near Wrest Park. The young Lord Tavistock was a member of the Dunstable Hunt when he was thrown from his horse in 1767 and mortally wounded. His portrait by Sir Joshua Reynolds shows him in the blue and silver uniform of that hunt.

The life of the middle rank of clergy like that of the squirearchy was sedate and pleasant. There was no longer the shadow of religious controversy to darken their doors, the gentle pace of village life was not yet touched by enclosures or the Industrial Revolution, no serious conflicts or social upheavals had to be faced. If the living was adequate and the incumbent had married well, there was little to choose between the parson and the gentleman, except that the former could not pass on his land and the latter owned substantially more.

A typical eighteenth-century parson is the Revd Benjamin Rogers (1686–1771) of Carlton (only a few miles from Hinwick), who was rector of the parish for fifty-two years. Rogers' life demonstrates how little movement there was even among educated people, for he was born in Bedford, schooled at Houghton Conquest and Bedford and spent the whole of his life in the county. The son of prosperous Bedford vintners, Rogers went up to Sidney Sussex College, Cambridge in 1702 and, without taking a degree, was appointed usher at the Bedford School in 1707 at an annual salary of £13 6s 8d. He was ordained deacon and priest and became rector of Stagsden in 1712 and rector of Carlton in 1720, when he resigned his first living. Rogers' rectory house is no longer there and the system of open fields that he knew has vanished, but his straggling riverside village with its outlying parish church still retains many of the features he would have known. Rogers' life only differs from those of hundreds of other Georgian clergymen of eighteenth-century Bedfordshire in that he recorded his sedentary life in a diary. [*B.H.R.S.*, Vol. 30, 1950.]

This diary breathes added life into the landscape that Rogers loved and cared for: the woods, open spaces, the neighbouring parish of Chellington and the tortuous road down to Bedford, nine miles to the south. In many ways he is Bedfordshire's Parson Woodforde, although his journal is much earlier, much shorter and not so concerned with food! One gains the impression of Rogers at the centre of his little flock, acting as farmer, legal adviser, quack and friend, perhaps because there was no resident squire in the parish. He emerges as a personage of almost Fieldingesque dimensions, who could have stepped from any of that novelist's works.

Rogers cultivated the glebe lands himself, but paid a 'hayward' or parish official to look after the repair of fences or parish boundaries and to impound stray beasts. He made wills for his parishioners, organised apprenticeship indentures and arranged settlement certificates for those who came to reside in the parish and had to come into the jurisdiction of its poor relief. He is an avid reader of *The Gentleman's Magazine* and he supplements his library by buying up the books of deceased clergy friends. His son is not a reader and is only interested in equine pursuits, continually attending local horse fairs and trading in ponies and mares. Parson Rogers is entertained by his patron, Lord Trevor of Bromham Hall, and all the local gentry and his society is made up of visits and returned calls in a radius of about ten miles. He is always immensely proud of his own husbandry:

> November the 3rd [1727] I cut a Colliflower in my Garden as large as both my fists, and Sent it to my Lady Wolstenholme.

> June the 7th [1728] Sent to Mr Chaderton by my Daughters Jane and Mary a little Basket of Beans, being the first I gather'd; having a little before been presented by him with strawberries and pickled Jack.

It is interesting to note that cauliflowers were much smaller than today's varieties and even cultivated strawberries were very tiny.

> 17th [February 1735] John Hannah grafted a Golden Roussett Cyon upon a Stock the Fruit of which I did not like. *Succedat.*

Rogers' concern for the village was always uppermost in his thoughts, particularly when disease was introduced by newcomers into a virtually static congregation.

> [1736] Yesterday, being Sunday and the 4th day of this Month, the Small Pox broke out afresh in this Parish in 5 Families, viz., Molly Rey, daughter of Mr John Rey Junior; a daughter of Thomas Sharman; a Daughter of the Widow Rey on the Moor; in Thomas Partridge's Family; and John Britain of William Wharton's Family. This new breaking out of them was occasioned, (as they say) by Mrs Rey's Funeral Sermon, Notice of which being given long before it brot a vast Number of People to the Meeting from all Parts to hear it, and amongst the rest a good many People from Olney, which is now and has been of a long time afflicted with the Small pox, and these, it is thought, brought the Infection.

The parson was zealous in collecting remedies for his patients and patent remedies for destroying pests. In July 1736 he copied out the

> Scottish Receipt for the Cure of the Bite of a Mad Dog. Take Rue without the stalks, 6 ounces; Garlic plant from the Skins and well beaten, and Mithridate of each 4 Ounces; Ash-colourd Liverwort, one Handful: Boil all three in 12 or 14 Quarts of Old Ale till half is consumed, then strain it, and keep it in Bottles for Use. Let it be close stopt while you boyl it.

This was taken from the *Northampton Mercury*, the only paper of the district for a hundred years. Also taken from this newspaper, I suspect, are the accounts of murders and suicides recorded with choice detail in the parson's diary. Crime in his own parish seems to have been almost negligible except for the occasional drunken brawl.

Brother clerics lived well, even too well, as is the case of his friend and neighbour the Revd Vere Alston of Odell.

> August 28th [1729] Mr Vere Alston had a fall from his horse which endanger'd his life; it was in Pavenham lane, having been at his Brother's and (as it is said) Drank too much ... upon my enquiry of him at his home when I went to see him, he told me that the day he had been so unhappy as to fall from his horse, he had been at Mr Lamb's at Sharnbrook, where he din'd, and assur'd me that they had but 2 bottles of wine, which however disorder'd him ...

It is not surprising to find Parson Rogers travelling considerable distances around Bedfordshire on a horse. More surprising is the visit to London in 1734. He and his friend, Mr Berry, set out from Carlton early and reached Luton at noon, where they dined at The Bell, arriving at four o'clock at Barnet where they stayed. It was to be a visit of less than a week, but they visited the Duke of Marlborough's house where they drank tea with the housekeeper and Dr Mead's 'Library and Curiosities'. The Duchess of Marlborough was the daughter of Roger's patron, Lord Trevor, and Dr Mead, physician to George II, was related to the Alstons and had his country home at Harrold Hall.

Rogers was a Tory in Whig country, so that his comments on elections both parliamentary and municipal are interesting. In January 1731 he journeyed into Bedford for the three days of election for a new member. Malpractice and graft were common at that time and Rogers records the Whigs' efforts to stifle the opposition. Sir Jeremy Sambrook, a newcomer to the county was the Tory candidate against Dr Thomas Brown of Arlesey, who was supposed not to be a valid candidate due to his debts. 'The Election was carried out with great Partiality on the Doctor's side. After the Writs bore date, the Mayor (Mr William Staines) with a Majority of Aldermen agreed to make a great Number of Burgesses and Freemen to strengthen the Party; 84 were said to be Nominated and Voted ... A good many of which were sworn during the Election.' The Whigs further tried to invalidate certain categories of voter, including those of 'Town House' status, those gentry who had houses in Bedford but only came in from their country houses occasionally. There was also a flurry of letters from a prominent citizen promising money or the payment of debts for a vote. 'The sum of the Poll on both sides,' recorded Rogers, 'was 719, Sir Jeremy having, after all their tricks and foul practices, a Majority of 31 according to the check-poll and 29 according to the Mayor's Poll. Note: there was the greatest appearance of Noblemen and Gentlemen that was ever known at any Election, and as many people out of the country as is usual at a County Election, the Town being extremely ful of people.' The following autumn he returned for the Mayoral election and was quite jubilant. 'But it was wonderful to see so many Tories come to Town upon the Election Morning from all Quarters, even Lincolnshire, Essex etc, so that very few of the Out-of-Town votes were absent; when the Whigs had none but Town votes, being secure of the Election. For they could not imagine how the Tories coud be brot out, they having, as they thot, a Majority both in the Upper and lower House.' He reports that Countess Granville of Hawnes influenced some voters for the Tory cause: at this moment her son Lord Carteret was plotting against Walpole.

Such electioneering could not only be ruinous to the characters of local gentlemen but have a devastating effect on their pockets. The most outstanding case was that of the Gostwicks of Willington who were actually brought to their knees by political expense and corruption. The Gostwick baronets had not been prominent in public life since the beginning of the seventeenth century, but Sir William Gostwick, 4th Baronet, married well, became sheriff of Bedfordshire in 1679, and acquired the manor of Cople Woodend where Samuel Butler's *Hudibras* is believed to have been written in 1686. Setting his mind on a political career, he became a focus of Whig support in North Bedfordshire after the departure of King James in 1688. He was entertaining Whig gentlemen at Willington in 1697 and courting the Earl of Ailesbury. When the general election was called in 1698, Gostwick went to great lengths to ensure that he and his fellow candidate, Lord Edward Russell, were successful. He sent his bailiff to every inn in Bedford, explaining with a wink that the Gostwick faction would not pay bills for the electors entertained there, this in the presence of witnesses! On polling-day, waverers were cajoled or bribed into voting for the Whig candidates. At

The White Horse, sixteen or seventeen voters were entertained by Sir William's collar-maker, the expenses probably being repaid in kind at a later date. The Whigs were returned, needless to say, and the baronet began a fifteen-year career at Westminster. But unhappily for Sir William, there were elections in 1701 and 1702, another in 1708, and altogether seven during his time as M.P. for the county. The outlays were terrific and by 1713 he was owing £26,700 to the Duke of Marlborough and the estate was so debt ridden that the poor old man had to seek payment from the Whig party. He obtained a pension from Walpole for the rest of his life, but when he died in 1720 there was little left. The poverty-stricken heir had to sell off the Willington property and seek his fortunes in the army; a five-hundred-year connection with the county was broken at last.

As is noticeable from the electioneering accounts of Rogers and Gostwick, Bedford town was immensely important to the gentry as a social and administrative centre. It was not on the two major north-south routes (a fact noted by Torrington at the end of the century) but it was on a navigable river. The route to the sea had been opened up early in the seventeenth century by a Cople gentleman, Arnold Spencer, whose company built sluices in the 1620s and obtained a patent to make rivers navigable in 1628. Spencer had hoped to gain an Act of Parliament that would open the river right up to Bedford with that part of the waterway leased from Bedford Corporation. The Civil War, the depletion in trade and the resulting decay left Spencer financially embarrassed. The task was taken up after the Restoration by the Ashley family, who benefited from the Navigable Rivers Act passed in 1665. The tolls for using the improved river up to Great Barford were shared by the Ashley and Jemmatt families, but in 1697 when the trade was at its height, one family tried to blockade the lighters authorised by the other, and the constables had to be called! The Ashleys were estimated to make about £400 per annum from their franchise.

It was very important for Bedford to have this artery; carriage by water was far cheaper than carriage by road, and with the increase in the use of sea-borne coal, the Ouse became vital. Prominent Bedford families traded on the river including the Wilkeses, Faldoes and Isaacs. Apart from coal, it is difficult to be sure what loads were carried, but it seems likely that they included agricultural produce from the county and stone for building. Two prominent diarists refer to the river at this time. Celia Fiennes in 1701–3 mentions 'this river beares barges' but prefers to concentrate on its other aspects. 'Bedford town is an old building its wash'd by the river Ouse . . . its stored with very good fish, and those which have gardens on its brinke keepes sort of trunck or what they call them (its a receptacle of wood of a pretty full size full of holes to let the water in and out) here they keep the fish they catch as pike perch tench etc, so they have it readye for their use.' In 1712, the Yorkshire diarist, Ralph Thoresby (1658– 1725), gives a rather different impression:

> Bedford, that gives name to the county, situate on both sides of the river Ouse, which is navigable for boats, from Lynn hither; there are two gatehouses upon the bridge, and near the river side has been an ancient castle, of which, scarce so much as any ruins remain; there being a bowling-green upon the height of all, whence a good prospect into the adjoining country; it is a clean town, but dead for want of trade and business; no spirit or life appeared; we could not procure a map of the county, either at the bookseller's, coffee-house or inn.

Maps had been available by Speed and Mordern since the early seventeenth century, but perhaps Thoresby visited the town on a bad day.

Although neither Celia Fiennes nor Ralph Thoresby would recognise the river at Bedford today, they might well have seen it as it still remains at Great Barford. It is fully navigable here and this particular stretch, with its wide reedy banks and flat meadows on either side, is delightfully unspoilt. Most of all, the landmarks are still in place at this point, the many-arched medieval bridge spanning the Ouse with the tall square tower of All Saints church. Further down the river at Little Barford is the timber-framed birthplace of the county's Poet Laureate, Nicholas Rowe (1674–1718).

Although the population of the county would appear from the diaries of men like Parson Rogers to be very static, it was surprisingly cosmopolitan. As early as 1681, George Abbot of Steppingley Park had a 'blackamoor' boy baptised at Steppingley church 'being about seven years old', presumably the son of one of his servants. In the Haynes parish register for 24 November

1771, there appears the burial of 'Jack Nightingale, An Indian Servant Boy of Earl Granville about the age of 15 or 16'. The retinues of these great houses contained many people of continental origin, mostly French before 1700, and then Dutch and Italian. Lord Ashburnham's tutor, Mr Moussac, and his gardener, La Tarte, were clearly French; the 2nd Duke of Bedford employed the Italian musicians, Nicola Cosimi and Nicola Francesco Haym, to be in his household permanently at a wage of one hundred pounds a year.

Bedfordshire folk on the main roads through the county must have been very used to passing travellers with their strange dialects and stranger clothes, in particular the Highland drovers, who brought their flocks down from Scotland to the London markets throughout this period. There was a good deal of suspicion of the Scots in the years before the 1745 rebellion and in May 1743, Lady Pomfret (the mother-in-law of Lord Granville) noted in her diary: 'At Eleven we sat out & arrived safe at Dunstable at about six in the Afternoon. Mr Roper was quarter'd in the same house who was Cornet of ye Guard that conducted the deserted Highlanders to London, we walk'd with him to see them in a large Barn sitting on Straw, some Singing, some playing Cards & most seem'd very merry, the Piper play'd us a Tune & my Lord gave him half a Crown.' These may have come from the Highland regiment that Walpole had tried to raise.

The landing of Prince Charles Edward in 1745 was much more serious and some Bedfordshire families, on learning that the Prince was at Derby, displayed panic. Mrs Sarah Osborn of Chicksands, whose son had immediately joined the Duke of Cumberland's army, was concerned enough to send her brother-in-law to retrieve her belongings. 'Dr Osborn was in town, thought it high time to remove the things from Chicksands. He went down that morning before the consternation was so great and sent Thomas Green with your two Boxes a Sunday, which are now here, and £100 from Denbigh. I begged the plate to be buried anywhere near him, for impossible to trust that road by the Wagon since we imagined the Highlanders would be at their heals.'[Emily S.D. Osborn, *Political and Social Letters*, p. 85]

There were Jacobite sympathisers in the county later than this.

The letter-writer Talbot Williamson recorded the death of Sir Humphry Monoux of Wootton in December 1757: 'the King has lost no friend in him, says a domestic of St James', for they used to drink the pretender's health from the master to the scullion . . .' [B.H.R.S., Vol. 34, p. 25]

It is not often that national events and a national scandal impose themselves on a small rural county, but sometimes such circumstances arise. They certainly did in 1756–7 with the trial and execution of Admiral Byng. The Byngs had settled at Southill in 1693 and by the 1720s had become a distinguished naval family, Admiral Sir George Byng being created Viscount Torrington in 1721 and holding the post of First Lord of the Admiralty from 1727–33. The 2nd Viscount was treasurer of the Navy and M.P. for the county and his brother John, born at Southill, had a remarkable naval career, becoming rear-admiral in 1745 and taking command in the Mediterranean in 1747–8.

Sarah Byng, the sister of the ill-fated admiral, had married into the Osborns of Chicksands and it is through her eyes that we see the Bedfordshire tragedy unfolding. The Osborns were by this time very well established country squires, they were making careers as diplomats and politicians and the 3rd baronet, Sarah's son was governor of New York State in 1753. They had begun to improve the old house at Chicksands and had employed the noted architect Isaac Ware to make alterations. Curiously enough Mrs Sarah Osborn seemed to know that the following years were to be difficult. Writing to Sir Danvers Osborn in July 1751 she says: 'I have a persentiment (sic) of coming evil . . . to our family, why I know not, but 'tis to be hoped I am mistaken.'

In 1756 the Government was repeatedly informed that the French intended to take the island of Minorca to strengthen their hand in the Mediterranean. It was strategically placed opposite the great French port of Toulon and those that controlled the island controlled the port. The Seven Years' War was about to commence and the men who decided its course were, surprisingly, mostly connected with this county. The Duke of Newcastle was not, but Lord Chancellor Hardwicke was the father-in-law of Lady Grey of Wrest, the lord President was Earl Granville of Hawnes, Lord Anson was a brother-in-law of Lady Grey and the Foxes were cousins of Lord Ossory of Ampthill.

Byng was appointed Admiral of the Blue Squadron and in April 1756 the fleet left Spithead. Byng's orders were unfortunately vague and did not take into account what eventually occurred: namely, a massive invasion of Minorca by 15,000 French troops. The Admiral weighed up the strength of the opposing forces and felt that the British were outnumbered. The fact that the French fleet could have been outmanoeuvred and attacked simply did not occur to him. A battle was fought, but the British fleet was withdrawn to Gibraltar by Byng before it had the chance to lay siege to the stranded French troops of Richelieu on the island. This was Byng's fatal mistake.

On his return in July 1756, Byng was arrested on the orders of the Admiralty by his own brother-in-law, Admiral Osborn, and was court-martialled on board the *St George* at Portsmouth docks in December 1756. He was sentenced to be shot with a recommendation to great mercy and it was anticipated that compassion would prevail. It is clear that in Bedfordshire he was expected to be reprieved. John Orlebar, writing to his daughter on 27 January 1757, said: 'I take it for granted that his Life will be safe; unless he should fall into the hands of an enraged mobb.' [C.R.O., OR 2071/230] But it was not to be and he was condemned to death. Sarah Osborn campaigned ceaselessly for her brother that month, appealing to the Duke of Bedford and the Lords of the Admiralty. The Duke gave her a rather non-committal reply. '. . . I shall be very happy if upon a strict examination into the proceedings of the Court Martial, I shall find myself at liberty to adopt those sentiments of mercy which the Court has so strongly recommended to His Majesty, as not one has a more real regard for yourself and Lord Torrington and his family than myself.' [Emily S.D. Osborn, *Political and Social Letters*, 1890, p. 117]

The most remarkable among the letters concerning the sentence is the one addressed to Admiral Byng from Voltaire, enclosing Richelieu's testimony of the admiral's innocence and always kept at Chicksands.

Sir, – Tho' I am almost unknown to you, I think tis my duty to send you the copy of the letter which I have just received from the Marshall Duke of Richelieu. Honour, humanity, and equity order me to convey it into your hands. This noble and unexpected testimony from one of the most candid, as well as the most generous of my countrymen, makes me presume your Judges will do you the same justice.

I am, with respect,

your most humble obedient Servant,

Voltaire

It was after hearing about the execution on board the *Monarque* on 14 March 1757, that Voltaire made his famous remark that it was done '*pour encourager les autres*'. Byng wrote to his sister from on board ship on the fateful day.

My dear, dear Sister, – I can only with my last breath thank you over and over again for all your endeavours to serve me in my present Situation. All has proved fruitless, but nothing wanting in you that could be done. God for ever bless you is the sincere prayers of your most affᵗ Bro.

J. Byng.

The Admiral, who was fifty-three, was buried at Southill, where his memorial records the 'perpetual disgrace of Publick Justice . . .' Mrs Osborn elsewhere called it 'Political Martyr-dom', for Byng's irresolute judgement was made an excuse to get a weak government out of trouble.

A glimpse of life slightly lower down the social scale from that led by the sociable Parson Rogers is shown in the diary of John Salusbury of Leighton Buzzard (1713–87), a respected minor official, charity trustee, turnpike trustee, militia officer and justice of the peace. He lived in modest circumstances at Leighton with one maid and one handyman, enjoying the company of bachelors like himself in games of commerce, cribbage, quadrille, whist and backgammon. His diversions were fishing and shooting, and an occasional visit to the races at Bedford or Aylesbury. He took the *Cambridge Journal*, suggesting that this paper was more popular in the south of the county than the Northampton one, and enjoyed plays when strolling players visited the town hall in 1759. One of his most charming vignettes is of an early game of cricket which he saw in Woburn Park in August 1757. Salusbury is clearly more interested in the takings of the betting man than in the skill of the game.

Aug. 15 . . . After breakfast rode to the circle in Woburn Park, where the match made on Saturday was finished. The first innings was greatly against Lord Sandwich, but on the second the odds was for him, his party leading the other 54 notches which was the number Mr St John's side got, so it was a tie. They then began the same match. All bets made on the former not declared off were to stand on this. The first inning over, two to one was laid on Mr St John, which I took in ½ crowns of Mr Ramsey; but the second inning Lord Sandwich got 100, by which he led the other side 67, which altered bets greatly. Mr St John got but 65 notches, so that he lost it by two, to win which he had two hands to go in, who were both bowled out by Doggett. I won my bet with Mr Ramsey, but lost my original ½ crown with Mrs Scott, so I won but 7s. 6d.

By a strange coincidence, one of the earliest recorded paintings of a cricket match is by a Bedfordshire artist. This is by J. R. Reade of Bedford, a sporting painter who kept a 'twopenny museum' of curiosities in the town, a primitive art gallery that was visited by the diarist Lord Torrington and supported by the Duke of Bedford. Perhaps the artist was asked by his patron to depict the cricket match scene in Woburn Park?

John Salusbury rides round the western side of the county and stays with various friends on militia business, notably Capt. Wingate of Harlington, Capt. Hutton of Leighton and Major Tupman of Great Brickhill. On 26 June 1759, he gave a dinner party to his friends when they consumed 'green pease soup, 3 boiled chickens, bacon etc., & a hunting pudding; 2d course, couple of ducks roasted, neck of veal, pease, tarts & custards'. [B.H.R.S.,Vol. 40, p. 86]

The south of the county, where Salusbury spent his life, was also the setting for an extraordinary series of benefactions in the town of Dunstable. Many merchant families from other parts of England prospered in the City of London and gave their wealth to their native boroughs. This was not common in Bedfordshire, but Dunstable with its strong connections with the capital is the exception. The Marshe family of Dunstable was prominent in the seventeenth century and started a dynasty that was to be important there for over one hundred years. William Marshe's daughter, Elizabeth, married Thomas Chew (1614–86), and their sons became London merchants in the distillery trade. Their sisters married well, one to a haberdasher, Henry Aynscombe, another to a distiller, William Ashton, and a third to a merchant, James Cart. The grandchildren of these families also distinguished themselves: one, Francis Dickinson, was a member of the East India Company and another, Marshe Dickinson, was Lord Mayor of London in 1757.

Their wealth flowed back into the town of their origins, first in the foundation of the handsome Chew Grammar School in High Street South in 1719, then with the lovely range of the nearby Cart Almshouses in 1723, and, later, the handsome pedimented range of the Marshe Almshouses in Church Street in 1743. These buildings are all outstanding and give modern Dunstable that civic dignity which its neighbour Luton so conspicuously lacks. The Marshes, Chews, Carts and Dickinsons also gave themselves a magnificent series of memorials in the Priory Church which are definitely the finest group of merchant monuments in the county. They were highly thought of even in the eighteenth century, and Lady Pomfret records in her diary the fine tombs of private citizens. It is a great pity that the finest of all, that to William Chew of 1712, is practically inaccessible. The two surviving sisters, Mrs Cart and Mrs Ashton, made another handsome gift to the church in 1722 when they presented an altar piece of the Last Supper by Sir James Thornhill (1675–1734). This great example of baroque painting hung at the east end until the late nineteenth century when it was discarded, damaged, and finally fell to bits in a period of neglect!

A few miles to the north at Eggington, one finds one of the most perfect early eighteenth-century houses, also the residence of a London merchant. Eggington House was built between 1710 and 1717 by John Reynal, a native of the French town of Montauban, in Languedoc, who may have been a Huguenot refugee. He began to purchase land around Leighton Buzzard in 1707 and is described as a tailor in the parish of St Andrew's, Holborn. His son, another John Reynal, was a member of Lincoln's Inn and the grandson J. S. W. Reynal was High Sheriff of Bedfordshire in 1777.

It would be nice to feel that the landowners were great supporters of the Bedfordshire sons who had gone to London and prospered, but this was not always the case. I can find only one instance of a Bedfordshire family buying a watch from the famous Thomas Tompion (1639–1713) the 'father of English watch-making'. Tompion was born at Ickwell, the son of the village blacksmith and worked there until he was twenty-five years of age. His move to London may have come as a result of the Olivers putting in the magnificent heraldic window in Northill church; the City was encouraging apprenticeships after the Great Fire of 1666. Tompion flourished as an apprentice watchmaker, becoming a journeyman clockmaker in 1672. He had been introduced to Robert Hooke of the Royal Society the year before and made a spring balance watch from Hooke's designs. Tompion went on to be the most celebrated clock and watch-maker of his day, was elected Master of the Clockmakers' Company in 1704, and is buried in Westminster Abbey. In February 1696, Lord Ashburnham wrote from Ampthill Park about his repeating watch that he had evidently bought from Tompion and which was out of order: 'It goes too slow foure houres in Twelve and sometimes stands still, I have mounted the spring as stiff as it will beare, and all will doe noe good.' He had also purchased an 'ebony pull clock' from Tompion and was enquiring about a 'white watch' which would 'hold its going true and well in the roughest exercises by sea or land'. [*Ashburnham Letter Books*, 2nd February 1696] It is possible that he was responsible for the turret clock at Ickwell Bury, 1683, but opinions are divided. A plaque marks the cottage in which he was born at Northill, and his name is inscribed on the bier in the church where his father was churchwarden. [Chris Pickford, *Bedfordshire Clock & Watchmakers*, B.H.R.S., Vol. 70, 1991, pp. 211–12]

The finest squire's church in Bedfordshire is All Saints, Sutton, the perfect country church, superbly situated at the end of its village. Here is the squire's pew of the Burgoyne family in the north aisle and behind it the monuments of all the Burgoynes from 1604 to 1938. They include a Jacobean columned memorial to John Burgoyne who appears in effigy, the handsome memorial to Sir John Burgoyne (1679) attributed to Grinling Gibbons and a splendid classical one with cherubs to John Burgoyne (1709). In the gallery is a Sacred Barrel Organ of 1830, still in perfect working order. Older parishioners can still remember the last baronet, Sir John Burgoyne, sitting in a chair in front of his ancestors, dozing in the services. There are no longer any baronets at Sutton, but the village has their legacy of good building, order and preservation. Many of the houses are timber-framed and attractive, and here and there there is an estate cottage. The pack-horse bridge over the stream is the only surviving medieval footbridge in Bedfordshire. It is first mentioned in 1504 and was kept in repair by the Burgoyne charities.

Farmers are often too busy to keep diaries, but John Pedley, who lived all his life at Great Barford, kept this sort of record in a rather terse matter-of-fact way. His life was one long round of fairs and markets; Bedford every week, Potton, Biggleswade, Ampthill and Higham Ferrers frequently, as well as smaller village fairs at Ickwell, Wilden, Bletsoe and Elstow. In December 1777, he attended Baldock fair from Barford, rising at five o'clock in the morning to travel by horse, and returning home by six o'clock in the evening. He notes: 'Was a little fatigued.' In fact Pedley was rather a hypochrondriac and continually refers to his ailments. He was much concerned with the making of a new road between Cardington and Barford bridges and constantly meets the commissioners of the road, Samuel Whitbread I and John Howard, the philanthropist. In 1773, John Howard visited him at his house; much later, in 1784, he mentions: 'Had a great dispute with Mr Whitbread.' It is interesting that a small-minded man like Pedley could argue on equal terms with one of the great landowners of the day. The new road was to link up with the Great North Road and would therefore become a vital artery for Bedford trade and traffic.

Though not a particularly educated man, Pedley sent his son to a private school at Aspley Guise. This had been founded as a classical academy in about 1720 and run first by the master, Thomas Gressam, and later by Robert Sawell. The school was situated at Guise House, the handsome red brick dwelling next door to Aspley House. Young Pedley would have been educated there along with the younger sons of the gentry, it being customary for only the older sons to go to Eton, Westminster or Harrow. Little is known about the earlier years of this academy, but in 1723 its numbers were depleted by smallpox, and in the 1780s it contained ninety-seven boarders and a staff of eight ushers. The school was probably of an Anglican persuasion, but the diarist Pedley was typical of this period of tolerance in that he was not bothered about which denomination he attended. He records going to nonconformist chapels after attending divine service at his parish church in the morning.

Pedley was obviously much concerned with bettering the lot of his family and of mankind in general. At Bedford for the Assizes in 1779 he notes: 'Saw many people from Elstow that has lately been innoculated for the smallpox – the Lord my God protect me from it.' His most ambitious expedition seems to have been in March 1785 when he journeyed to London to give evidence at Westminster Hall about the disputed county election of 1784. The contest had been so close that Andrew St John had one vote over Lord Ongley. Ongley challenged the vote of a certain William Lugsden of Little Staughton as being intended for him. St John petitioned and every single vote had to be scrutinised. Pedley was extremely reluctant to go to London and was worried all the time that he was at Westminster Hall about catching the smallpox. He met many Bedfordshire friends gathered there, but was very relieved to be paid off with six guineas expenses and allowed to return to Bedford!

Some squires and parsons were concerned about the founding of parochial libraries. There was apparently a parochial library at Cranfield as early as 1715, probably kept at the church for the use of the clergyman and church officers. In 1740 the Bromham Parochial Library was established by Thomas, 2nd Lord Trevor and was fitted up in its own room over the church porch. A slab let into the wall states: 'This small library was founded and freely given for the use of the Minister and Parish of Bromham By Thomas Lord Trevor in the Year 1740. No book to be taken out without leave of the Minister or Lord of the Manor.' In the much later volume, *Bromhamensis* (1792), Robert, 4th Lord Trevor states in a rather quaint way why his brother began it. The translation from the Latin runs like this: 'If perchance the rain lord hanging above watches over the fish, making wintry the sky which is shortly to be covered, then may the learned contents of these shelves give refreshment. The devotion of my brother proclaimed in the past that this should be publicly used by the ministers pledged to the sacred office, less a good supply of books should be lacking.'

The collection which comprises eight hundred and sixty books is fascinating because it reflects the taste and concerns of the time. Many of the volumes were from the library of Trevor himself or his wife, containing their signatures, and many show their pursuits of gardening and travel. Among them are Bacon's *The Wisedome of the Ancients* (1619), *The Office & Authority of a*

Justice of the Peace (1707), *Rapin Of Gardens* (1718), *The Clergyman's Companion* (1709), and *A Tour Through Holland* (1788). Sadly, the library has not been housed at the church since 1984.

At Caddington a library was established for the parishioners before 1770 'usually kept in the Vicarage house' but one of the vicars, Mr Champness, 'took them out of the parish'. The Cardington parochial library was begun in 1788 by John Howard and Samuel Whitbread and this still remains in the old vicarage house in the pedimented bookcase originally made for it. The Yelden parochial library was founded considerably later under the will of the Revd E. S. Bunting. [W. J. H. Watson, 'Community Libraries in Bedfordshire' 1830–1965, PhD thesis at Bedford Library]

A few of these local parsons were authors and some of the more distinguished ones funded their learned volumes by subscription. Dr Zachary Grey (1688–1766), rector of Houghton Conquest, published his edited version of *Hudibras* in 1744. He had gathered a formidable list of 1600 subscribers and nearly one hundred of these names were men and women with Bedfordshire connections. One expects to see the names of Sir Roger Burgoyne of Sutton, William Beecher of Reynold or Mr Brandreth of Toddington; more surprising readers are 'Mr William Webb Draper in Bedford' and 'Mr John Bryddal Apothecary Ampthill'. The one I like best is 'Honest Tom Martin'. Grey was a scholar of Trinity Hall, Cambridge and well-to-do. He rebuilt his rectory house in a modest Palladian style, although he preferred to winter in Ampthill among his learned friends such as Sir Simon Urlin, Recorder of London, also a subscriber to the book, who had rebuilt his handsome house in 1725. Grey's wide acquaintance must have included the artist, William Hogarth, who illustrated the book with magnificent copper plates.

No book is recorded as being printed in Bedfordshire before 1719. In that year, Mr Underhill Robinson, a member of the Stationers' Company and a freeman of London, printed his *Vindiciae Verae Pietatis Or Evangelical Sanctification truly Stated and Vindicated* at Milton Ernest. Robinson was a trained printer and the son of the Revd John Robinson, curate of Elstow and then rector of Colmworth. The printer was born at Elstow and died at Milton Ernest the same year that his book was printed. It was not until 1766 that a professional printer Bartholomew Hyatt set up his press in Bedford. [*Beds Magazine*, Vol. 20, p. 235]

VIII

Country House Ascendancy, 1700–1800

For Bedfordshire and elsewhere, the eighteenth century was the great age of the country house. For more than one hundred years, the majestic classical mansions that were rising in Portland stone or native brick in various quarters of the county became the background for a political, social and cultural life of a very high order. In most cases, the desire to build, consolidate and embellish had arrived at that precise moment when there was sufficient wealth to do so. Some families like the Russells were benefiting from political favour allied to great returns from their London estates, others, like the Ashburnhams, from judicious marriages that brought in funds from Wales and the West Country, indirectly augmenting their Bedfordshire properties. The Greys of Wrest Park had enjoyed immense privilege under Queen Anne, and the Carterets of Hawnes were to receive the same patronage under George I and George II. The lesser gentry like the Osborns of Chicksands, the Orlebars of Hinwick and the Monoux of Wootton, all benefited from the political stability of the last Stuart and the first Hanoverians, creating grand houses and gardens on a lesser scale.

The only house not to flourish in this way was poor Houghton, standing magnificently on its ridge, its turrets and gables visible for miles, but now architecturally out of fashion and vacated by its owners. Lord Ailesbury had left England for the last time in February 1698 to escape anti-Jacobite legislation and Houghton remained empty for forty years, presided over by a skeleton staff and the occasional tenant.

All the great advances in country house design, decoration and use were stimulated by the fashion of the various Hanoverian courts. The Bedfordshire aristocracy spent the season in London and were only on their estates in the summer, during the hunting and shooting months and at the New Year, but they undoubtedly felt their roots to be in the countryside. There was a great tradition of hospitality, strengthened perhaps because Bedfordshire lay on the routes northwards and was a suitable stopping place for friends and relations.

But the principal reason behind these schemes of luxury and aggrandisement was to create a suitable base for political power, dynastic liaisons and territorial control which were the bywords for success in the eighteenth century. A country house of suitable proportions, displaying both wealth and taste, impressed one's friends and enemies alike and was the focus of much trade and agriculture in the local community (see Chapter IX). It was an excellent place from which to patronise and control the local elections and to influence the handful of accredited voters in small and vulnerable seats at both county and borough elections. This was linked to the ownership of land because one's tenants were expected to vote for the cause of their landlord or state the reason why not!

The ownership of church livings was also an important ancillary to the great estate and the landowner's nominee was a crucial influence in elections and a powerful ally in the byzantine workings of the Established Church. Lord Ashburnham of Ampthill Great Parke had a private chaplain who acted as his messenger and conveyed letters as a go-between with the bishop and archdeacon. By the end of the eighteenth century the Dukes of Bedford were patrons of some thirty livings, about half of them in Bedfordshire, the Greys of thirteen, five of them in Bedfordshire. Lord St John owned five Bedfordshire livings, Lord Holland one, and the Orlebar family one. Well endowed livings were desirable and the best form of sinecure for a younger son of the country house with few other prospects.

Although rents were the mainstay of the great estates, wealth also entered the leading Bedfordshire families through judicious marriages and carefully placed investments. The wife of the 1st Lord Carteret of Hawnes Park was an heiress in her own right and owned large estates in the West Country. Her extreme longevity and the careful nurturing of her properties meant that there was a handsome inheritance for her son, the 2nd Lord, when she finally died. The 2nd Duke of Bedford married the daughter of a city merchant and acquired the funds that enabled his son to purchase all the neighbouring estates and villages near Woburn in the 1740s. Lord Trevor of Bromham Hall and the Harveys of Ickwell were descended from wealthy legal families; Sir Samuel Ongley of Old Warden was a Cornhill linen-draper and director of the East India Company, as was Sir Gregory Page-Turner of Battlesden. Both the Pym family of Hassells and the Antonies of Colworth were Dutch or India merchants and the Whitbreads of Southill were to found their fortune on the celebrated brewery. Large fortunes were to be made from prizes taken by the Navy and it was this which established the destiny of the Byng family in the late seventeenth century. Sir George Byng took part in the successful exploits against the Spanish and was created Viscount Torrington in 1721.

Late in the century, the landed families were increasingly involved with the Turnpike Trusts and therefore had interests in the development of roads, commerce and transport. By and large, their political and business influence stopped short of the towns, although the 4th Duke of Bedford began to buy property in Bedford by the middle of the century.

All of the great houses of the county were beginning to take shape by 1700. Their locations were often historical, monastic lands appropriated by private ownership in the case of Chicksands and Woburn, the site of ancient dwellings as in the case of Melchbourne, or former castles as with Odell and Ampthill. They were improved or rebuilt to cater for parade and hospitality rather than compact family living, although this was to change at the close of the eighteenth century when comfort became the essence of country house life. Their collections, like their heraldic achievements, represented a continuity of distinction which any visitor would immediately recognise. The great line of family portraits at Woburn dating back to the sixteenth century was a social birthright both impressive and awe-inspiring. The celebrated 'Warming-Pan Bed' at Chicksands, in which James II's son was supposed to have been 'introduced', reminded the county of the Osborns' royal service when the bedstead was handed down as a perquisite of office. The Duke of Kent at Wrest commissioned a magnificent state portrait of his patroness, Queen Anne, from Jacopo Amigoni (still *in situ*) and his great-grandson Earl de Grey commissioned a portrait of *his* patroness, Queen Victoria, more than a hundred years later.

Fresh ideas, new styles and a more sophisticated approach to these great inheritances were usually inaugurated after the Grand Tour of a son and heir. The seriousness of travel had been set down by Francis Bacon: 'Travel, in the younger sort, is part of education; in the elder, a part of experience.' That was the Renaissance view. Samuel Johnson's view was the general one in the middle of the eighteenth century: 'Sir, a man who has not been in Italy is always conscious of an inferiority, from his not having seen what it is expected a man should see.'

The Grand Tour was considered to be a necessary part of a gentleman's education from the middle of the seventeenth century, and almost all of the great Bedfordshire houses developed after such a Continental visit. The earliest Bedfordshire landowner to make a foreign cultural tour was probably John, 1st Lord Ashburnham who travelled through France in 1673, although he was not then resident at Great Parke. The same year, Lord Bruce visited Paris and was accompanied by Mr Arrowsmith, a fellow of Trinity College, Cambridge, as his tutor. Others followed in quick succession, usually taking the traditional routes to France and Italy, but sometimes varying this to travel through Germany and the Low Countries. They include the Earl of Kent (Wrest Park) in 1690, the 2nd Duke of Bedford (Woburn Abbey) in 1698–9, Mark Antonie (Colworth House) in 1699–1700, Lord Harrold (Wrest Park) in 1715–16, the 4th Duke of Bedford (Woburn Abbey) in 1731, the Marquess of Tavistock (Woburn Abbey) in 1761–2, Lord Ossory (Ampthill Park) in 1763–4, John Osborn (Chicksands Priory), partly a diplomatic mission, in 1766–7, the 4th Earl of Bute (Luton Hoo) in 1766 and the 3rd Earl in 1769–71, and Lord Grantham (Wrest Park) in 1801. The homecoming of the 2nd Duke of Bedford was commemorated in an ode by the Dunstable-born poet, Elkanah Settle (1648–1724). He celebrates the young man's erudition in *Sacellum Honoris* (1700): ' 'Tis Thou set'st Knowledge at a Light more fair / To See's to know, to Judge is to Compare.'

The lesser gentry tended not to go on the Grand Tour but there are exceptions. John Harvey of Ickwell Bury travelled to Italy as early as 1688–9, keeping a copious diary and noting down the pictures that he saw in Florence.

Among the dozen or so country houses that have been

mentioned, a majority survive in slightly altered form, but only three have the same family in residence from the eighteenth century. Their broad acres and handsome interiors have done much to enhance the development and importance of the county, and their privileged but beneficial culture certainly raised some remarkable figures. Bedfordshire's landed estates produced two prime ministers, Lord Goderich and Lord John Russell, a lord president of the council in Lord Carteret, an ambassador to France in John, Duke of Bedford, a secretary of state in Lord Bute, two viceroys of Ireland and, at a later date, an acting viceroy of India, Lord Ampthill. They also provided notable opposition politicians like Samuel Whitbread II, reformers like John Howard and agriculturalists such as Francis, 5th Duke of Bedford.

Probably the most fascinating and complete of these houses, whose development can be traced through a series of letters, is Ampthill Park (now Park House), then Great Parke, which was painstakingly rebuilt for the 1st Lord Ashburnham between about 1690 and 1710. The mansion still stands today, magnificently set below the greensand ridge, and looking out to the Bedford plain northwards and obliquely eastwards towards the dramatic view of Houghton a mile distant. It lost its northern park in the early twentieth century, and the great oaks that gave the place its fame in the seventeenth and eighteenth centuries are depleted, but the grandeur of the siting and the sophistication of the design are self-evident of its importance.

The Ashburnhams were a Sussex family of antiquity and significance and it was John Ashburnham, who had served Kings Charles I and II, who was rewarded with the former royal park of Ampthill in 1661. This Ashburnham never lived in Bedfordshire, but his son let the estate to the Dowager Countess of Ailesbury of Houghton and she began to build a house there in 1689. Her second son sold the new house and the remainder of the lease back to the Ashburnhams for £6500 in February 1690.

The Ashburnham who succeeded to the property and decided to live in Bedfordshire was John, 1st Baron Ashburnham (1656–1710), a grandson of Charles II's groom-of-the-bedchamber. He was described by a contemporary as a 'small dark man' but that he was also astute, able and energetic is shown by his letters. These eight volumes give a remarkable insight into the running of a great estate in the years of Queen Anne, but also a very personal glimpse of the capable and efficient peer who owned it. He was a stickler for detail, punctilious over the minutiae of farm management and intolerant of fools or knaves. Everywhere he travelled his letter-books went with him as a record of day to day transactions and woe betide the clerk or agent who was slack enough to leave them behind! There was no scrap of information omitted, whether it was the price of rabbits in Bedford market or the availability of cod-fish in London, his lordship wanted to know about it. If the letters reveal a rather dictatorial character, instructing and demanding, they also show the compassion and interest of a great landlord for his servants and dependants, the relationship with his agent, John Hutton, and his valet, Joshua Hague, being touching and humorous. Lord Ashburnham knew well that his position of wealth and influence in Bedfordshire gave him great power, but equally that the scale of his enterprises left him wide open to abuse from tradesmen and tenants. It was probably this that made him check every price and every tenancy agreement and consult with aristocratic neighbours about the wages they were paying.

Ashburnham was a sound supporter of King William III and the Protestant cause, deeply suspicious of any popish influences and no friend to anyone who did not toe the line. In 1698, when he learned that the vicar of Maulden, Thomas Pomfret (1667–1702), a minor poet of distinction, was recommended for the living of Ampthill he informed the Lord Chancellor of his disapproval in no uncertain terms.

> I think myself oblidged to aquaint yr Lordsp that Mr Pomfract is a most scandalous man to the present government as well as in his life and conversation, and that in such a place as Ampthill the consequences of such a Minister might be worthy of consideration. This little Markett Town is a place of accesse being in the heart of the County, and I have observed as many impudent passages upon all occasions against the government as I have heard off in any other part of the Kingdom and frequent meetings of discontented people have been there such I meane as the publique look upon discontented & dangerous.' [*Ashburnham Letter Books*, 28th May 1698]

Thomas Pomfret was an appointee of the Earl of Ailesbury and had served him at Houghton as page. Ashburnham had no wish to be associated with the Earl's dangerous Jacobite

Stained Glass of Princess Elizabeth and Lord Fanhope, Ampthill Church (*Hunting Engineering Ltd.*)

Lady Margaret Beaufort
(*National Portrait Gallery*)

Catherine of Aragon, *c.*1530
(*National Portrait Gallery*)

Chicksands Priory, Shefford

Chicksands Priory, Shefford, Gothic Hall

Ruins of Houghton House, Bunyan's 'House Beautiful'

Woburn Abbey, Canaletto Room (*Philip Heley*)

Woburn Abbey, Holland's Library

Vale of Woburn by C.W. Bamfylde 1750 (*Woburn Abbey Collection*)

Woburn Abbey Sheep Shearing by George Garrard A.R.A. (*Woburn Abbey Collection*)

Old Bedford Bridge by George Arnald A.R.A. (*Samuel Whitbread Collection*)

Harrold Village by Thomas Fisher, 1815

John Bunyan by Thomas Sadler, 1684 (*National Portrait Gallery*)

below left:
John Howard by Mather Brown (*National Portrait Gallery*)

below right:
Arnold Bennett, resident at Hockliffe

Luton Hoo from the air (*Harold Cox*)

An airship over Cardington, 1925

sentiments. He had other reasons to dislike the Ailesburys, although he had been on good terms with the old countess. In 1693, he had entertained the Governor of the Tower while Lord Ailesbury was incarcerated there and passed on some idle gossip. In 1695 there was a celebrated row between the two families which shook the county.

As a newcomer to Ampthill, Lord Ashburnham required a special pew in Ampthill church, distinct from that of the Earl, to accommodate his growing family and retinue. He therefore conceived the idea of constructing a gallery over his pew and the two nearest pews to provide extra seating, with an exterior staircase in the churchyard which would lead through a window and not breach the church walls. Lord Ailesbury, hearing of this, protested to the Bishop of Lincoln that the church would be darkened and the fabric damaged. Not to be outdone, Ashburnham sent a letter to a close friend of the Archbishop of Canterbury describing his intentions in great detail. He then sent his chaplain to see the Bishop of Lincoln, but the prelate was unwilling to be drawn into a dispute and recommended the advice of the Archbishop together with that of Sir Christopher Wren. Ashburnham wrote at once to the architect.

October 14th 1695

Sir
By our Bishops and my owne desire you are requested to apoint a fitt person to come downe hither on Saturday next; we survey the Church of this Parish in order to the erecting a galerie therin without prejudice to the fabrick or the inhabitants. I will take care to see the expense of this matter defrayed, and as I know you to be most capable, soe in your direction will be answered the intire satisfaction of all . . .

Wren selected his assistant Nicholas Hawksmoor (1661–1736) to visit the site and the younger architect could see no objection to Lord Ashburnham's proposals. Ashburnham replied to Wren about the certificate.

I have received your very obliding letter by Mr Hawkesmore who has taken a view of the Church and will show you the practicability of what I have proposed about a gallerie. I shall cause my Chaplain to wayte upon you tomorrow in the evening at seven o'clock at Wills Coffee House and doe now send him from hence for that purpose That he may have your Certificate to shew to the Archbishop on Tuesday morning and be back with me on Wednesday that I may direct the building the gallerie before I goe to Parliament where I must speedily attend.

Ashburnham entered in his letter-book a copy of Wren's certificate:

I doe hereby Certifye unto his Grace of Canterbury and the Right Reverend the Bishop of Lincolne, that a gallery may be erected in the Parish Church of Ampthill over the seate of the Right Honoble the Lord Ashburnham and over two small pewes adjoyning to the said seate, which said gallery may containe sixteen foot nine inches and halfe in length, and nine foot four Inches in Breadth, and that the same may be built without any prejudice to the fabrick of the said Church or impediment to the other seates therin, and that a doore allsoe may be made through one of the windowes to land into the said gallerie without any prejudice to the said fabrick. All which I have caused to be specially & carefully viewed & surveyed, By my clerk Nicholas Hawkesmore and John Crook my workman and agent upon the place. Octr 19th 1695.

The archbishop sent a covering letter to recommend the adoption of Sir Christopher Wren's ideas, but Lord Ailesbury was not prepared to take this lying down. He persuaded Dr Foster, the Commissary for Bedford, not to sign the document because technically the dimensions had to be shown. Even when this was completed Foster refused to sign and shortly afterwards the Ampthill churchwardens reported that the rector of Ampthill had received a threatening letter from Lord Ailesbury's steward. That peer now came out into the open and listed a series of objections to the gallery which were in turn answered by the other. The wretched Bishop of Lincoln was caught in the middle of this cross fire and preferred to play for time and offend nobody. Ashburnham therefore despatched his chaplain once again with the following letter to the bishop.

27th October 1695

My Lord
    This I hope will be the last time that ever you will heere further of a gallerie to be built at Ampthill for me or mine, except it be in my thanks for the lycence that I desire. Inclosed is the case of this galleries stated. My Chaplain, Mr Cunningham, is instructed soe farr as to be able to give some answer, and I hope satisfactory, to such interagatories as shall be put to him; having been an eye witness in the whole concern, he is able to make good the case which I begg your Lordsp will peruse fully, if you

have any remaining doubt or difficulty. I was indeed surprised when I read your letter and saw not the lycence but that a Caveat in your Lordsp's Court was the reason it was not granted. But at the same time I could not but admire Your Lordsp's great wisdom and justice in giving me so cleare satisfaction of the reasonablenesse of your proceedings and caution especially at this time, that more than an ordinary circumspection was necessary to cleare both your Lordsp and myself from the least colour or imputation of taking any advantage whatsoever over the circumstances of any one in the world to the prejudice of their just rights of interest.

Having had little success with the bishop, Ashburnham then tackled the archbishop once again, sending an account of his actions to his friend, the courtier Brian Fairfax. 'I have sent my Lord Arch Bp a fatt doe against the approaching festivalls, and as I used to send some venaison to his worthy predecessor soe I hope his grace will accept it from mee kindly now as I intended it. My Deer used to be counted very good; I wish this may prove soe, with my humble service which I hope & desire you will make acceptable to his Grace.' The 'fatt' Ampthill doe seems to have succeeded where letters did not, for the permit was granted at the end of 1695 and the gallery designed by Wren. By the time that Lady Ashburnham was choosing the green velvet and tassels for her cushions in 1696, Lord Ailesbury was already under suspicion and progressing towards a political exile which would have no need of pews in Bedfordshire!

Perhaps because Ashburnham had inherited a partly built mansion, perhaps because he was a veritable architect *manqué,* he watched over every detail of the building work with a careful professional eye. During the twelve years of its most active construction his lordship seldom let a day go by without cross-questioning a craftsman about his work or a contractor about his prices. 'I blame nott tradesmen for seeking good bargaines', he wrote in October 1697, 'but I abhor trickes and knavery of all kinds in bargaining or bargaines I am offered . . .' Lord Ashburnham discussed the merits of one marble or another, investigated the most economical and speedy methods of transportation and discovered the prices paid to his neighbours, so as not to be overcharged.

In the earlier years he was more concerned with the gardens than the house, planning a fountain court on the south side of the house below the great lime avenue, devising terraces, and pallisades and small garden buildings for the sloping site on which the house is situated. He consulted Queen Anne's gardener, George London, as well as the nurseryman, Nicholas Parker, about the varieties of fruit trees and plants. The lay-out of the gardens must have been on the formal French plan; this is underlined by Ashburnham's demands for box hedges to be planted and plantations to be laid out. Figs and vines were imported from France and he was meticulous in his instructions to Parker over every batch of fruit trees ordered. 'I desire you will take care that the things be all of the very best that can be had for money.' [*ibid.*, 6th March 1696–7] Parker and his son held three acres of land at Strand-on-the-Green in the early eighteenth century and received a great tribute in John Lawrence's *The Clergyman's Recreation* (1714).

Parker was also expected to provide gardeners from among his acquaintances and Ashburnham seems to have been unfortunate in his choices. George Masters was a case in point: '. . . he has suffered my gardens to run into a wildernesse notwithstanding that he has beene constantly allowed two men and a weeder woman, & that all digging planting & seeding the ground was all done and over before I went into Sussex soe that there was very little to doe of any kind . . .' [*ibid.*, 30th July 1698] Perhaps the terrain made it more difficult to work. He complains bitterly in one letter to his agent at Ampthill that the garden at Great Parke cost three times as much as his Sussex estate. [*ibid.*, 16th July 1697]

With the construction of the house, Ashburnham's energy and restlessness quite literally left no stone unturned. Within the space of ten years he had gone through most of the principal architects of the age, usually to seek advice, hesitate, and finally reject the conclusions of these professionals. In the mid 1690s he was employing Alexander Fort, a surveyor and joiner associated with Sir Christopher Wren, in 1704 he was consulting Nicholas Hawksmoor again, and in 1706 he was writing to Captain William Winde (*d.*1722). The same year he approached Thomas Archer, the best exponent of Italian baroque in England, who was soon to be employed at Wrest Park. He was also anxious to enlist the services of the statuary, Van Nost, and the decorative painter, Louis Laguerre (1663–1721), but such whims did not come to fruition. He seems to have been most successful with the Midlands architect John Lumley, who had been recommended to him by Lord Nottingham. Here he had a lesser figure of the architectural profession who was more pliable and could provide him with what he wanted. Lumley's creation must have looked very much like the famous Buckingham House in St James's Park, with balancing wings, cupolas and screened forecourt. No pictures of it survive, but an early map does give a rudimentary outline of the main front. The cental block of the mansion today is substantially Ashburnham's house although altered by Chambers sixty years later.

Ashburnham was critical of the timber he found in Bedford-shire and wrote to his Sussex agent to enquire what was available from those estates. He was contemplating the felling of 200 tons of timber at Ashburnham which would be transported to Cowden on the coast and taken to Kings Lynn by boat. It would then be brought down the Ouse to within two miles of Bedford and transported to Ampthill. It is not clear whether this amazing plan was ever put into effect. [*ibid.*, 16th May 1698] He was also using the presence of Oxford clay in Ampthill Park to enable him to start kilns for the baking of bricks on the site, a normal practice in the area.

These letters reveal how much travelling took place between the various estates, how much movement of staff there was between houses and how much the different properties supple-mented each other. Ampthill Great Parke with its rolling ridges, great oak plantations and deer was principally for recreation. One of these fascinating letters concerns the moving of Ashburnham's hounds from Sussex to Bedfordshire and is a splendid example of the peer's concern for his family and servants. He is always firm, but also persuasive, equally interested in the route to be taken as in the eczema suffered by his little son. The scene is set like a great sporting painting by Pieter Tillemans or John Wootton, one can practically hear the horses' hoofs and the jangling harness!

London Jany 31st 1697/8

Palmer
    I have inclosed sent you the perticulers of the things that I would have you send me upp hither by Joshua on his return with my sonne Jack from

Ashburnham from whence I would have him sett forth upon fryday next in the morning, soe as that he may come that day earlye in the evening to Sevenoak: I am satisfyed that Joshua will be carefull of my sonne and other matters intrusted with him in every circumstance, and I know Mr Moussac will not be wanting in the governing the child to his advantage upon the way, and I hope Jacky himself will be tractable and complyant in every thing with those that love and serve him. You must furnish Joshua with what money you think necessary for the expence of this journey, who will give me an account of it at his return, and you must allsoe advance unto Lenn the Huntsman in money sufficient to carry himself, Tinker and 16 couple of hounds to Great Parke. A Perticuler of the Crosse roads my sonne sends you in his letter as he informs mee: for I will not have the hounds come by London: Lenn will lye out two nights and noe more, and for that he must have allowance. You must give him a great charge to be careful in all his businesse. Be sure, Palmer, that a perticuler care be had of my sonne Bertram's face, and that you give me an exact account of it by Joshua. Lett Lawrence take care that Jacky's Bedd at the Inne at Senoak be well ayred and that he lye by his beddside in a Pallet Bedd.

A note of things to be brought upp by Joshua
My Black velvet Cap and Cape of the same.
Two pair of Hunting Boots and Spurs. One Hunting Whipp and
one hard Whipp. My Perruques left at Ashburnham.
My spotted muff. My large Sylver hilted Sword.
My new Quilted night Capp with Mrs Hague.

Notes of the horses to come upp and Riders on fryday next

1. The Thunder Horse.	Joshua Hague
2. The White mare	The Porter
3. The Gutts horse	Monsr Moussac
4. The welwyn horse	La Riviere
5. The Lanyns horse	Thomas farrer
6. The little Lightning horse	My sonne Jack
7. The old Padd	Lawrence

Saddles, Bridles, Armes &c as Joshua shall inform you. Lenn & Tinker Lenns Horse; and 16 couple of hounds on Monday next.

Alas, this feverish activity so vividly re-enacted through his letters was brought to an end with the death of the 1st Baron in 1710. In 1710 and 1711, the young 2nd Baron and his wife, Miss Taylor of Clapham, a Bedfordshire heiress, died successively of smallpox. These tragedies marked the end of the Ashburnhams' activities in this part of the world.

Great plans were also afoot at a country house four miles away from Amphthill, Wrest Park, already mentioned as the scene of royal visits. Here, the ancient family of Grey was rebuilding its fortunes and, interestingly, employing some of the same architects, gardeners and craftsmen that Lord Ashburnham had his eye on for Great Parke. A generation later, the grandson of Ashburnham was to marry the daughter of Wrest Park, Lady Jemima Grey in 1724.

Henry Grey, 12th Earl of Kent (1671–1740), inherited the house of his ancestors and wished to aggrandise the property and make his family the first in Bedfordshire. Being an assiduous courtier, he very nearly achieved this. Lord Chamberlain to Queen Anne (1704–10), he was created Viscount Goderich, Earl of Harrold and Marquess of Kent by 1706, and Duke of Kent in 1710. In recognition of his increased status he began to beautify the grounds at Wrest and to lay plans for redesigning the old house in a more fashionable and continental taste. Although the mansion was not greatly altered and later demolished, the gardens remain an outstanding example of early eighteenth-century formality and hold their own with any in the country.

The seventeenth-century gardens at Wrest must have been striking, even if they were not well known. The Cavalier poet, Carew, wrote of the spring that 'Pours forth her waters' into 'spacious channels' in 1641. The presence of water made the grounds particularly attractive to late seventeenth-century gardeners and the small park north of the mansion, laid out by the 11th Earl, was now increased with extensive grounds to the south, put in hand by his ambitious son, the Duke. This was formed on an axial plan, the house standing at the head of a vista which included the straight lines of the canal and an important eye-catcher at its termination. The Duke (then Marquess) of Kent was formulating his schemes from about 1706. His boldest move was to commission Thomas Archer (1668–1743) to design the Pavilion at the canal's end, which faces the house and provides the whole scene with a sophistication of French proportions. The Duke's early Grand Tour must have given him a decided taste for the Italianate and the baroque, an unusual development at the time. Archer, who had travelled to Italy a few years after the Duke, would have known his employer at court. Archer's diminutive banqueting house is a complex piece of geometric planning, a fascinating problem of a hexagon with segmental and rectangular attachments on alternate sides of it. The plan probably derived from Michelangelo's project for S. Giovanni dei Fiorentini at Rome and more closely to Borromini's S. Ivo. The immediate impression is of a chapel, and yet this building is a pleasure pavilion full of baroque grandeur and movement, with its central dome, pediments and giant order of pilasters. It is also a pleasing combination of textures, the main building being in a local yellow brick but the angle pilasters in red brick. The interior, beautifully detailed, contains ravishing trompe l'œil murals by Louis Hauduroy of 1712, fluted columns and medallioned busts in grisaille and gold. Small staircases ascend and descend to tiny servants' rooms, offices and kitchens and a regal three-seater water-closet! This building has a justifiably honourable place in an engraved plate in Colen Campbell's *Vitruvius Britannicus* (1715).

The pavilion can be seen not only from the main *clair voie* but from a number of rides that radiate about it, each in turn punctuated by clearings or small buildings. Thomas Archer designed the Hill House in 1717, another focal point which has since vanished. At the end of the Duke's life, the architect, Batty Langley (1696–1751), designed the splendid Bowling Green House of about 1740 and the first truly Palladian building to arise in the county.

The Duke used the Grand Tour of his eldest son Lord Harrold in 1715–16 to make contact with Italian architects at the Piedmontese court. Giacomo Leone drew up plans for the rebuilding of the house in 1715 and these schemes were shown to other Italian architects on the journey, notably Filippo Juvarra who prepared his own plans. The fact that the Duke did not proceed with these ideas was partly due to his loss of money in the South Sea Bubble in 1720, but also because of the death of his two sons, Lord Henry Grey in 1717 and Lord Harrold in 1723. The young widow of Lord Harrold remarried as Lady Gower and became the correspondent of the celebrated Mrs Delany. The Greys also laid the foundations of an important picture collection, the 11th Earl having bought Van Dycks from Sir Peter Lely's sale and Lord D'Arcy's in 1682–3. The Duke must have ordered the fine statue of William III by Andrew Carpentiere in front of the pavilion. Later members of the family were patrons of Gainsborough, Reynolds, Turner and Bonington.

Wrest Park is a remarkably enduring place and despite the vicissitudes of the twentieth century has retained its dignity, tranquillity and magic. Part of this is due to the tact and grace with which succeeding members of the Grey family treated their inheritance, blending new with old but skilfully retaining the bones of what had gone before. Within a few years of the Duke's death, the taste for formality had gone and the Marchioness Grey implemented a naturalising plan for the grounds in the hands of 'Capability' Brown in 1758–60. Such masterpieces as the pavilion were totally out of favour, and in 1776 Mrs Boscawen, the Admiral's daughter-in-law, called it 'an immense heavy ugly building'. But it was allowed to remain. Similarly, the Marchioness's grandson, Earl de Grey (1776–1859), created the new early-Victorian mansion in a complementary style to that of his great-grandfather's gardens. He built the new house (1839) on a drier site to the north of the old building, greatly increasing and enhancing the perspective of the ground and the pavilion to a lay-out of almost Versailles dimensions. It was small wonder that Victorian visitors thought the grounds had been laid out by Le Nôtre! Lord de Grey was not only an able politician and landowner, but an amateur architect of talent, the first President of the Institute of British Architects and the virtual begetter of the French-inspired mansion.

Today, despite the mushrooming of uncompromisingly ugly buildings to the north, the necessary appendages of the thriving National Institute of Agricultural Engineering, the grounds in the lee of the house to the south are worthily preserved by English Heritage and open to the public. The quiet rides still border the canal and intersect with here the dominating view of an urn, there the intriguing shoulder of a statue, that urge you to explore further. The high segments of trees between the walks are impenetrable and it is easy enough to lose the crowds or find oneself in a remote seat near a piece of water. Rabbits, pheasants and a few waterfowl are one's only companions and it is easy to fancy oneself back in the period of Rocque's great Plan and Views of 1735 and 1737 with its clipped yews, pleached walks and arbours.

At the gates of Wrest Park, Silsoe village straggles along the old main road from Luton to Bedford with the ironstone parish church on the park side of it. This was also paid for by Lord de Grey and carried out by the Hertford architect, T. Smith, probably with de Grey's aiding and abetting because it is an early Gothic pastiche of 1829–31. But the Greys themselves do not lie at Silsoe, but a further mile to the west, in a mausoleum attached to the parish church of Flitton. This handsome, unspoilt church has a fine wrought-iron screen in its chancel through which one gains access to the Greys' Valhalla. The first portion was established for Henry Grey, 5th Earl of Kent in 1614 and the other three interconnecting chambers added by the Duke of Kent one hundred years later. A whole school of monumental effigies open up for the visitor from the sombre magisterial tomb chests of the 9th Earl and Lady Elizabeth Talbot to the baroque pyramids of Lord Harrold and Lord Henry Grey and the splendour of the Duke and Duchess of Kent, the Duke's figure attributed to J. M. Rysbrack. (The sculptor is known to have done busts of them.) The theatrical presentation of the chapel makes one wonder who its architect was: the plan of a cross is simple enough but the disposition of the later monuments is rather ambitious. Could the instigator have been Thomas Archer who was working at Wrest during this period? This is easily the most exciting mausoleum in the county, the perfect postscript to a great eighteenth-century estate. It is often open in the summer months.

Hawnes Park, a little to the north, was the home of John, Lord Carteret (1690–1763), a man of outstanding quality. A brilliant scholar, he came away from Christ Church, Oxford in 1708 with, according to Dean Swift, 'more Greek, Latin and Philosophy, than became a person of his rank'. [*Sundon Memoirs*, Vol. 2, 1847, p. 32] He was a fluent German speaker and so became the favourite of George I and acted as his envoy to Sweden in 1719. He was at first a supporter of Sir Robert Walpole, and under his administration was Lord Lieutenant of Ireland from 1724 to 1730. During this time he became the intimate of Jonathan Swift and frequently debated with him. On one occasion Carteret defended the action of the Government so logically that Swift burst out: 'What brought you among us? Get you gone – get you gone. Let us have our boobies back again.' [*ibid.*] Popular in Ireland, Carteret was suspected of not being a real Whig and siding with the Tories and Jacobites. Years later, when asked how he governed Ireland he replied: 'I say, that I pleased Dean Swift.'

Carteret, who became Earl Granville in 1744, advised George II and was lord president of the council for twelve years till 1763. He used his beautiful Bedfordshire home for relaxation rather than political debate, a new west front was built on to the Tudor house by Ripley and he laid out drives in his grounds. His library was probably the finest in the county and he indulged himself in fishing and billiards. The great walled garden that he created is still there and produced the most magnificent fruit. 'You are vastly good to think abt fruit for Me,' Lady Granville wrote in 1745, 'but as I think None equal to ye Hawnes fruit I sh'd be sorry had ye any ripe to rob you of it.' Granville's declining years were spoilt by an addiction to the bottle, but he was sober enough in 1763 to read the Treaty of Paris on his deathbed and give an opinion!

Although Ampthill Park, Wrest and Hawnes were important aristocratic houses and Wrest was celebrated for its gardens from an early date, they were not great political houses on the model of Houghton in Norfolk, or Stowe in Buckinghamshire. Woburn Abbey, on the other hand, became increasingly important as the century progressed and the influence of the Russells reached its peak.

John, 4th Duke of Bedford (1710–71) consolidated his great inheritance through his energy and acumen in the middle of the eighteenth century. He succeeded a wastrel brother in 1732, at the age of only twenty-two, to discover that the great house at Woburn was in a state of decay and that the London properties were not producing the revenues expected of them. The young Duke was an excellent businessman and he was soon involved in shipping, in the East India Company, and in capitalising on his Bloomsbury properties. London was progressing westwards and by the 1740s Covent Garden, at the hub of the Russells' little kingdom, was the most fashionable meeting place in the city. High rents could be obtained in this now popular area and the political ascendancy of the Whigs made it an ideal climate in which the Duke could invest and profit. The increased revenues and the increased status gave him both the wealth and the will to improve the Bedfordshire estates.

In the collection of Woburn Abbey, there is a panoramic landscape watercolour of Woburn by the amateur artist Coplestone Warre Bampfylde (1719–91). In the foreground, the artist, two of his friends and a dog, stand or sprawl on a grassy knoll contemplating the great sweep of countryside before them. It is obviously high summer, the trees are in their full July leaf, docks and daisies flourish in the foreground and great heads of cloud spring up from the horizon. Just below the artist group is the old manor house of Birchmore, the home of the Stauntons in the sixteenth century; further to the right, and in the middle distance of a heat haze, is the little town of Woburn, with a wooden cupola to the church and a lantern above the market house; the date is about 1762.

But the fascination of this landscape lies in its natural features, for Bampfylde has depicted it between the age of the common field and the beginning of the enclosed estates. It is noticeable that the countryside is made up of great swathes of open land, bordered by hedges where the roads or boundaries run east and west, but before the advent of small fields. In the middle distance the folds and undulations of the ridge east of Woburn Abbey are dark with trees, while gashes of light between them denote the rides that were designed through them with a systematic formality. These are the 4th Duke's plantations, only a few years old; his too are the Palladian lodges and walls garrisoning his park and marking out the territory of his Grace's preserve, which will shortly absorb all local villages.

The Abbey is visible in the distance, gleaming white with the new Ketton stone of Henry Flitcroft's rebuilding in 1747–61 and the dimmer outline of his stables beyond. Other features start up out of the paper, in particular the Chinese fishing temple on the lake, only recently completed, and the Duke's galleon on the lake. This drawing, so redolent of the peace, quietude and order of Georgian ducal Bedfordshire, must have been painted within a year or two of the visit of the editor of *Defoe's Journey Through Great Britain*, 1761 edition. He gives an excellent summary of the scene and the changes.

The Park is fine and large, as I have said; but its great Beauty consists in the tall Woods, of which there are upwards of 500 acres; and his Grace is now planting every Year vast Quantities of Trees, and the Hills of this park, which were covered with Heath and Broom, are many of them planted with Firr-trees, whereby the black, disagreeable Prospect, is altered to a perpetual Verdure; and by this means the Duke will furnish a Supply of this Timber to his Successor, sufficient for half the County.

On the North-side of the Park his Grace has made a Plantation of Ever-greens, near two Miles long, with a fine Riding thro' them; where, in the Depth of Winter, he can ride in shelter, and through a perpetual Verdure. At the end of this Plantation is a noble Piece of Water, with an Island in the Middle, upon which is a *Chinese* Building, where, in Summer, his Grace often dines with his Company; and, on one side of this Water, the Hills, which rise to a considerable Height, are planted with Ever-greens, theatrically, which has a noble Effect when viewed from the Building.

There is also another very commodious thing in this Park, which is rarely to be found in others; that is, a great Number of small Roads through the Woods, whereby a Person may either walk or ride to every part of the Park in the wettest Time, without meeting the least Dirt. [*A Tour thro' Great Britain*, 6th Edition, 1761, Vol. 3, pp. 51–3]

This book refers to the galleon which Bampfylde had carefully put in his picture.

Before the House is a very large Bason of water, surrounded with a fine broad Gravel-walk, which is bounded by Posts and Iron Chains. On the Water is a beautiful Yacht, of between 30 and 40 Tons Burden, elegantly carved and gilt, and completely rigged, and mounts 19 Guns, which are fired on Occasion of Entertainments, &c given on board her by his Grace. There is also an elegant Boat, with a fine Awning over it; a Wherry of the common shape, and a Skiff, which are very neat, and make a beautiful Appearance on this noble Bason of Water. [ibid.]

Ten years later, Arthur Young notes of this lake somewhat laconically: 'formerly a large yacht swam in it, but rotting, it has not been rebuilt'. [Young, *Six Months Tour Through Northern England*, 1779, p. 42] Young also makes a cogent point about the lack of eye-catchers in the park. Instead of water, he writes 'what might be much easier gained, are buildings scattered about it, which would give a pleasing variety to the ridings, and for want of which, most of them are very melancholy'. This is still true today, although interest is supplied by the variety of animals.

The 4th Duke was also a great builder. Various schemes were put before him in the 1740s for improving Woburn Abbey and turning it into a seat worthy of the greatest family in the county. The Duke's chosen architect was Henry Flitcroft (1697–1769) who had worked on the Bloomsbury estate. Much of the structure of the old monastic building survived (as at Chicksands) and the difficult task with which Flitcroft was presented was the remodelling of an awkward old house that had historical or sentimental associations for the family. Therefore the work that began in 1747 saw a total remodelling of the west and south fronts of the house, but the retention of most of the early features on the north side. This immense undertaking took thirteen or fourteen years, the great rooms of parade being under construction from 1755 to 1758, the paired stable blocks in 1757 and the architect still pressing for payments as late as 1762.

It is clear that the Duke had experimented with house building in the 1730s at Stratton Park, Hampshire, which bears some resemblance to Woburn and he felt himself to be a competent judge by the 1740s. The handsome span of Flitcroft's west front with its pedimented 'middle break' and balancing end pavilions was a typical Palladian solution. It masks a central court with linking wings and the approach is through a main arched doorway into a columned entrance hall. This is not particularly striking in scale or richness and Arthur Young, visiting in 1769, calls it neither 'well-proportioned' nor 'elegant'. The rooms on the piano nobile are both, however, and are in that dignified well-behaved Palladianism one associates with the followers of Lord Burlington. Flitcroft's rather stately interiors are enlivened by some exuberant rococo details and ceilings attributed to G. B. Borra (1712–86). This slight change of style is beautifully contrasted with the traditional looking-glasses of Samuel Norman and the far more fanciful ones by Whittle and Norman, c.1755. Despite later alterations, the majority of the rooms on the west front retain the stamp of their day, particularly the lavish decor of the State Salon with its lofty coffered ceiling and Corinthian doorcase.

The Duke also saw to it that a greater degree of comfort was introduced for his household. The original drainage system was renewed, fresh reservoirs were created for the water supply and, most revolutionary of all, a water-closet was installed for the specific use of His Grace in 1748–9. This was situated in the

North Garden away from the house, later to be embellished with fine woodwork, brass and tiles. By 1760 there were three other water-closets in use including one inside the house for Lord Tavistock. There was also a 'cold bath' and a 'hot bath' for the use of the family, but most of the household had to use portable tubs in their rooms. A great innovation was the importing of French earthenware stoves for heating the staircases and corridors; although they were termed 'Dutch stoves' they were purchased from Paris in 1756 and must have greatly improved the comfort in winter.

The Continental bias of the Woburn collection not only reflects fashionable enthusiasms, but the Duke's interest in European culture. He had made the Grand Tour in 1731 before succeeding to the title, so that his interests were registered more by his memory than his pocket. He was obviously dazzled by the virtuoso performance of Canaletto's paintings in Venice and by 1732 was in a position to order an important series from the artist. This commission was worked on by Canaletto for a number of years and resulted in the breath-taking group of twenty-four pictures destined for Bedford House, Bloomsbury and eventually Woburn. As was the case with most Canaletto works for the English market, the deal was handled by Consul Smith of Venice and bills exist for substantial sums in 1734 and 1736. The whole series is on view in the Canaletto Room at Woburn Abbey.

The Duke was an important patron of the young Thomas Gainsborough (1727–88) as well as of the marine artist, Samuel Scott, and the landscapist, George Lambert. As a devotee of the portrait, the Duke was also a patron of Sir Joshua Reynolds (1723–92), first President of the Royal Academy, whose portraits are still in the house.

The Duke's public life was busy, raising a regiment against Prince Charles Edward in 1745, as Secretary of State for the Southern department 1748–57, Lord Lieutenant of Ireland 1756–60 and Ambassador to France 1762–3. This last appointment, which involved the fitting up of three grand houses in France *à la française*, probably resulted in the purchase of much of the French furniture and objects of art still at Woburn. The Duke and Duchess were francophiles, popular with Louis XV and Madame de Pompadour, and patrons in a small way of the Sèvres porcelain factory. After the successful negotiations of the Treaty of Paris by the Duke (to conclude the Seven Years' War) the Duchess was presented in 1763 with the celebrated *bleu lapis* dinner-service, comprising 183 separate pieces, most of which survive.

The Duke had inherited a notable library and this was now supplemented by the latest works on architecture, art, shipping and travel. He acquired the gardening books of Philip Miller, who was director of the Chelsea Physick Garden and was employed by his grace at £20 per year 'for inspecting my garden, hot houses, pruning the trees etc, and to come to Woburn at least twice a year, oftener if wanted'.

Woburn was a show place from the beginning and as with Wrest and Luton Hoo, accredited visitors were admitted to the grounds and house at certain times. Mrs Boscawen visited Wrest in this way in 1776 and Dr Samuel Johnson walked round Luton Hoo in 1781 making aphorisms. Strangely enough there was no guide to Woburn Abbey before Stephen Dodd's *History* of 1818 and nothing on Wrest before 1899.

The 4th Duke's second wife was Gertrude Leveson-Gower whom he married in 1737 and it was her younger sister Lady Evelyn Leveson-Gower who became the new chatelaine of the Ampthill estate in 1744. She married the head of the Fitzpatrick family, the 1st Lord Gowran. It may have been an intentional act of the Duchess of Bedford to settle her sister in the centre of Bedfordshire, strengthening the Bedford interest. Between 1732 and the end of the century, the Whig party dominated the county and the Bedfords' relations or friends were normally the members of parliament. The Fitzpatricks, who had bought the Ampthill estate, were certainly politically allied to the Russells and, as it turned out, shared many of their cultural and sporting enthusiasms as well. Lady Gowran's son was created 1st Earl of Upper Ossory in 1751 and was succeeded by his son as 2nd Earl in 1758. The young Earl therefore had the Duke of Bedford as both his uncle and guardian and the ties between the two houses were very strong until the young man came of age. Cambridge and a great preoccupation with the turf were followed by the Grand Tour and a great interest in the arts. The 2nd Lord Ossory was in fact to spend more money on Park House than anyone since Ashburnham. Ossory was considered a very promising youth and was spoken of highly by Horace Walpole who met him in Paris. David Hume (1711–76), the philosopher, met him on the same occasion, a fact that is recorded by the scurrilous C. Piggot in *The Jockey Club*. 'Many years ago,' wrote Piggot, 'when David Hume was Charges des Affaires at Paris, he pronounced him the most promising young Nobleman of all the English then abroad; yet he has represented the county of B-d in several Parliaments, and never given any specimen of his abilities.'

This is rather unfair criticism of someone who devoted his life to the interests of Bedfordshire in Parliament, in the Militia and in local affairs. He was M.P. for County Bedford 1767–94 (as an Irish peer), Lord Lieutenant of the county from 1771 and a Colonel of the Bedfordshire Militia. The circumstances of his married life were somewhat unusual and in many ways affected his life at Ampthill Park and his place in society. Lord Ossory had an amatory relationship with Anne Liddell, Duchess of Grafton, the estranged wife of the 3rd Duke of Grafton in 1767. A daughter was born to them in August 1768 but it was March 1769 before the Duchess obtained a divorce by Act of Parliament allowing the Earl to marry her. This scandal had considerable reverberations and the couple were not accepted at court, nor much seen in London, and had to make their own life in Bedfordshire. Piggot refers to Lady Ossory as a 'slippery damsel' [*Jockey Club*, 1792, p. 21] but also adds of the Ossorys 'they have always enjoyed a considerable portion of domestic happiness'. [*ibid.*, p. 90]

Anne, Countess of Ossory (post 1736–1804) was a woman of exceptional abilities, wit and charm. Her isolation in the country and her clever receptive ear made her the ideal correspondent for that voluminous letter-writer Horace Walpole (1717–97). For twenty-seven years until his death, the countess received these flattering, informative and amusing epistles in her post-bag, Walpole coming himself on numerous occasions to stay with her. 'Keep the Graces and the Duke of Dorset at Ampthill', Walpole wrote to her in 1773, 'assemble everything that is agreeable round you, shine at the head of them, and do not imagine that your sisters will improve by being educated in London, where, what will they see that are better models?' [*Letters*, Vol. 6, 1906, p. 38]

Lady Ossory took Walpole at his word, and her country house became a centre for some of the most brilliant men of the age. Ossory created a wonderful environment for his Countess, remodelling the Ashburnham house, giving it a much updated entrance front and replacing the old balancing wings with more classical versions. Probably on the advice of the Duke of Bedford, Ossory employed the influential neo-classical architect, Sir William Chambers (1726–96), to carry out the work, including a magnificent salon with a ceiling by Joseph Rose. All this survives.

The Ossorys were considerable patrons of the arts and it was no accident that Chambers, the first treasurer of the Royal Academy should have been their friend. He was followed shortly afterwards by the sculptor, Joseph Wilton R.A., and then by Sir Joshua Reynolds himself to paint the Ossorys' daughter as 'Sylva' and 'Collina'. In fact, the infant days of the Royal Academy of Arts were planned here in the Ossorys' rooms. Horace Walpole wrote in December 1780, 'I dote on Ampthill.' [*Letters*, Vol. 7, 1906, p. 470] Well he might, because at one house-party in October 1776, the guests included Edward Gibbon (1737–94), David Garrick (1717–79) and his wife, as well as Walpole himself! The Ossorys' cousin Charles James Fox (1749–1806) was another visitor. The Earl was a supporter of the theatre and organised amateur theatricals at Ampthill; his wife regaled Walpole with details of these frivolities. Later, in 1779, Lord Ossory was a pall-bearer at Garrick's funeral. A great intimacy too existed between Lady Ossory and Sir Joshua Reynolds; she embroidered him a waistcoat in the house and her husband was remembered in the artist's will, being left the first choice of his studio. Many of these guests, Gibbon and Walpole in particular, were impressed by the comfort of the house and its splendid library.

Wrest Park was not so powerful in these later years. The house was occupied by the Marchioness Grey who had followed the Duke of Kent and she was elderly and surrounded only by widowed daughters. The Greys were intellectuals and many important foreigners visited the house, but the family were less and less radical as time passed and further and further away from their neighbours politically.

If Ampthill was frequented by the artists, writers and actors of the age, Woburn Abbey was increasingly a political house at the end of the century. Under the young bachelor 5th Duke of Bedford, it was a focus for the Whigs and particularly that brand of Whiggery fostered by Fox and adopted with enthusiasm by George, Prince of Wales and the Carlton House set. They broadly approved the changes in France, following the Revolution, they were unashamedly francophile and came to be admirers of Bonaparte. This divide from the court party and the Tories was almost as much cultural as political; they preferred French style, French art and liberal learning. Henry Holland was their architect and very soon after coming of age, the 5th Duke was tearing down Chambers' neo-classicism at Woburn and replacing it with the purer Louis XVI style of Holland.

The other characteristics of Francis, Duke of Bedford are provided by such observers as Horace Walpole who witnessed the young Adonis going to court in 1791. 'The Duke of Bedford eclipsed the whole birthday,' he wrote, 'by his clothes, equipage and servants: six of the latter walked on the side of the coach to keep off the crowd – or to tempt it: for their liveries were worth an argosie.' [Walpole to Miss Berry, 8 June 1791, *Letters*, Vol. 9, 1906, p. 323]

The Duke, so serious minded in some respects was an odd mixture of plain living and great extravagance. His resplendent appearance at court contrasted with his modest attire in the country and his great alterations at Woburn were chiefly for his male friends and his mistresses as noted in 1789 by Isabella Elliot.

'The house we could only look at from without, for it is only shown on Mondays,' she comments. 'The Duke is altering and enlarging it at a great expense, although nobody ever inhabits it but Mrs Hill, an old madame.' [*The Life and Letters of Sir Gilbert Elliot*, Vol. 1, 1874, p. 301] Piggot notes that the Duke had gone on the Grand Tour with one lady friend before installing Mrs Hill at the Abbey. It is an odd conclusion that the superb interiors at Woburn by Henry Holland, the decorations by George Garrard and Signor Biagio Rebecca, and the richly exotic Chinese Dairy were created for a succession of actresses and females of the demi-monde like Mrs Hill and Nancy Parson, Lady Maynard. The Duke's circle was cosmopolitan and libertine, including the then Duke of Devonshire and his mistress, as well as Lady Elizabeth Foster, Sir Harry Fetherstonhaugh and Richard Brinsley Sheridan, not to mention the Prince Regent himself. Sheridan records a houseparty in July 1800 when almost the entire Opposition were staying at the Abbey. The Duke also had a retreat at Oakley House in the north of the county, over-looking the River Ouse, also beautifully transformed by Holland; this was mostly lived in by his brother Lord John, afterwards 6th Duke.

The political constituents of Woburn Abbey were equalled by the Whig stronghold of Southill Park, fifteen miles away. Samuel Whitbread (1720–96), a Bedfordshire man, had founded the famous brewery in Chiswell Street and returned to the county in 1795 when he bought the Southill estate and the manor of Gastlyns. His son, Samuel Whitbread II (1764–1815), was the distinguished radical statesman, M.P. for the borough of Bedford from 1790 to 1815, and a close ally of Charles James Fox. It was under his direction that the mansion was remodelled by Henry Holland, a fine working library established and an important art collection begun. The interiors at Southill, which remain intact, are probably the most perfect surviving rooms of the Regency, not merely in the county but in England. Here one can see the original silk curtains and pelmets in the windows, the original furniture by Marsh and Tatham, and portraits by Gainsborough in the setting for which they were designed.

Whitbread was one of the few Bedfordshire figures of this time to move on a national as well as a county stage. He was a leading opponent of William Pitt, a prime mover in the trial of Lord Melville, a friend of Princess Caroline of Wales and a promoter of the Drury Lane Theatre. His country mansion with its strange retinue of important politicians and stray hangers-on was a forcing house for ideas and party loyalties. Thomas Creevey captures this atmosphere in his diary entry for 30 October 1809: 'Arrive at Whitbread's – Southill, Bedfordshire, – Whitbread and Lady Elizabeth Whitbread (sister to Lord Grey) quite delighted to see us. Nothing but politicks between Whitbread and me from the moment we meet just before dinner till bedtime.' [Creevey, *Memoirs* Vol. 1, 1904, p. 109] Whitbread was deeply involved with the county at a local level, but we must leave that to the next chapter.

IX

The Land and the Landscape

Francis, 5th Duke of Bedford was a vigorous and able man, a patron of art and agriculture, but also addicted to the excesses of his age. The great interiors of Woburn Abbey were being created for his exclusive use rather than for the use of a family, and the library and its ante-rooms were ideal for the kind of gatherings that the Duke most liked to host. These would include the great landowners of the period, but also the foremost agriculturalists, the inventors of ploughs and harrows, the breeders of cattle and sheep, men engaged with experiments on grass, wheat or oats. The Swiss writer Marc-Auguste Pictet (1752–1825) describes the rather informal atmosphere of Woburn in its heyday.

> The drawing room where one usually meets is the Duke's library; we found there an interesting gathering but of men only. Dinner which was more like supper as it was nearly eight o'clock, was merry without being noisy. General and private conversation was well sustained, we came back to the drawing room for coffee and tea, which, in this country quickly follows, then each one left as they pleased; We stayed amongst the last talking round the fire. [Houfe *Through Visitors' Eyes*, 1990, p. 173]

This meeting of minds among men with common interests was the background to the Duke's celebrated agricultural shows held in Woburn Park. From the middle of the 1790s, he held Sheep Shearings which were agricultural gatherings at which experiments were carried out and machinery was demonstrated. These rather modern events were preceded by breakfasts, and the open days received considerable coverage in the press as well as visits from such noted authorities as Arthur Young (1741–1820). In 1794, four acres of the park were divided by hurdles and different breeds of sheep placed behind them and fed on turnips or grass. They were then weighed and the South Downs were found to have done best, closely followed by the Leicesters.

The Sheep Shearings were something of a social occasion, best commemorated in the handsome oil paintings and engravings by George Garrard A.R.A., which were published as 'Woburn Sheepshearing' in May 1811. This shows the various divisions of the exhibition taking place near the Woburn Model Farm with the distinguished visitors looking on. This includes the shearing itself, the display of hides and inspection of broad cloth, the showing of oxen, the demonstration of ploughs and waggons and the sale of animal models by an artist. The company includes portraits of all the most distinguished agriculturalists of the day as well as an envoy from the Russian court and representatives of the Board of Agriculture and its Secretary, Arthur Young. The Duke of Clarence is present, so too are the Revd Henry Bate Dudley, Mr Fary, Secretary to the Smithfield Club, Sir Watkin Williams Wynn, Sir Joseph Banks K.B., Thomas William Coke of Norfolk, Sir Harry Fetherstonhaugh, Lord Egremont and the Duke of Manchester. Among the local grandees who were agricultural improvers one finds Lord Ossory, Lee Antonie, Samuel Whitbread, Mr Higgins, Sir George Osborne, Sir John Sebright, Mr Thomas Gibbs, the Ampthill nurseryman, and William Salmon, Surveyor of the Woburn estate.

Arthur Young's earliest visit to Bedfordshire had been in 1769 when he recorded his impressions of its countryside in *A Six Month's Tour Through The North of England*. Young questioned the farmers about their soil, their crops and their rotation in every village he entered. He was quick to commend innovations and equally quick to condemn slovenly work. At Houghton Regis he noted the chalk on the high ground, black clay on the low land and a rotation of fallow land with wheat, peas, beans or oats, then turnips and barley. He was critical of the lack of hoeing and the yields. 'When beans alone, they stir twice, sow some broad cast, and some after the plough; 2½ bushels per acre, but never hoe; twenty-five bushels the medium produce. They give two tilths for turnips, hoe them twice, and always feed off with sheep. So few for this crop cannot be too much condemned.' [*Tour*, p. 27] He found the farms round Milton Bryan much smaller than in the Dunstable region and lying on a mixed clay and gravel ground. They grew mostly wheat and barley and few oats, the wages for the labourers varying according to the season. 'In harvest, 35s. a month and board and carriage of a load wood. In hay time, is 1s.

4d. a day, and small beer. In winter, 10d. a day, and small beer. Reaping wheat, 3s. to 4s. 6d. Mowing grass, 1s. 4d. and 1s.6d.'

It is interesting to note that although this was in the days of the 4th Duke of Bedford, improvement was already in the air. Young commends the Duke for raising large crops of carrots on the sandy part of his property where nothing else grew: 'it is to be regretted that the neighbouring farmers do not follow so excellent an example'. [*Ibid.*, p. 32] He was also impressed by the experimental ground in Woburn town, where a Mr Bramstone had developed trefoil and lucerne grasses as well as types of bird grass, fox-tail and dog's-tail.

The Woburn Sheep Shearings were usually held on about five consecutive days in the middle of June and those of 1799 and 1800 were particularly well reported in *The Annals of Agriculture*. Although the competitions and premiums offered by the Duke were taken up nationally, there was a strong Bedfordshire element and several prizes for Bedfordshire men and Bedfordshire experiments alone. In 1799 for example 'Mr Potts' Bedfordshire plough from Silsoe' was highly recommended because 'with two middle-sized mares' it 'ploughed two roods and nine poles in three hours and three minutes' and was thought a better performer than the Norfolk plough. [*Annals*, Vol. 33, p. 311] Another premium of 5 guineas was for the 'best two-shear fat weather' sheep 'bred in Bedfordshire' – the winner being Mr Butterfield of Potsgrove. At this meeting the great rivalry developed between Mr Coke of Norfolk and the Leicestershire Tup Club over the superiority of the new Leicester breed and the South Downs, neither side accepting the challenge of the other. This controversy spilled over into the columns of the Leicester and Northamptonshire newspapers with letters signed 'A Friend To Truth' and 'Leicester'. The editor considered that bets placed on these trials of different breeds over four years would be more worthwhile than horse-racing. 'The attention of the farming world would be strongly excited, and the consequences in general would be excellent, whatever the result might prove upon the particular question.' [*ibid.*, p. 435]

The 1800 meeting was particularly successful, with two hundred farmers and landowners dining at Woburn on every day except the last. Visitors came from Ireland, Northumberland and

Shropshire as well as from neighbouring counties and representatives from Prussia. There was a large number of local clergy among the exhibitors, many of whom held glebes and had taken a keen interest in the enclosure of the common lands or had considered the agriculture of their parishes scientifically. The Revd Markham of Northill, writing to Mrs Harvey of Ickwell Bury in June 1800 said: 'I attended the sheep shearing, & I believe was thought a knowing one with *my own spur*, for Sir John Sebright came up to me and very seriously asked my Opinion concerning the Weight of two Devonshire Heifers wch were exhibited.' [C.R.O. HY93/2]

The Duke's chief experimenter at Woburn was also a clergyman, one of those brilliant eccentrics that the Anglican church throws up from time to time. Dr Edmund Cartwright (1743–1823) had been a fellow of Magdalen College, Oxford, was rector of Goadby Marwood in Leicestershire, but more interested in inventions than in his ministry. He was the reputed inventor of the power-loom for weaving and a wool-combing machine, but went bankrupt as a result of his inventions in 1793. By 1800 he was being retained by the 5th Duke and was living at Woburn and working on the Model Farm. Marc-Auguste Pictet met him there in 1802, describing him as 'very knowledgeable in agriculture and mechanics'. Pictet also mentions the Duke's more elaborate schemes which were interrupted by his untimely death. 'On the way back [from visiting a threshing mill] we saw a very pretty house which the Duke is having built with the intention of turning it into a boarding school or a college of agriculture to be headed by Mr Cartwright. The art of farming could not be studied in any better way.' [Houfe, *Through Visitors' Eyes*, 1990, p. 172] Later, in 1804, Arthur Young wondered whether the outlays which the 6th Duke of Bedford was incurring on some of his experiments were really worth it. 'Cartwright has built him a steam engine (£700) for threshing and grinding,' he comments, '12 per cent interest in the least to be calculated, or £84, and yet a one-horse mill, price £50, would thresh all the corn that will ever be brought to this yard.' [*Autobiography of Arthur Young*, Ed. M. Betham Edwards, 1898, p. 396]

But in 1800, Young's plaudits in print for the Woburn Sheep Shearing were unequivocal, whatever feelings he may have harboured privately. 'May the new century open auspiciously to the plough! May the spirit of this sheep shearing improve the flocks of Britain! May her fields smile again with ample harvests, her wastes by a GENERAL INCLOSURE covered with cultivation, her farmers rich, her poor well fed and happy: and may we all, by reverence of THAT BEING from whom all blessings flow, endeavour to deserve them!'

Arthur Young continued to make his yearly visits to Woburn in the 1800s, although with a growing distaste for the extravagant living of many of the participants. His strongly held Christian views made him more and more a champion of oppressed people and his compassionate spirit was aroused on a visit to a Bedfordshire village in 1800.

'My adventures increase and have a strange similitude,' he writes in the privacy of his diary.

Passing through Millbrook, near Lord Ossory's, some cottages with corn in their gardens, on the slopes of a narrow sandy vale, caught my eye, but speedily passing it was a second thought to stop the horse and walk down to them. There are thirteen of them, and all inhabited by owners. A hemp weaver, who lives in the first I entered, gave me an account of them all, and amongst the rest he named Underwood's, who had a large family, and was sadly poor. I went to it. Poor indeed! the cottage almost tumbling down, the wind blowing through it on every side. On a bed, which was hardly good enough for a hog, was the woman very ill and moaning; she had been lately brought to bed, and her infant was dead in a cradle by the bedside. What a spectacle! She had four children living: one, a little girl, was at home, and putting together a few embers on the hearth. My heart sank within me at the sight of so much misery, and so dark, cold, tattered and wretched a room. Merciful God, to take the little child to Himself, rather than leave it existing in such a place. What a sight! I entered another cottage, which was lately built, neat and cheerful, the Widow Scarboro's; she earns something, by washing, but her smoky chimney most uncomfortable. No wonder, with the old broad high fireplace. In the depth of winter the door must be open. I told her how to cure it, but I wished to give her a Rumford grate and see it fixed. Impossible! and her evils are nothing to poor Underwood's.

. . . These poor people know not by what tenure they hold their land; they say they once belonged to the duke, but that the duke has swopped them away to my Lord [Lord Ossory]. How little do the great know what they swop and what they receive! What would be a blessing poured into their hands if they knew how to use it. What a field is here! How very trifling the repairs to render these poor families warm and comfortable! Above their gardens on one side there is a waste fern tract now enclosed, from which small additions might be given them, yet would enable them to live from their ground at least much better than at present. What have not great and rich people to answer, for not examining into the situation of their poor neighbours?

To Woburn Abbey. Here is wealth and grandeur and worldly greatness; but I am sick of it as soon as I enter these splendid walls. I had rather be among the cottagers at Millbrook had I but the means of aiding them. I will see Lord Ossory, and try to do something for them.'
[ibid. pp. 331–3]

It is still quite easy to look down on the village of Millbrook from the high road as Young must have done two hundred years ago. It is a less open landscape than in those days, the 'fern tract' is now an evergreen wood, but the cottages or their successors still cluster at the bottom of the dingle and the church sits dramatically above on its hill crest. There are still a few cottages of the 1800s but most are the estate workers' houses of a mid-Victorian date. Perhaps Young's strictures had some effect on Lord Ossory; the surviving cottages might have been rebuilt by him, but more significant is another row in Woburn Street, Ampthill. These were built by Lord Ossory between 1812 and 1816 in a *cottage orné* style with thatched roofs and half timbering, very picturesque and of an early style for the county. Here perhaps is an example of Ossory trying 'to do something for them'.

Still earlier in date are the charming grouped and dated cottages at Cardington, all built by the philosopher squire and prison reformer, John Howard (1726–90). They are dated 1762 and 1764 and are in a pleasing vernacular style, not in the least ornamental, but simply traditional. They include the former almshouses behind the church and the original workhouse, and with such a benevolent landlord it is hardly surprising that such excellent work was done. In 1782, a census of Cardington was carried out at the instigation of John Howard and Samuel Whitbread, probably by the village schoolmaster, James Lilburne. Its exact purpose is not known, but it seems to have been a survey into the condition of the cottagers and their lives with some scheme for betterment. Such work was a sign of increased interest in the estate village and the rural population in general. [*B.H.R.S.*, Vol. 52, 1973] Ebenezer Maitland, travelling through in September 1783, called it 'the prettiest village I ever passed through'. In particular, he said: 'The church is exceedingly

neat, as are all the Houses, which are plaster and all numbered.'
[Houfe, *Through Visitors' Eyes*, 1990 (p. 112].

At this time Cardington was partly owned by Howard and partly owned by the Whitbread family. Lord Torrington wrote that they 'strive which shall most benefit and adorn it, for what cannot the riches of the one and the charity of the other accomplish'. '[*Torrington Diaries*, Vol. 4, p. 109] The Cardington and Southill estates were united in 1820 and this may account for the great similarity of style in the estate cottages at Southill, 1796–7, 1800 and 1815, with their honey-coloured rendering and thatch. It is certainly the case that Samuel Whitbread II cared about the condition of his tenants as much as any landowner in the county, and generally more than most. He was a justice of the peace and also an overseer of the poor in the parish of Southill from 1806 till his death. In these roles he was able to look into the condition of the workhouses, obtain legal advice where necessary and order overseers to act in cases of sickness. Many applicants made the journey to Southill Park to put their cases to Whitbread in person in his justice room. He was particularly interested in housing, and cases came before him of slum dwellings at Clifton, of a woman 'living in a mud cottage' at Maulden and a poor family at Houghton Conquest whose home had been unroofed by the landlord. Whitbread copied all these cases meticulously into notebooks, eighty per cent of the earlier entries being in his own hand, although later years are in the hand of a clerk. As a justice and humanitarian he was very prompt in arguing on behalf of hardship cases, but he was equally dismissive of applicants who were not truly needy. He was progressive in medical matters, recommending that the whole parish of Langford be vaccinated after an outbreak of smallpox and sending diseased parishioners to the Bedford Infirmary. [*B.H.R.S.*, *Samuel Whitbread's Notebooks, 1810–11, 1813–14*. Ed. A. F. Cirket, Vol. 50, 1971]

At about this period (1804), the Board of Agriculture was offering premiums and a gold medal for 'the best and cheapest cottage' for a labouring family on an estate with one third of an acre of land for their own use. The line of cottages at Melchbourne known as The Street are estate workers' cottages, neat without being particularly ornamental, built at the end of the eighteenth century by Lord St John. The 12th Lord St John had married Emma Louisa Elizabeth, the sister of Samuel Whitbread, and her money was beautifying the village. Improvement often went hand in hand with a deep religious conviction and this was the case with Lady St John, a dedicated evangelical, and friend of William Wilberforce. She entirely rebuilt the church of St Mary Magdalene in the village, leaving the medieval tower, but creating a handsome Georgian preaching house. It is a unique eighteenth-century interior in this county, nothing like it surviving elsewhere, its box pews, family pew, pulpit and classical arcading exactly as conceived in 1780. She also presented to the church a Wedgwood black basalt font, similar to the one presented by the Whitbreads to Cardington. This no longer survives at Melchbourne but the set of neo-classical communion plate, the gift of Lady St John, does.

Country landowners may well have been keen to put up new dwellings in place of old, for the new ones had no obligations of common rights connected with them. During the whole of this period from 1750 to 1840, parish after parish was being enclosed by local Acts of Parliament. The enclosure of the common land removed a valuable asset from the farm labourers who happened to have common rights handed down to them. To an eighteenth-century day labourer the possibility of grazing a few sheep on the common or collecting firewood in winter without charge was a great addition to his meagre wage. Although small independent farmers tended to decline after the enclosure acts, there is little evidence that the new measures wiped out a sturdy yeoman class. Most philanthropists like Arthur Young felt that this rationalisation of the land made economic sense for landlord and tenant, the fields were correctly managed and the yields improved. When the commissioners came to look at individual villages, many of the common rights were already in the hands of absentee landlords or local tradesmen. However, a village that was enclosed often came into the hands of just one landlord, who preferred to lease his land out in large parcels to substantial farmers. This tended to lock out the small man from climbing the social ladder to independence and ultimately a smallholding of his own.

Unrest resulting from Parliamentary Enclosures of common land was mercifully rare in Bedfordshire. At Harrold in 1770, the steward of Marchioness Grey had some trouble with villagers who claimed partial rights on land when it was not being used for arable farming. The steward could have settled the dispute by paying the cottagers off with money, but as this was not done some violence took place.

A more serious incident occurred at Maulden in 1796 where the parliamentary commissioners had decided to enclose land on the moor that was used by cottagers for grazing cattle and cutting turf for fuel. Although the commissioners had set aside an allotment for this purpose, the villagers were not appeased. A crowd of about two hundred people obstructed the land and prevented a survey from taking place. A local magistrate appealed to the War Office and a troop of cavalry was sent to Ampthill in case a riot should break out. Maulden was a very independent village on the greensand ridge, made up chiefly of small market-gardeners who would be more concerned about preserving their trade.

This was the background to the years that saw the French Revolution on the other side of the Channel. During the last decade of the eighteenth century there were exceptionally poor harvests and the price of bread rose alarmingly. In 1800, Pawsey, the Wrest Park steward, noticed that even respectable farmers were eating barley bread and he ordered old does to be killed in the park and given to the poor. The same year he ordered barrels of herrings from London to feed the needy in Silsoe, at first an unacceptable alternative to meat, which they gradually agreed to eat. [Godber, *History of Bedfordshire*, 1965, p. 415] It is noticeable, however, that the surviving Regency country houses and farms in this area still have bars across the windows of their larders and kitchens rather than their living-rooms and libraries!

The problems were exaggerated by a massive growth of almost fifty per cent in the population of the county between 1801 and 1831. This was partly due to the spread of inoculation against smallpox, a tremendous blessing in itself, but it did not mean that the ordinary person was better housed or fed.

The new breed of landowner was probably aware of all this even if he did not have the religious zeal of Lady St John. He probably wanted to house his employees well, but at the back of his mind was the desire to create a Gothick hamlet that was part of his park scenery and generally redolent of a feudal well-being. The Gothic

Revival had not come particularly early to Bedfordshire although Lady Pomfret had planned a Gothick farm at Westoning in July 1755 to suit her 'Gothick Imagination'. That year, Mr Wade-Gery had asked Isaac Ware to design a Gothick mansion at Bushemead Priory and the fine model for it still belongs to the family. Neither project had come to fruition. More successful were the Gothick alterations by Ware for Chicksands in 1749 and the Catherine Cross in Ampthill Park, designed by James Essex for Lord Ossory, with a verse inscription by Horace Walpole. This last, charming monument, commemorating Catherine of Aragon, still stands sentinel in its park landscape.

Two amusing experiments in Gothick design were carried out in the centre of the county in the early 1800s, both single buildings rather than schemes. Humphry Repton (1752–1818), the well known landscape gardener, had remodelled Woburn Park in about 1806 in accordance with the most advanced principles of picturesque gardening. In 1811, he designed Aspley Wood Lodge for the Duke of Bedford, on the extremities of the estate near Woburn Sands and now almost on the county boundary. This little vernacular building was designed at the Duke's wish as an example of architecture 'prior to the reign of Henry VIII'. Details were taken from Lynn, Kelvedon and St Edmondsbury and the cottage garden was designed for flowers that appeared in the Tudor portraits at Woburn Abbey. It survives miraculously today, although the knoll behind is now densely wooded and the position rather dark and gloomy for what must have been conceived as a witty jeu d'esprit. It is easily seen from the main road from Woburn Sands to Woburn.

In 1808, Sir Gregory Osborne Page-Turner employed Repton to lay out the gardens at Battlesden, only half a mile from the ducal estate. Page-Turner was an immensely rich young baronet who commissioned architects and artists in a wild and capricious manner and was slightly mentally unbalanced. In 1818, he paid the artist George Shepherd (1784–1862) to paint an elaborate watercolour of the completed gardens. This shows iron conservatories and treillage buildings set in luxuriant flower gardens, but incorporating a rustic cottage and the tower of Battlesden church as part of the scene. The painting also shows Page-Turner, his bride, his mother and his brother and sister-in-law strolling through the grounds in the height of fashion. It is not perhaps surprising that Page-Turner was declared bankrupt in 1823 with liabilities of £100,000. The mansion and the gardens have vanished, but Battlesden still remains one of the most forgotten and remote of the Bedfordshire villages.

Humphry Repton had been laying out landscapes in the county from the 1790s and Lord Torrington gives an amusing glimpse of him in one of his diaries. Torrington had grown up at Southill and continued to haunt the inns of Biggleswade and Eaton Socon after his family had ceased all connection with the place: his penetrating eye missed no detail of his fellow travellers!

> . . . At 10 o'clock I intended my ride (Garwood to go alone, and prove his horse, and his horsemanship) but Mr Repton – the now noted landscape gardener – came in, and delay'd me for ½ an hour: he is a gentleman I have long known, and of so many words that he is not easily shaken off; he asserts so much, and assumes so much, as to make me irritable, for he is one (of the many) who is never wrong; and therefore why debate with him?
>
> I wondered that he should not keep his own post chaise, and he wondered at my riding; so wonders never cease! I left him at breakfast; and took my ride to Gastlings, and More Hall Farms; but both the Mr W's were gone to our fair. I had left word at the inn, that I hoped they would dine with me.
>
> At 9 o'clock Mr R[epton] return'd from his visitation in this neighbourhood; to draw his plans, and to relate his journies, his consequence, and his correspondence. Scarcely any man who acquires a hasty fortune, but becomes vain, and consequential; tho' Mr R – being now sought for, has a professional right to dictate, and controul; and being Nature's physician, to tap, bleed and scarify her. [*Torrington Diaries*, Vol. 3, pp. 10–11]

Repton was probably visiting Francis Pym of the Hazells, near Sandy, where he laid out the grounds in 1790–2. He records making a Red Book of the property, one of his prized sketchbooks, showing the effects before and after his landscape transformations. This fascinating object does not seem to have survived. Torrington also records that Repton visited another nearby landowner, Mr Thornton of Moggerhanger, whose house was to be rebuilt by Sir John Soane in 1809–11 in an advanced classical style. It is known that Repton improved this landscape and another property at Beeston Lessowes for which Red Books have survived. Surviving plantings certainly suggest his hand.

A more elaborate and concentrated example of the rustic estate village is that of Old Warden, certainly the best known as well as the best maintained in the county. It is difficult to date this artistically arranged series of cottages, lodges, pumps and public buildings, but it was probably built at the same time as the celebrated Old Warden Swiss Garden in the 1830s. The 3rd Lord Ongley who succeeded here in 1814 was a dedicated picturesque gardener and this enthusiasm clearly spilled over into the village at his park gates. In 1800, the 2nd Lord and Samuel Whitbread had swopped land in their two parishes to give the two estates tidier boundaries. Perhaps this gave the new Lord Ongley an incentive to redesign the village with vernacular buildings in the *cottage orné* style. The majority of the estate houses are thatched, rendered and with attractive diamond-leaded lights set into bays or casements, their roofs punctuated by dormers. They are all exceptionally well sited on the village street and on a bank behind it, offering great visual and architectural variety.

Early visitors to Old Warden, like Emily Shore the diarist, write reams about the garden but seldom mention the village. The Swiss Garden grew on a site north-east of Old Warden Park and is an interesting survival of Regency gardening, although it was added to by succeeding generations. Apart from a diminutive Swiss chalet for summer picnics, decorated with rustic wood and cones, there is little enough that is Swiss about it. It is a creation of mounds and walks and ponds which typify early nineteenth-century romantic gardening. Pieces of Greek revival ironwork form pergolas for climbing roses and here and there a glade reveals a fountain or a statue or a thatched seat round a tree bole. Perhaps the most interesting building is a fernery approached down a long grotto with dazzling effects of light. Emily Shore recorded her disapproval in 1835. 'The whole of this garden is in very bad taste, and much too artificial. The mounds and risings are not natural; the ornaments, such as vases, statues, lamps, arches, etc., are altogether out of place. Even the Swiss cottage is ill-imagined, and the quantity of linen furniture in the arbours and tents looks ridiculous.' But for us it is a rare glimpse into Regency methods and hundreds of tourists visit it every year.

The preoccupation with the land which created new machinery, new farm buildings and picturesque estate villages, also gave birth to a new kind of agricultural literature. The fashion for romanticism in painting and architecture had its counterpart in poetry and there was a rush from the artificial to the natural in verse. The Bedfordshire gentry and clergy (like Legh Richmond of Turvey) made trips to the Lake District, and those less fortunate bought books about it. George Crabbe's poetry, and in particular his 'Village' (1783), had created a taste for rural poetry that described the life of the ordinary people and revealed some painful home truths. Bedfordshire had its own rural rhymester, Thomas Batchelor (1775–1838) of Lidlington, a minor poet and a trenchant writer on agricultural matters. Batchelor was born at Marston Moretaine but brought up on his father's tenanted farm at Boughton End, Lidlington. Although well educated for his time, Batchelor had difficulty in his quest for knowledge as books were not readily available. 'In 1795, or 1796,' we read, 'whilst literally guiding the plough, he composed some short poems; and, in the spring of 1799, a solitary journey through Marston . . . furnished him with materials for his *Village Scenes*.' This was published in 1802–3 as *Village Scenes: the Progress of Agriculture; and other Poems*, a delightful little book, full of charm and feeling. Batchelor was befriended by the family's landlord, the 5th Duke of Bedford and more interestingly became a correspondent of Bedfordshire's other more celebrated rustic bard, Robert Bloomfield (1766–1823). Batchelor presented a copy of *Village Scenes* to Bloomfield and I have recently seen a copy of the same work owned by Lady Byron with her name in Byron's hand; truly Thomas Batchelor reached high! Batchelor is best remembered today for his major work, *General View of the agriculture of the County of Bedford* (1808) the first real treatise on the subject. He also published a substantial work on phonology.

Robert Bloomfield came to Bedfordshire for the best of reasons; he had visited the county in 1810, had been well received, and he liked the place. He had been living in modest prosperity in the City Road, London, writing small books of verse and being well supported by admirers such as the Duke of Grafton. His popularity began with *The Farmer's Boy* (1800) *Rural Tales & Ballads* (1802), *Good Tidings: or, News From the Farm* (1804) and *Wild Flowers* (1806). He was blessed with a phenomenal memory and when invited to Carlton House by the Prince Regent, was asked to look at an unseen book of verse and memorise it in a few minutes, a trick that he never failed to accomplish. Bloomfield's indigent relations and the ill health of his family were always a drain on his resources, and after unsuccessfully trying to work in the Seal Office, he escaped into Bedfordshire. In 1810 he had been well treated by the Whitbreads of Southill and the Osbornes of Chicksands Priory, so that when he was offered a small neat house in Bedford Street, Shefford, (now North Bridge Street) he took it with alacrity. He was destined to spend nearly twelve years in the county that he described as 'a fine and fruitful country' and the first four of these were very happy. Bloomfield fitted quite easily into the small town atmosphere of Regency Shefford and his letters are filled with excellent descriptions of its fairs and celebrations, strolling players and local characters. He was able to inform the banker poet Samuel Rogers in 1819 that he had composed a long poem of nearly a thousand lines. This was his *May Day with The Muses*, published in 1822 and the only poem composed by him during his time at Shefford. Bloomfield was sometimes accused, as a self-made son of the soil, of holding deistical and radical views. He was known to have a statuette of Napoleon in his home during the Napoleonic Wars, an eccentricity he shared with the Hollands of Ampthill Park House. The portrait of Bloomfield by John Hoppner R.A. (1758–1810) now in the Robert Bloomfield School at Shefford shows a nervous and sensitive face over the blue coat and cream waistcoat of the romantic poet.

Bloomfield's description of the peace celebrations in 1814 are colourful and spirited:

> The street from Weston's to Inskips's was a perfect grove, interspersed with white flags of all sizes and shapes and 'flowers of all hues' . . . At 2 in the afternoon peace was proclaimed in form by a large party (between thirty and forty) of the townsmen on horseback with white favours (for we all mounted the cockade) preceded by a Herald on a white horse. The former dressed in a fine jacket, very large military hat trimm'd with silver and bearing in his hand a roll of paper by way of Truncheon. This worthy was no other than Mr Weston who read the proclamation at all corners followed by his troop and a band of music . . . to accommodate that band a boat was procured from Chicksands, placed upon a carriage and surmounted by boughs of oak and laurel, and in the front rode Judy

Basterfield in white and crown'd with a wreath, as the emblem of Peace. In the procession rode Mr Williamson, Mr Walker (the Church parsons), Mr Poiter the Catholic priest, and Briggs the Methodist preacher, and all who could procure horses or wish'd to join the cavalcade. [Mary Phillips, *Beds Magazine*, Vol. 8, No. 57, pp. 9–10]

Bloomfield died on 19 August 1823 and he was buried at Campton, a fitting resting place for a rural poet. His poor wife hung on in insanity for a further eleven years and died in Bedford Infirmary on 10 June 1834. She lies in St Mary's churchyard, Bedford.

A slightly different aspect of rural life was given in the tracts written by the Revd Legh Richmond (1772–1827), vicar of Turvey. This gifted evangelical preacher carried on the spirit of John Wesley and John Berridge in the north of the county, but he was best known as a writer. He set down his experiences as a curate on the Isle of Wight, in a series of tracts, *The Dairyman's Daughter*, *The Negro Servant* and *The Young Cottager*. They were collected in 1828 as *The Annals of The Poor*. Although these religious stories do not have Bedfordshire settings, they were all written in Turvey Rectory.

It was not only poets but artists who were able to succeed from rather unpromising beginnings. A case in point is the Bedfordshire landscape painter, George Arnald A.R.A. (1766–1841). He was the only early local artist to become a member of the Royal Academy and achieved a considerable reputation at home and abroad. He was born at Farndish, the tiny village in the northernmost corner of Bedfordshire – so far north that the gardens on the north side of its High Street are in Northamptonshire! Arnald came from yeoman stock which had fallen on hard times and it seems scarcely credible that he would have been encouraged as an artist in so remote a place. However, he had a precocious talent and was helped in portrait painting by a local man, perhaps the Revd Orlebar Marsh, the antiquarian vicar of Stevington.

Arnald was educated at Leighton Buzzard and lived at various times at Houghton Regis and Wingfield where he had relations, before moving to London. There he studied under the moonlight painter William Pether and imitated his style very convincingly. Arnald studied at the Royal Academy School and in the 1790s he was taken up by influential patrons such as Sir George Beaumont and Sir Thomas Bernard. He travelled to Ireland and on the Continent and became a friend of Benjamin West, the President of the Royal Academy, and of Joseph Farington, its Secretary. As a result of his contact with Beaumont, he became a correspondent of William Wordsworth and John Constable and in 1810 he was elected an Associate of the Academy.

Arnald continued to return to Bedfordshire to paint and a sketch-book containing local views and an autobiographical poem are in the County Record Office. His landscapes are usually in the romantic tradition, with blasted trees, ragged rocks and great cloud formations, but they are always well conceived as topography and full of light. Perhaps his most significant local view was not a landscape but a townscape, *Bedford Old Bridge in state of demolition*, exhibited at the Royal Academy in 1812. This was bought by Samuel Whitbread of Southill for sixty guineas and appears to be the only example of Bedfordshire patronage. Arnald's greatest triumph was in winning the competition at the British Institution in 1825 for a painting of the *Battle of the Nile*. This huge canvas carried with it a prize of £500 and found a home at the Greenwich Hospital where it can still be seen. Arnald died at Pentonville on 21 November 1841.

If humble origins were no deterrent to Arnald, nor were they for the son of a bailiff at Battlesden. Joseph Paxton (1801–65) was born on 3 August 1801 at Milton Bryan, where his father William Paxton was superintendent of Sir Gregory Page-Turner's estate at £65 per annum, with a servant and a horse. Paxton attended the Woburn Grammar School for some time and was first apprenticed in Hertfordshire before returning to work at Battlesden in 1818. He must have impressed his employer even at this stage, because Sir Gregory allowed him to create a lake in the grounds. It was only a short time before he was appointed in 1823 to the Horticultural Society's gardens at Kew where he met the Duke of Devonshire for the first time. In 1826 he was put in charge of the Duke's gardens at Chatsworth and began on his spectacular career as one of the great engineers of his age. Between 1836 and 1840 he was constructing the 'Great Stove' at Chatsworth, a conservatory nearly 300 feet in length and the prototype of the Crystal Palace. When the Great Exhibition was being planned in the late 1840s, Paxton was a natural entrant for the competition, but it was a surprise to the public when his 'palace of glass' was selected from 233 entrants. The building covered nearly twenty acres and was opened by the Queen on 1 May 1851, when Paxton was knighted.

This remarkable man was already a Fellow of the Horticultural Society (1826), the Linnaean Society (1833) and a member of the order of St Vladimir of Russia (1844). He was also an extensive author, writing the *Practical Treatise on the Culture of the Dahlia* (1838), the *Pocket Botanical Dictionary* (1840), and editing the *Horticultural Register* and the *Botanical Magazine*. His public career was to extend into railways and he was the M.P. for Coventry from 1854 until his death.

Paxton continued some contacts with his home county after his early success. In 1837 he was in correspondence with J. T. Brooks of Flitwick Manor, a noted gardener, on specimens of *Musa Cavendishii*. In 1843, Brooks confides to his diary that he would like to engage Paxton for advice, but realised that he was already out of his reach. [*The Diary of a Bedfordshire Squire, B.H.R.S.* Vol. 66, 1987, p. 39] At the end of his life, Paxton returned to Bedfordshire to design the Victorian mansion at Battlesden for the later Page-Turners.

The more scientific approach to the study of flora at the close of the eighteenth century is reflected in the first serious botanical work on the county. Its author was the Revd Charles Abbot (1761–1817) who was born at Blandford in Dorset and educated at Winchester and New College, Oxford. His Oxford connections brought him to Bedford in 1788 as usher at the Grammar School and he eventually added to his salary the vicarages of Oakley Reynes and Goldington and curacies at St Mary's and St Paul's, Bedford. Abbot was first and foremost a field botanist and keen to classify Bedfordshire plants on the new system. He was also an entomologist, numismatist and archaeologist. His great work was *Flora Bedfordiensis Comprehending Such Plants As Grow Wild in the County of Bedford, Arranged According to The System of Linnaeus with Occasional Remarks By Charles Abbot M.A. F.L.S.*, published at Bedford in 1798.

There were amateur botanists about before Abbot. Lord Bute of Luton Hoo made an extensive collection in his garden there in the 1780s and classified it by his own system, the *Tabular Distribution of British Plants* (1780). Mrs Delany had mentioned the blue iris on a roadside at Bedford in 1784, and in his *Flora* Abbot thanks the Countess of Upper Ossory 'for the very generous occasional loan of books from her Ladyship's collection'. In his dedication to the Queen, Abbot makes clear that the book is intended for ladies' use, listing and describing the plants with their Latin names and identifying their locations. He had ranged far and wide in his quest, noting the Sweet Woodruff at Aspley and, in King's Wood near Ampthill, the Common Comfrey on the 'Banks of the Ouse', the Water Violet at Eaton Socon mills and the Least Water Moss at Oakley. The book was embellished with delicate copper-plate engravings, coloured by hand but unsigned, and clearly done by either the author or his wife, who made a herbarium which is still in existence. Abbot corresponded with the leading botanists of his day and some in his own neighbourhood, such as Thomas Martyn (1735–1825), rector of Pertenhall, who edited Miller's *Gardener's Dictionary*, and John Hemsted (1746–1824), vicar of St Paul's, Bedford.

The 6th Duke of Bedford was an important collector of botanical books and many of the ladies in the country houses must have made collections or drawings. One of the most charming to survive is an album from the north of the county 'Wild Flowers from Odell Wood, Bedfordshire by Emma M. Alston & Caroline M. Alston'. They were the daughters of Mr Alston of Odell Castle, and their watercolours, dating from the late 1830s, are of willow-herb, garden nightshade, pimpernell, white bryony, moth mullein and many others delicately rendered in watercolour. [*C.R.O.* X 48/5]

We have already encountered the independent market-gardeners of Maulden, defending their rights in 1796. At about the same time, Lord Torrington was noticing the superb cultivation of these market gardens between Beeston and Sandy where the Great North Road runs through otherwise flat country. 'Passing thro this neighbourhood,' he writes on 19 May 1794,

> any observer would be astonish'd at the culture, and gardening of the fields; surpassing every thing I ever saw, but just about London; for every field is cropp'd by peas, carrots, parsnips, French beans, cucumbers, &c &c even the very open fields; and you cannot prevent your horse from

smashing the cucumbers. (I once told this to a friend of mine, who smiled contradiction, till I led him into this garden of a country; and then he owned his surprise and conviction.) [*Torrington Diaries*, 1936]

The country was perfect for this sort of production and for the growth of nurseries. One such nursery which developed a great reputation in the Regency was started by the Gibbs family of Ampthill in the old walled garden of Houghton House. Robert Gibbs (*c*.1734–1814) was a Scotsman who had become head gardener to Lord Ossory in about 1773. He had married an Ampthill girl and they had a numerous family, including three sons who were involved in horticulture. The eldest son, Thomas Gibbs (1771–1849) founded the seedsman's business at Ampthill and Old Brompton with a retail outlet on the corner of Half Moon Street, Piccadilly. He was educated at the private school at Aspley Guise, an important step up the ladder for so many aspiring Bedfordshire boys at this time. Later, in 1799, he made an important marriage to Sarah Prosser Brandreth of Houghton Regis, a member of a wealthy family, and this may have affected his career. That year he was made seedsman to the Board of Agriculture, and in the 1800s he conducted a number of experiments on grasses and became a member of the Smithfield Club. By this time he had many important clients including Lord Somervile and the Duke of Bedford. He was a founder member of the Horticultural Society and of the Medico-Botanical Society, and on his death a marble tablet was placed in Ampthill church recording his work. He had built a handsome house opposite the church and his son Humphrey, who succeeded to his uncle's estate at Houghton Regis, became a prominent member of the gentry and was High Sheriff for Bedfordshire. His grandson was Sir Thomas Brandreth Gibbs, Honorary Secretary of the Smithfield Club and Director of the Royal Agricultural Society of England.

It was not only professionals like the Gibbs family, or grandees like the Bedfords and the Whitbreads, who indulged in agricultural experiments. The small landowners like Dr Macqueen of Segenhoe Manor tried out traditional building crafts and John Foster of Brickhill, Bedford and St Elizabeth's, Jamaica created new implements. Foster combined great energy with great curiosity, a typical outlook among the evangelical landowners of the county. His commitment to new science went hand in hand with a commitment to the gospel and the desire to improve the lot of his fellow men. He was part of that wide circle which enabled him to entertain at his Bedford house both the preacher Charles Simeon of Cambridge and the American novelist Washington Irving at the same time.

Foster won high praise for his development of the fluted iron roller for farms in 1807. He was chairman of the Central Agricultural Society for many years and in 1827 was presented by the Society with a magnificent silver gilt trophy in the form of the Warwick Vase for his services to agriculture. This superb piece of neo-classic plate was designed and made by the renowned silversmiths, Boulton of Birmingham. Foster attended the Holkham agricultural gatherings as well as those at Woburn and was a pamphleteer, writing *Six Letters On The Corn Question* in 1827. With typical generosity, he comes out in favour of Catholic emancipation in this document!

The years following the Napoleonic Wars were difficult ones for those working in the countryside. The disbanding of the forces, the increasing population and the uncertainty of agricultural depression, created an atmosphere of unrest. Many Bedfordshire villages had a residue of agricultural labourers who were unable to find work. These unfortunate men became 'roundsmen', unemployed labourers who were taken on by the farmers as rate-payers, a proportionate number to the rateable value of the farm. This was a new variant of the historic Poor Law system but was unpopular and inadequate. Roundsmen could take their complaints to a magistrate although they seldom did so. In January 1822, six Keysoe labourers were taken to the Quarter Sessions for conspiring to increase wages for themselves and others. They were said to have visited farms with the 'intent to alarm and terrify'.

Haytime and harvest could also be a time of brooding discontent. Itinerant labourers were employed, often the Irish who roamed the countryside looking for work in the harvest fields. There was some trouble with the Irish at Felmersham in the August of 1824, when a mob of thirty men with bludgeons in their hands attempted to attack the newcomers.

During the 1820s, the disaffection began to show itself to an alarming extent in the damaging of parish property and assaults on parish overseers. At Ampthill, for example, in 1829, the whole of the work force was based upon agriculture, with only the women and children being engaged in lace or straw plait. There were therefore no alternative trades to alleviate the plight of this depressed majority. Some labourers refused to work at what they were put to. Threshing by hand brought wages so they were later to take their vengeance on threshing machines. An alternative was to work on repairing the roads, but these gangs were said to breed grievances and the task fermented their discontent. There were outbreaks of hedge-breaking, tree cutting, poaching and sheep stealing, and the robbing of farmers' premises. The Eaton Socon overseer was threatened in 1828 and the following year an overseer's deputy was assaulted with stones at Eaton Bray. The Duke of Bedford's estates suffered very badly from poaching in 1828 and after his gamekeepers had been brutally attacked he offered £100 rewards for the apprehension and conviction of the offenders. He instructed his steward: 'I wish it to be clearly understood that it is on account of the barbarous and brutal attack on the men, and not for the destruction of game, that I offer this reward.' [B.H.R.S., Vol. 57, p. 81] The keeper requested a Bow Street Constable to be sent down, the Duke replying that they were 'useless out of London, and a good active and intelligent Constable at Bedford or in the neighbourhood of Wootton and Kempston will be much more efficient'. At Luton there were some ugly incidents when discontents, disguised with blackened faces, tried to set the house of a hat manufacturer on fire.

By 1830, the mood of revolution throughout Europe was sufficient for the landowners and the gentry to feel very uncomfortable. Things seem to have been unpleasant in the centre of the county, with a riot of more than one hundred persons at Millbrook the previous year, a magistrate threatened and two parish constables having to show pistols. Things were not improved by rumours and reports of the so called 'Swing' riots in Kent in June 1830, when many threshing machines were destroyed and there were ugly demands for higher wages. The Woburn Abbey fire insurance arrangements were reviewed and shortly afterwards the Woburn steward reported to the London steward on the first serious incidents. 'I am very sorry to inform you that the disgraceful proceedings which are taking place in Kent and Sussex, etc. have I fear reached our neighbourhood. Last night several ricks of Corn at Mr Hoare's new farm near Holcutt were destroyed by fire.' The London steward replied to say that dogs and geese should be kept on the farms as alarms; the recommendation was also made to take on the unemployed in piece work 'to secure a fair day's labour for a day's wages, which no superintendance can do if day wages are paid'. [ibid., p. 90]

It was all very well for the parish to push the unemployed on to the responsibility of the tenant farmers, many of whom were in a very bad way in the 1830s. The Woburn accounts show that several were insolvent. J.&S. Batchelor, for example, of Boughton End, Lidlington, were in debt to the tune of £498 11s. These were the brothers of the Bedfordshire poet and the man who had written the first agricultural book on the county!

A serious arson attack took place at Wootton Pilinge (now Stewartby) on 27 November 1830, when all the buildings and rick yard were destroyed. That day, the Lord Lieutenant, Lord Grantham, held a Special Sessions at Bedford and elsewhere to look into measures for the preservation of public peace. Those concerned included the high constables of the various Hundreds, the Clerk to the Magistrates, together with local magistrates and solicitors who were authorised to swear in special constables for the local districts. At Toddington it was suspected that many of the work force so sworn in had little respect for anyone's private property. Many of them had been incited to unruly behaviour by the owner of one of the recently legalised licensed beer shops in the village.

There was some disorder at Stotfold and quite a serious riot at Flitwick on 6 December. About twenty or thirty labourers went round the Flitwick farms in a band, forcing those sworn in as constables to come out with them. They were debarred from entering Priestly Farm, and about eighty returned to the centre of the village with sticks and bludgeons. There they were met by a force of constables and Lord Grantham. He urged them to disperse. One labourer was reported as saying: 'we want more Money and more Money we'll have and damn'd if we won't'.

Before dispersing, they called on the squire, J. T. Brooks, who had personally called out thirty constables who were paid two shillings for their work. Brooks comments rather tersely on this episode in his diary: 'Rural Riots, mob at the House . . . all passed off well.' There was evidently no panic at Flitwick Manor.

But the events had frightened the upper classes and a more charitable attitude followed. At Great Barford, a subscription list was opened. 'The Vicar, Churchwardens, Overseers & Farmers of Gt Barford have thought it adviseable to enter into a voluntary subscription to supply the labouring class . . . with a few Coals gratis when the severity of the Weather may render such a supply most desirable & most acceptable.' [*Ibid.*] With similar ends in view, some landowners made allotments available. Acts of arson and vandalism continued and I have always heard that Samuel Swaffield, Lord Holland's steward, ascended to the leads of Ampthill Park House to survey the landscape for rick fires.

The Poor Law Commission of 1834 went into the underlying problems of this discontent, agricultural riot and burnings. The result was revised Poor Law legislation which set up the Union Workhouses by Act that year. This was designed to ease the burden of individual parishes by grouping them all together under one roof in a single workhouse under a Board of Guardians. Logical and economical on paper, the scheme was very unpopular in practice, because it penalised the poor by moving them away from their place of origin and divided families up in the segregated wards of the new institutions. Outside relief was abolished and no payment was made unless the unfortunate worker was inside the rather forbidding walls of the place.

At Ampthill, serious trouble broke out in May 1835 when the officer of the Union was attacked by a mob at Lidlington and forced to hand over his money; he received the same treatment the following day in Millbrook. The crowd then moved to Ampthill and broke the windows of the House of Industry, despite the reading of the Riot Act. The justices were in session at The King's Arms and the crowd moved on there, flooring the High Constable in front of the inn. The Assistant Poor Law Commissioner was despatched to London and brought back with him an inspector, two sergeants and eighteen men of the Metropolitan Police. One hundred and fifty specials were sworn in and four troops of yeomanry were sent to Luton, but the trouble spread no further. A year later the handsome Union Workhouse was opened in Ampthill from the designs of James Clephane. [Underwood, *A Goodly Heritage*, 1976, p. 109] Similarly large Workhouses rose elsewhere in the county, notably the one at Biggleswade with an octagon centre and spreading wings by Thomas Gwyn Elger (1835–6).

X

Clerical Interludes,
1820–60

If the eighteenth century in Bedfordshire is remembered chiefly today for its country mansions, streets of elegant town houses and fine bridges, the nineteenth century is remembered for another sort of building. Church building was one of the main preoccupations of the gentry, enlightened townsmen and benefactors at this time, and in the climate of public service that prevailed, schools, infirmaries and almshouses came in their wake. There were, it is true, a number of exceptional country homes being built, but it is the extraordinary range of churches that impress as one moves about the county. Towers by Clutton and steeples by Sir George Gilbert Scott (1811–78) emerge from treetops, a tomb by Burges or a porch by G. F. Bodley will catch the eye, and a medieval exterior will give place to a nave or chancel in rich Victorian clothing. A similar lustre and singularity attaches itself to many of the incumbents, ministers and self-styled prophets who instigated and beautified such places. Among them were writers, academics, popularisers, artists, fervent ritualists and ardent evangelicals, the arrangers of music and the arrangers of stained-glass, eccentrics, reprobates and fanatics. The one thing that is common to them all is a ceaseless and obsessive energy!

There had always been a band of progressive, hard-working clergy in Bedfordshire from the days of John Wesley. Wesley was a frequent visitor in the 1750s and 1760s, criss-crossing the county by horse to visit his remote congregations. His great friend had been the Revd John Berridge (1716–93), the unconventional vicar of Everton. He was much disliked by the gentry for his Methodism, but Torrington, the diarist, defended him: 'His Face appears to me abundant of Honesty, Zeal and good works . . .'

In the early nineteenth century, conscientious patrons of livings, like the Greys of Wrest Park, encouraged young and progressive clergy into their churches. Flitton, where the Countess de Grey did not own the living but may have had influence, welcomed the Revd J. T. James, later Bishop of Calcutta, as incumbent in 1818. A little further to the north, the Revd R. P. Beechcroft held the living of Blunham from the Countess. In July 1821, he reported to his patroness how the village had celebrated the Coronation of King George IV, a somewhat controversial crowning because of the King's estrangement from his wife.

> I therefore take the liberty of giving you some little idea of our Loyalty on the day of the Coronation in this village & its vicinity. Mr Thornton, Mr Campbell, my mother, & myself, united in an order to every family for 1 Quartern Loaf & 3 lb of Meat. This gave us the opportunity of leaving home for Biggleswade, when reaching the Parish Church with a Band of Musick, I was requested to read Morning Prayer & Preach. We had Anthems & every appropriate peculiarity which could mask the day. At ½ past 2 the whole Population dined at Tables beautifully arranged – Unanimity was the order of the day. I, adjourned, for so we must term it, at Moggerhanger House. In the Evening, the Tenants were invited to a dance of young people upon the Lawn, Fireworks followed, and then a Supper. By a little good management, & a conciliatory spirit, all those evils were avoided which have unhappily occurred at Huntingdon & other places, where King's folk & Queen's folk have engaged in battle array. [C.R.O. L30/11/200]

The Sunday School movement began soon after 1780 in Bedfordshire and by 1787 there were fourteen schools at such varied places as Melchbourne, Dunstable, Biggleswade and Clophill. The landowning families supported the idea, the Whitbreads and the Russells financed the schools, and by 1851 the county had more children enrolled than any other in the country. [*Beds Magazine*, Vol. 20, p. 256]

Houghton Conquest stands at the crossing of two by-roads and about equidistant from the main trunk roads from Luton and Ampthill to the county town. Few villages could claim to be more centrally situated in Bedfordshire than this one, and yet it is not a typically Bedfordshire village and its history and traditions before the twentieth century marked it out as rather a special place. This elusive quality of distinction was quite apparent to anyone passing through, even as late as the Second World War. Old houses and closes remained intact, the church was centrally placed and the village street passed solid brick houses on its meandering course, as well as substantial eighteenth-century inns and one or two sizeable farmhouses still within the boundaries of the settlement. Half-way along the street, the eye was drawn to a row of trim seventeenth-century almshouses in brick with a central gable containing an inscription, a building that lent great importance to the scene. Here, one instinctively realised, substantial people had lived and left their mark: people with some pride of place and sense of perpetuity, but the casual onlooker would be hard pressed to say whether they were of the seventeenth or eighteenth centuries. They had all left a rich patina of their lives on the village, but for nearly forty years in the nineteenth century the village and the rectory house were the home of a group of scholars who typified all that was best in the Victorian parsonage.

Archdeacon John Henry Rose (1800–73), his brother, his son and his two brothers-in-law enjoyed the seclusion of the Rectory to write poetry, study art, compose theological works and investigate the archaeology of the county. But that Christian peace and serenity spread out, too, in more practical ways to the village and the neighbourhood, expressed in a love of people, place and landscape.

The reason that Houghton attracted such people dated back to a time well before the Roses themselves. The living of All Saints church was one of the richest in Bedfordshire, standing at £828 per annum in 1856, well above that of any of the Bedford town parishes. This may have been the result of a bizarre legacy from the Middle Ages when Houghton consisted of two rectories, two parish priests, but only one church. The two rectories were Houghton Gildable and Houghton Franchise, with separate patrons and separate powers to appoint. This strange state of affairs lasted until 1641 when they were most sensibly amalgamated. The gift was then in the hands of the dominant family of the village, the Conquests of Conquest Bury, but by 1720 it had been purchased by the scholar Zachary Grey, who was therefore patron of his own living. He sold it to St John's College, Cambridge in 1725. Grey built himself the handsome rectory, which still stands behind an avenue of limes in a very secluded part of the village. Its grounds stretch away to the foot of the greensand ridge which forms a natural backdrop to the village and is commanded by the gaunt ruins of Houghton House.

It was to this almost idyllic setting that the young Cambridge cleric, J. H. Rose, came as rector in 1837. Like Grey before him, he had prefaced his move to Houghton by being elected a Fellow of St John's, but he had also been vicar of St Edward's, Cambridge and Hulsean lecturer in 1833. Rose had established himself in the Cambridge of the 1820s and 1830s, the Cambridge of the fiery evangelical preaching of Charles Simeon of Holy Trinity, but also the Cambridge of a rising tide of Tractarianism. He was by no means an evangelical, but neither did he follow the course of his High Church elder brother, Hugh James Rose (1795–1838), scholar, polemicist and founder of the 'New Biographical Dictionary'. Both brothers stressed the 'beauty of holiness', the importance of Christian architecture, the adorning of churches and the sacredness of the crown, but J. H. was altogether a gentler person, an able administrator, a good writer, but happy in the simpler pastoral duties of a rural parish.

In many ways Rose represents a change in society at the beginning of the Victorian age. The dissolute ways of the Regency were frowned upon, the period of absentee clergy was over, and if the ministry was rather different from the Revd Berridge of Everton in the previous century or the Revd Legh Richmond of Turvey in the previous generation, it was none the less earnest. The unique quality of Anglicanism was to be restored, the liturgy powerfully upheld and the gospel furthered by education, architecture and art as well as by improving the lot of ordinary people.

The previous incumbent at Houghton had been the Revd Thomas Barber, a most pious man, who had prepared the ground for Rose, but whose zeal had been upstaged by the non-conformists. 'The result of his endeavours,' wrote Rose's brother-in-law, years later, 'the very moment of the revival which he effected in the parish, was the Wesleyan Chapel, (it almost broke his heart), which bears on its front the date 1832, and which was built and endowed, out of mere spite, by a farmer named Armstrong – the decayed representative of what had been a gentle family hereabouts . . . the standard of Rebellion was forthwith planted beside the road leading to the Rectory by the disciples of John Wesley'. [C.R.O. 11/28/2] It can be seen from this that the truce between Anglicanism and nonconformity that had partially existed under Georgian broad churchmanship was at an end!

The chatelaine of Houghton Rectory was Sarah Caroline Rose, whom Rose had married in May 1838. She was the elder sister of the Revd J. W. Burgon (1813–88), Fellow of Oriel College, Oxford and vicar of the University church of St Mary's in the same city. Burgon was naturally a bachelor, as all resident dons had to be, and so spent all his vacations at Houghton Conquest. Rose and his younger brother-in-law made a very good partnership in nurturing the parish, planning publications and investigating the history of the neighbourhood.

Rose must have been among a minority of the clergy in Bedfordshire who had made the Grand Tour, visiting Bavaria, Austria and Italy in 1824–5. He was a German speaker and may well have come across the German artists living in Rome, as well as seeing their works in the Munich Gallery on his way south. At Houghton Conquest, he and Burgon soon developed a plan of furthering the faith by introducing high art to the villagers. They compiled and had printed at Oxford a modest book entitled *Cottage Prints* whose prospectus explained that they were 'to supply prints for the Cottage'. The intention was to bring the Christian message to the poor in acceptable illustrations by renowned artists. They were later to advocate illuminated and framed prayers for the same purpose. The title-page to the book was designed and possibly drawn by Burgon (no mean artist) and the volume contained tinted lithographs after Raphael or Angelico da Fiesole, but more notably by the German Nazarene artists, P. Veit, Carl Müller and J. von Fuhrich, whom Rose had admired on his tour. They stated that the prints should be used as Sunday School rewards or to decorate the barren walls of labourers' homes. The twelve-part work was issued in paper covers in 1849–51 and bound with 'a peck of letter-press' that year.

By a coincidence, one of the new bound volumes with P. Veit's 'The Heavenly Stranger' was displayed in the window of the High Church bookshop of Messrs Hering & Remington at 137 Regent

Street, London, in December 1851, for the Christmas market. It was seen by the Pre-Raphaelite model, Elizabeth Siddall (later Mrs D. G. Rossetti), who mentioned it to William Holman Hunt (1827–1910), the Pre-Raphaelite painter. He was already working on a picture based on the biblical text, Revelation III, 20: 'Behold, I stand at the door and knock . . .' The print in *Cottage Prints* was also based on this text and Hunt went to look at it, summarily dismissing it as a quite different subject. He did however considerably alter his famous painting, *The Light of the World*, as a result of this, so that the Houghton Conquest prints have some claim to having altered the meaning of this great nineteenth-century masterpiece.

Burgon was a minor poet and is most celebrated for his poem 'Petra', a Prize Poem recited at the Sheldonian Theatre, Oxford on 4 June 1845. It contained the famous lines which every Victorian schoolchild knew:

> The hues of youth upon a brow of woe,
> Which men called old two thousand years ago!
> Match me such marvel, save in Eastern Clime,
> A rose red city – 'half as old as Time!'

There is no certain proof that the poem was actually composed at Houghton Conquest, but it seems very likely that it was. Burgon was there in the spring, and again in the summer of 1845, when he wrote and dated his sonnet 'To The Flower "Peristeria Elata" ' for which he drew a charming frontispiece in the second edition of his *Collected Poems* (1846). Burgon wrote of this Rectory house with affection: 'In the chamber which for upwards of 30 years he called his own, – (the large bedroom which looks down upon the orchard and the avenue, and is furnished with a narrow window to admit the setting sun,) – in *that* room he has spent, as he thinks, the happiest hours of his life – *There* he produced most of his works, such as they are – *There* he always seemed to himself to study more successfully than anywhere else.' [*Houghton Conquest Common Place Book*, p. 163, C.R.O.]

J. H. Rose found the church in a very sad condition: 'by the year 1838, [it] had fallen into a state of the most deplorable decadence, by reason of the utter neglect which it had experienced for nearly 200 years. The tower arch and the chancel arch had both been walled up with lath and plaster, the upper half of the East window had been blocked up in a similar way, three wooden mullions having been introduced below.' [*ibid.*, p. 155] Rose was equally shocked by the silver – 'the appointments of the Holy Table were all of the most sordid type' – and he quickly replaced them by communion plate of good Gothic design by William Eaton (1836–7) between 1842 and 1846. Burgon also described the state of the music: 'The village minstrelsy when Henry Rose first knew the place was certainly of a type which would now-a-days be pronounced fabulous.' [*Twelve Good Men*, 1891, p. 150] Rose organised a public subscription for the church and contributions came from neighbours like the Duke of Bedford and Lord John Thynne of Haynes Park, enabling the rector to instal a magnificent pipe organ. But neither Rose nor Burgon was ritualist, and when the latter was briefly British chaplain at Rome in 1861, he penned his inner thoughts. 'The gorgeous externals of public worship in which the Romish Church delights, – rich dresses, gay colours, lighted candles, – must sicken any one who is on the look-out for true Religion; and loves it far far more than wax and millinery.' [*Letters from Rome*, 1862, p. 113]

A few years after his arrival, Rose became one of the founder members of the Bedfordshire Architectural and Archaeological Society with like minded clerics such as the Revd William Airy of Keysoe and the Revd Beatty Pownell of Milton Ernest. Appropriately enough, their President was Earl de Grey K.G. of Wrest Park, amateur architect and first President of the Institute of British Architects. At the inaugural meeting on 21 March 1848, Rose read papers on 'Conventual Seals of Bedfordshire' and, in succeeding years, on 'Jewish Shekels', 'Lombardic Inscriptions' and 'Architectural Devices on Ancient Coins'. His chief interests were design, lettering and the Gothic inheritance.

In the middle of his time at Houghton, Rose busied himself about the restoration of its old buildings. In 1852, he employed the well known architect Thomas Leverton Donaldson (1795–1885), Professor of Architecture at University College, London, to restore the Clerke almshouses in the main street. This was an enlightened piece of conservation of seventeenth-century buildings, not common among the Victorians. At a later date, in

1869, shortly after Rose had become the Archdeacon of Bedford, he undertook the complete restoration of All Saints Church under the direction of Sir George Gilbert Scott. This took two years to complete, and in Burgon's words 'at an expense of considerably more than £3000 – of which, one third (the cost of restoring the chancel) was entirely sustained by the Rector'. [*Houghton Conquest Common Place Book*, p. 155, C.R.O.] This had included a project dear to Rose's heart, the unblocking of the original east window.

The family at Houghton Conquest, the scholarly brothers-in-law with their books, the ladies with their painting and good works, the children amusing visiting dons with their sayings, seem to mirror the world of Trollope, the exact scenes of *Framley Parsonage* or *The Vicar of Bullhampton*. Rose's 'secluded dwelling', as Burgon calls it, was a retreat for many international scholars in the 1850s and 1860s, among them Temple Chevallier (1794–1873) the astronomer, W. H. Mill (1792–1853) the orientalist, and H. L. Mansel (1820–71) the metaphysician. 'The best traditions of an English country parsonage were to be witnessed at Houghton in perfection,' wrote Burgon in later years. 'Real learning and sound Divinity, pure taste and graceful hospitality – flourished there and abounded. Within doors, there was unfailing loving-kindness, unbroken peace and joy: without, there was (with all their faults) a God-fearing, well-disposed and affectionate peasantry.' [*Twelve Good Men*, 1891, p. 150]

It was rather less secluded after the opening of the railway at Millbrook in 1846, but even so much of Rose's ministry was carried out on foot. In the diary of J. T. Brooks of Flitwick Manor there are accounts of Rose and Burgon walking backwards and forwards to Flitwick, Ampthill and Westoning, thinking very little of ten or twelve miles a day. With Brooks they could share their love of horticulture and the latest theological works with the other clergy.

'The surrounding scenery must surely be of the very best type,' Burgon was to write, 'for we never, any of us, to the last, grew tired of it. I think on the contrary we enjoyed and admired it every year, more and more. There is not a walk to be taken in any direction within a reasonable distance of the Rectory, but will be likened with some sweet, some tender recollections so long as memory shall discharge its office.' [*Houghton Conquest Common*

Place Book, p. 163, C.R.O] J. T. Brooks leaves us a picture of the great Oxford don teaching in the Houghton Conquest Sunday School in 1843 and comparing the 'insignificance of worldly grandeur' to 'the simple wild flower.' [*B.H.R.S.*, *Brooks Diary*, p. 16, 11 Jan. 1843.] Burgon's country walks, his love of people and interest in nature, had a surprising result and he gradually became intrigued by local words and meanings, becoming the county's first etymologist.

Burgon had studied Anglo-Saxon with two friends at Oxford. In their vacations, they met together in the evenings and collected dialect words and unusual pronunciations. Making Houghton Conquest his base and Bedfordshire his study, Burgon devoted a lifetime to collecting these expressions and meanings on his country tramps. Burgon called them 'Bedfordshire Provincialisms', and in two scrapbooks [Bedford Museum, B.M. 5308 M.L. 293] he described the way they were collected. 'I need not record here – nor indeed anywhere else – the slow progress by which the list of words has grown. Now, one of the dear Children, – now, another, has brought me my materials: & how often has it given interest & meaning to the visit to the Cottage or the Farm, to call to mind the mass of papers in a corner of the drawer.' Ably assisted by his niece, Miss A. C. Rose, and his nephew, the Revd W. J. Rose, the glossary was published in the *Bedfordshire Times* by sections in 1868. Burgon relied on the clergy and gentry to listen for this vocabulary in context and he garnered a rich harvest. 'Unkid or Unked', an adjective for sad or desolate; 'hoddydods', the dialect name for snails; 'moke', a donkey: 'slipe', a thin stretch of land; 'flitty-mouse' for bat, 'maggy', a scarecrow, but, equally, an 'untidy graceless woman'. Happily, some of these still survive in the villages. Burgon also collected place names and even the traditional May songs that survived at Keysoe and Bromham.

In 1853 the Roses acquired another Bedfordshire relation when John Burgon's youngest sister, Helen Eliza, married Charles Longuet Higgins, the squire and benefactor of Turvey. Longuet Higgins (1806–85) was another remarkable churchman and landowner whom Burgon was to christen 'The Good Layman'. He affected in the north of the county the same sort of traditionalism and conviction as the Roses at Houghton Conquest, but as a country magnate and forthright committee man was able to do much more in his own village as well as in the secular life of Bedfordshire.

Longuet Higgins was the son of John Higgins of Turvey Abbey, who had inherited the rambling manor house from his uncle. He was a keen landscape gardener, a collector of books and lover of paintings, and Charles grew up in this civilised atmosphere. During his boyhood, Legh Richmond was the parish priest at Turvey and the Higgins family, and particularly the sons, came under his evangelical influence. The two families shared a tutor, so that all the boys might learn Latin and Greek, but the curates appointed dallied so much with Richmond's daughters that little progress was made. Charles apparently went up to Cambridge with the rector of Turvey's son, Henry S. Richmond and both of them attended Charles Simeon's receptions at Trinity church. Higgins's churchmanship must have changed somewhat between his undergraduate days in the 1820s and his marriage in 1853, because for that ceremony he had invited Dr Pusey to celebrate, although the famous High Churchman declined. Influenced by the rise of Tractarianism in the 1840s and agreeable contact with the Rose family, Higgins's standpoint seems to have altered towards a reverence for the beauty of holiness, a respect for tradition and a strong social sense. What he had certainly inherited from Richmond and Simeon was searching enquiry, thoughtful discussion and earnest devoutness, the features of evangelicalism.

It was said that Longuet Higgins went up to Cambridge at twenty years of age in 1826, determined to rebuild the parish church at Turvey, to provide new cottages and schools for the village and to found a library for the clergy. If this was the case, he must have been a very single-minded young man, for he eventually succeeded in all these ambitions. He returned from Cambridge in 1829 and began to study law at Lincoln's Inn from 1830 to 1833 and medicine at St Bartholomew's Hospital in 1836–8 under Sir James Paget. He returned to Turvey to serve as an able magistrate and as a voluntary physician to the destitute poor in the surrounding villages, functions that he performed for years.

Succeeding to the Turvey property in 1846, Charles Longuet

Higgins laid some of the plans for the village that had occupied his mind since undergraduate days. But suffering from asthma, he decided to take a tour of the Middle East with his brother, visiting Alexandria, Cairo, the Nile and Jerusalem for the benefit of his health. Before his departure, he had organised the building of a National School and Schoolhouse for the village, following this with a 'Museum' to contain books for the clergy and a reading-room for the working men with a cottage for a matron. Between 1849 and 1851, he built forty-nine 'substantial cottages' as well as shops, completely transforming the character of the place. This was a model village rather than an estate village like Old Warden; it was not built on picturesque principles but to improve the lot of the villagers and give them airy and hygienic residences. The designs are all in a simple vernacular cottage style, but well constructed and well planned one with another. The pairs of cottages cost £300 each and, as Burgon stated, were 'placed for the most part on a raised terrace, and provided with every requirement for decency and comfort, as well as furnished severally with a small garden, – in room of the squalid tenements which skirted the public way when first I knew Turvey'. [*Twelve Good Men*, pp. 444–5]

The surviving plans are all drawn out in a pleasant, amateurish manner, and one concludes from this that they were all the squire's own designs with the help of an estate steward and the local masons. Charles Knight, the prophet of popular education, wrote in 1865: 'There is probably no such pattern village in England as this of Turvey. Its cottages are newly built of stone, each containing four rooms, with outhouses and a good garden, of which the rent is fifteen pence a week.' [*Passages From A Working Life*, 1865, pp. 203–4]

Like his brothers-in-law, John Burgon and Revd J. H. Rose, Longuet Higgins wished to raise the standard of musical appreciation among the parishioners. As early as 1838 he had been anxious to change the musical cacophony at All Saints. As Burgon recalls: 'The traditional clarionet, flute and bas-viol; all these in the hands of old men who exercised a prescriptive right to render "Brady and Tate" after their own peculiar fashion, and to lead voices of the congregation according to their own queer will, – effectually blocked the way.' [*ibid.*, p. 437] This reads very much like the disputes between the old order and the new order in Thomas Hardy's *Under the Greenwood Tree*, and one has a certain sympathy for the home-grown music and traditional instruments of the village. But the pattern of worship was changing, and discipline and high standards were cornerstones of the Victorian church in everything from its art and architecture to its singing and flower arranging. A relative bequeathed a small organ to the church and Higgins immediately presided at it, although he wished that the old instruments could have been retained in some way so as not to offend the villagers. He gradually winkled the singers out of their gallery into the chancel of the church. In 1840 he produced his own hymnal, *Psalms and Hymns adapted to the Services of the Church of England*, printed at Bedford, anticipating *Hymns Ancient and Modern* (1861 and 1889) by more than twenty years. He played the organ three times every Sunday and scarcely ever missed a single service in forty-eight years.

He was a great supporter of the Victorian organ. A Hill organ was installed in Turvey church at the time of its restoration and he superintended the installation of another at Houghton Conquest. His advice was frequently sought on the subject and in 1868 he was asked for his opinion on an organ for St Mary's, Bedford. 'You do not want noise,' he replied, 'but music in your church with of course sufficient power to give all the expression which the service may require. You ought to obtain for Four hundred pounds, an organ which will make the young ladies' hair curl all over the church.' [C.R.O. P81/2//13]

From 1862, he was the instigator for sixteen years of Choral Festivals which took place in Turvey church and included choir members from thirty-four local villages, a pioneering achievement in itself. A contemporary recollection demonstrates the joy of these occasions:

> It was a Choir Festival – a beautiful day: and I well remember the eager happy faces of the villagers from all the Country round as they drove or walked into the village: the thanksgiving Service in the parish church, – and then the royal repast which awaited everyone in the School-room. It was one of those days which do not end with the revolution of the sun: but live on in the memory, and of which one says long afterwards, – 'I am glad I was there, that day!' [*Twelve Good Men*, p. 449]

In 1852, Longuet Higgins had begun the restoration of Turvey church at his own cost, using the services of Sir George Gilbert Scott as architect. He was able to reopen an old quarry near the church, which Scott maintained was the source for the old church walls, and this satisfied his historical sense. The vast number of interments and the unstable site of the church meant that the chancel had to be demolished and the whole of the nave lengthened and rebuilt. The great Tudor and Elizabethan monuments of the Mordaunt family were taken down and re-erected, great and reverential care being taken of the remains. The greatest care too was taken in restoring the thirteenth-century arcading, the piscina and sedilia and the earlier font. The fourteenth-century painting of the Crucifixion was carefully renovated and retained as well as the matchless iron scrolls of the south door. It is one of the finest pieces of Victorian restoration in the county and if the stained-glass by Hardman seems rather severely Victorian, one can feel very thankful that the benevolent figure of Higgins with his sensitive eye was watching over the building works for two years.

Scott's concerns about the restoration of churches in general and Turvey in particular were voiced in an important letter of 30 March 1852:

> I have, as you may possibly be aware, [Scott wrote to Higgins,] committed myself to a somewhat indignant published protest against the changes which are every day made in our ancient churches on which I have a strong and painful feeling. My opinion is that we are bound to hand down to posterity these venerable remnants of the architecture of ancient times with as little alteration as we possibly can. Of course this must give way in some cases to the interpretive claims of increased population, but I hold that we are bound to try every means of meeting these claims before we destroy the visible history and identity of an ancient edifice. Since I wrote my protest I find that the case has been taken up by others and much more strongly. With Mr Ruskin and Professor Willis at their head many now protest against all 'restoration' as having convicted itself of being only another name for *destruction*.

Having read a pamphlet printed by Parker of Oxford, Scott told Higgins it 'brought your church somewhat keenly in conscience'. [C.R.O. HG 12/6/46]

Higgins's collection of early books for the use of the Archdeaconry was gathered together over thirty years and housed in the 'Museum' in the centre of Turvey. He was an early enthusiast for town and village museums, where specimens of geology, minerology and antiquarian interest should be displayed 'to instil, foster, and develop in the minds of all classes of people an interest in the common objects of Nature'. [*Twelve Good Men*, p. 454]

Burgon was to outlive most of his Bedfordshire relatives and write their obituaries in his notable book of modern saints. Higgins was no exception: he died on 23 January 1885, mourned by the people of Turvey 'as for a parent'. He had always been a great patron of living painters and sculptors and it was fitting that his passing was commemorated by a handsome white marble and alabaster memorial by H. H. Armstead R.A.

All through the county, landowners were of a more serious persuasion than their immediate forbears; the irreligiosity of the 5th Duke of Bedford would have shocked his successors and the deep-thinking Flitwick squire, John Thomas Brooks (1794–1858). He confided to his diary in 1853:

> Lady Day and Good Friday. To church in the morning (prayers) and afternoon. Made all our people attend so that the Church was filled with labourers – the only day on which I can compel attendance to a place of where they ought to think it their highest privilege and happiness to be permitted to go to. With the rising good and zealous clergyman (so different from the old *drones* dying out) I trust the people will be taught to love and reverence and adhere staunchly to the Church as good men should do, but owing to the sad neglect of the old Foxhunting parsons the vile dissenters of all sorts have sadly gained ground. [*B.H.R.S.* Vol. 66, p. 167]

The Ecclesiastical Census taken in Bedfordshire in March 1851 fully justified Brooks's concern. It showed, much to the alarm of the Established church, that nonconformity was on the increase throughout the region. Bedford town had always been a centre of nonconformity and of proliferating sects. Dr Philip Hunt of St Peter's, Bedford referred to 'a melancholy variety' of chapels. As well as five Anglican parishes, there was the long-standing and respected Moravian congregation, the Bunyan Meeting, the Howard Chapel, the Calvinistic Baptists and the Wesleyan Methodists, the Particular Baptists, the Primitive Methodists, the Congregation of Jews, the Catholic Apostolic Church and the Christian Brethren.

Perhaps the most colourful figure to emerge was the Revd Timothy Richard Matthews (1795–1845). He had a conventional background as a Cambridge student and was a follower of the great evangelical preacher, Charles Simeon. He became curate of Bolnhurst and Colmworth in 1819 and soon developed an erratic and eccentric style of ministry, holding services when he felt like it and being influenced by the Methodism of the Fieldings, a local family of farmers. His marriage to Ann Fielding led him to conversion and a Wesley-style practice of preaching in the open air. In 1825, he became chaplain to the House of Industry in Bedford (later the Workhouse) and used this key appointment to support his growing family and develop an independent career outside the Church of England. He was resident from 1830 in Bedford, where his presence upset some of the Anglican clergy. His compelling preaching and physical presence gained him large congregations in the House of Industry Chapel and later in his own chapel of Christ Church in the Bromham Road.

Matthews was a fine figure of a man, with long hair and jutting brows, who was well known on the streets of the town, striding along in his black Geneva gown with his preaching bands waving in the wind. His custom was to blow a silver trumpet down the streets, a trick that his adversaries called 'the beggar's call', and so lead a crowd of people off to his services. In 1832, a visiting American consecrated Matthews a bishop of his own Primitive Episcopal Church, a scandal that led to his dismissal from the House of Industry. He continued to exercise his own unusual ministry, preaching all over England, but wishing to be taken back into the Anglican fold. In 1837, Matthews's brother-in-law returned from America as a Mormon missionary and founded congregations in the east and south of the county at Eaton Socon and Studham. Matthews himself dallied with this, although he gave more assistance to the Irvingites or Catholic Apostolic Church, which built a tabernacle in Gwyn Street in 1838. In the last five years of his life, Matthews preached 1446 sermons, a load that took a great toll on his health. When he caught typhus fever in 1845, he rapidly declined and died at the age of fifty-one. He was buried under a stone in his own chapel, but later moved to Colmworth churchyard.

The nonconformist element was particularly strong at Bedford, a mixture of that single-minded approach to life and belief in plain speaking which seem to grow well together in a county of small husbandry. A literature of nonconformity was ever present from the days of Bunyan, shackled to tracts and sermons, or more occasionally bursting out into rhyming couplets. It took the full liberalism of the nineteenth century to give this lurking presence the wings of a novel; in fact the nonconformist novel is the region's single contribution to modern fiction.

The great exponent of these books was William Hale White (1831–1913), who was born at Bedford and educated at the Commercial School (Modern School). His father was William White, bookseller and printer of the High Street, who was well read and cultivated, and was a leading member of the Bunyan Meeting. The elder White was an outspoken man of liberal persuasions and was vociferous on the rights of dissenters, particularly on their status and representation within the Harpur Charity. This made him unpopular in the town and later led to the loss and closure of his business. Influential friends, like Lord Charles Russell, were able to give the unhappy bookseller a post as Assistant Doorkeeper at the House of Commons. He left the town in 1852.

This background of provincial trade and chapel-going made a deep impression on the young Hale White and its introspective characters and cabals formed the basis for all his subsequent novels. At the age of seventeen, he was recommended for the ministry by the elders of the Bunyan Meeting (Old Meeting) and sent to study at the dissenting New College in 1850. White's intellectual ability and abundant imagination made him question the orthodox beliefs of his tutors and he was expelled from the college in 1852. His liberalism appealed to the publisher, John Chapman, and he was taken on as an assistant of the *Westminster Review*. Here he helped the assistant editor, Marian Evans, afterwards celebrated as George Eliot, and became a firm friend of this unconventional and brilliant novelist.

Like Trollope, White found a safe haven in the Civil Service where he worked diligently for years, first as clerk and then as Director of Contracts. His leisure was spent in writing and slowly

White metamorphosed into the novelist Mark Rutherford. Rutherford, as we may now call him, drew very heavily on his youthful days for the local colour of his novels, but their descriptions are more general than particular. One gets an excellent feeling of independent religion in early Victorian Bedford, but the locations are not easy to identify. The books began with *The Autobiography of Mark Rutherford* (1881), *Mark Rutherford's Deliverance* (1885), *The Revolution in Tanner's Lane* (1887), *Miriam's Schooling* (1890) and two further novels. Rutherford's forte is to reveal the tensions in these strict Calvinist communities, brought about by the effect of the new philosophies on the nineteenth-century traditionalist congregations. Good characterisation and an excellent narrative style have kept the works of this minor master perennially alive.

The Bedford skyline was changed at this time by the appearance of a number of new churches and chapels. The earliest was the 'Commissioner's church' of Holy Trinity, Bromham Road, an austere Gothic building by John Brown of Norwich, built in 1839–40. The only complete rebuilding was undertaken with the little medieval church of St Cuthbert. Here a neo-Norman edifice was erected on the site by the architect Woodroffe and bitterly criticised by the *Ecclesiologist* for its Norman derivation. The great town church of St Paul's was also considerably altered in 1865–8 by the Bedford-born architect R. Palgrave and his master G. E. Street, St Peter Merton also being altered. In Mill Street, the new Bunyan Meeting in an Italian style was opened for worship in 1849 and, with great haste in 1850, the Howard Chapel was refronted in classical dress to accommodate eight hundred persons.

In the county at large, numerous fine churches were being raised. One of the earliest country ones is All Saints, Ridgmont with its lofty spire designed by Sir George Gilbert Scott for the Duke of Bedford in 1854. A great contribution was made by an unusual architect who deserves to be better known. Henry Clutton (1819–93) was a pupil of Edward Blore and a partner of William Burges, who specialised in grand churches in the French style but also built two notable country houses in the county. Clutton made his debut here as a protegé of Francis, 7th Duke of Bedford, when he designed the estate church at Steppingley in

1859. It replaced the smallest church in Bedfordshire which was tumbling down. Was this perhaps a trial run for the grander projects to come later? The traditional ironstone of the area was used convincingly and, like many Clutton ensembles, sits well amid a school and schoolhouse also from his drawing-board.

The great ducal commission came in 1865, presumably from the short-lived 8th Duke or his cousin who managed the estate, to create a grand parish church for Woburn. This replaced the unspectacular but probably adequate ironstone church in the town centre. St Mary's is a vast and expensive Gothic building that originally had a soaring spire which could be seen for miles across Woburn Park. The lofty interior has got a later reredos by Caroë and stained-glass by Kempe, but rather lacks the mystery of a High Victorian church. In 1877, the 9th Duke, in mournful mood, took a party of ladies and the writer Augustus J. C. Hare to see the new church. 'The church was built by Clutton,' Hare writes, 'who was turned loose into a field and told to produce what he could. He did produce a very poor mongrel building, neither gothic nor romanesque. The Duke said, "Would you like to see what is going to be done with me when I am dead?" and he showed us the hole in the floor where he was to be let through "to the sound of solemn music," and then took us down into the vaults beneath to see the trestles on which his coffin was to repose!' [A. J. C. Hare, *The Story of My Life*, 1900, pp. 60–1]

Other churches were to follow: St Michael's, Aspley Heath, for the Duke in 1868, alterations for Willington in 1876–7, and Clutton had already undertaken the transformation of Souldrop church, in the north of the county, in 1861. Of all these surviving works, Sandy Lodge, (1869–77) built for a member of the Peel family, is the most charming. It is a Jacobean mansion with formal gardens, placed in a woodland setting, and now the headquarters of the Royal Society for the Protection of Birds. A few miles away at Old Warden is his other domestic work, Old Warden Park, a vast dissolute piece of neo-Elizabethan (1872), for the ironmaster Joseph Shuttleworth.

We have only briefly mentioned Clutton's work at Souldrop church, but this does give us the excuse of introducing a delightful clerical character and the only one to keep a diary at this period, the Revd George Digby Newbolt (1829–1907). Newbolt represents something rather different in Bedfordshire; an Oxford High Churchman, who had presumably come under the influence of Tractarianism while at Brasenose College in 1852. He was presented to the living of Knotting-cum-Souldrop in 1856 and in 1860 had the chance to rebuild the church and decorate it according to his own principles. The Duke of Bedford agreed to this 'on condition of the Rector being answerable for £500 to build the Chancel'. Newbolt was well connected, his family being important clerics and his second wife the daughter of Hollingworth Magniac of Colworth. It was therefore easier for him to collect benefactors for the chancel, as well as the kind of rich vestments and ornaments that went with his theology. The Revd John Keble subscribed £3 to the rebuilding of Souldrop. The result is a perfect, small, Early English-style building with lovely Victorian carvings and brilliant stained-glass by O'Connor.

Compared with the careless 'drones' mentioned by Brooks at the beginning of the century, Newbolt's regime was exceptional. There were frequent Holy Communion services, the celebration of saints' days and festivals, and the decoration of the interior with flowers. He was also pleased to have introduced a harvest festival, a revival to counter the godless harvest-homes and drunkenness. Like Turvey and Houghton Conquest, an organ was introduced at an early stage and the singing included chants. The list of offerings recorded by Newbolt reads like a lexicon of ritualism: 'A Pede Cloth . . .'; 'Two ruby velvet Alms Bags . . .'; 'Two brass Standards for Chancel (5 lights each) . . .'; 'Chalice Veil'; 'Sedilia Cushions'. In later years, the richness of vestments was increased to include 'a Dossal of red with green and gold orphreys', a 'green silk Veil and Burse' and 'a plate for Altar Breads', together with many silk stoles and altar frontals. The people of Souldrop enjoyed Newbolt's presence, especially as he helped them in practical ways, such as a Rectory Allotment scheme in the 1870s.

Incumbents could spend a lifetime in one place and frequently did so. The Revd Augustus Orlebar (1824–1912) was vicar of Willington for fifty-four years. He is now best remembered as the original of 'Tom' in Thomas Hughes's *Tom Brown's Schooldays* (1857). Orlebar entered Rugby School in 1838 and was in the same form as Hughes. It was Orlebar's fight with another boy that was fictionalised as the famous match with Tom and Slugger Williams. Hughes also based the character Arthur on Orlebar.

Further south, at Haynes, Hawnes Park had been inherited by an important cleric, The Revd Lord John Thynne. The 2nd Baron Carteret of Hawnes, a noted bibliophile, had died in 1849 and Lord John, a Canon and Sub-Dean of Westminster came to live in Bedfordshire in succession to his uncle. He was a good landlord and much loved in the neighbourhood, where he kept his mansion well and was immensely proud of the Carteret heirlooms that it contained. Rather surprisingly, he gave the magnificent pair of Flemish tapestries from Hawnes Park to Westminster Abbey in 1871. They depict 'The Meeting of Rebecca and Abraham's Servant at the Well' and 'The Healing of the Lame Man at the Beautiful Gate' and are seventeenth-century works from the studio of Wauters of Antwerp, both in a wool and silk weave. They were given to hang in the Jerusalem Chamber where they can still be seen, as part of its restoration in 1871.

If Lord John was a great cleric at Westminster, he was clearly a countryman when in Bedfordshire. Augustus J. C. Hare wrote of a visit in 1876: 'We met the old man riding in his park, and so much taken up with a sick cow that he almost ignored us. But when we had walked round by the charming old-fashioned gardens, we found him waiting for us on the garden doorstep, all courtesy and kindness.' The most lasting memorial to Lord John is his 'Thynne Chapel' in Haynes parish church, an intelligent Victorian creation following the death of Constantia (Lady John Thynne) in April 1866. This is formed out of the north aisle of the chancel, part of a rebuilding in the 1850s. It is all part of a piece by Sir George Gilbert Scott, with a painted roof by Poole's, an iron grille by Potter & Sons and glass by Clayton and Bell, who also designed the angels. What draws the eye in this ensemble is the marble tomb effigy of Constantia Thynne, carved by H. H. Armstead R.A. and under an alabaster canopy designed by Gilbert Scott. She is dressed in contemporary costume, a highly unusual feature for the time. This charming little chapel must have been sparkling in 1870; it could sparkle again if it was restored.

Lord John died in February 1881, when the *Bedfordshire Mercury* described him as 'a devoted son of the church and himself deeply valuing her ministrations'. As well as Haynes, he restored Wilstead, Houghton Conquest and Clapham churches in Bedfordshire, and Kirkhampton in Cornwall. After a funeral service at Westminster, his coffin was brought from St Pancras by train and interred at Haynes.

Bedfordshire was not known for its Anglo-Catholics, but the rector of St Paul's, Bedford from 1864–9 was the Revd Michael Ferrebee Sadler (1819–95), a populariser of tractarian doctrine and a strong high churchman. The alterations to St Paul's were carried out during his incumbency and he could have achieved higher preferment after Bedford, for he was actually offered the primacy of Canada. He left a lasting influence on Bedford by inspiring Miss Fanny Eagles, of an old Bedfordshire family, to found a sisterhood in the town. Sister Fanny trained as a nurse and was made a deaconess in 1869 and returned to Bedford as a parish worker in St Paul's and St Peter's, wearing a nun's habit and sharing a house with two other deaconesses. They opened a small orphanage in Bromham Road, St Etheldreda's, the first religious community in the county since the Reformation.

The Roman Catholics were developing from small beginnings throughout the eighteenth century, mostly in the Shefford area. A family of the name of Noddings were active in the town in the early eighteenth century and Mass was regularly offered in the top room over their butcher's shop. Mrs Noddings, the last of the line, left all her property in the High Street to establish a Catholic mission. The Noddings themselves were buried in the graveyard at Campton until 1743, and one of the Roman Catholic priests was also buried there in 1781. The small building was known as St George's Chapel and it was run by a succession of erudite and well travelled priests who were greatly loved in Shefford. When the Revd C. Taylor died at Shefford in 1812, he was described in the press as 'a benevolent man, who loved his country, and was a kind friend to suffering humanity, taking great pleasure to instruct the humble and illiterate'. [*Beds Notes & Queries* Vol. 1, p. 12] But the great figure at Shefford in the nineteenth century is Canon Collis, who was resolute in wishing to start a children's home and a community on the site. This began in 1869, but Collis's desire to create a church, fitting to the aspirations and status of the community was not immediately realised. Collis's pocket-diaries record a ceaseless round of visits with a begging bowl, desperately trying to finance the Shefford Home with its small staff and dependent boys. He visited the Duke of Norfolk and another Catholic lady with Bedfordshire connections, Lady Amabel Kerr, granddaughter of Lord de Grey. His great benefactress turned out to be Mrs Lynes Stephens of Lynford Hall, Norfolk, the immensely wealthy collector and philanthropist who did so much for the Roman Catholic Church in East Anglia. Collis wrote later:

> I had made a resolution that I would not commence the building of the church unless I had in hand the money to pay for it. The last fifteen years had made an old man of me, and I had no longer the strength of body required for the labour of raising several thousand pounds. As this was so, I had accustomed myself to the thought that it would not be permitted to me to see the new church. On my second visit to this lady – Mrs Lynes Stephens – I was led at once to say, 'A church is very needed – it would be a great work to do for God and his Orphans. How grateful they would be, and their prayers are of much account before God.' I did not say many more words than all put down here.
>
> Two months afterwards, I was informed this lady had written to the Bishop to say she would build the church. [H. E. King, *Ancient Catholic Mission And Its Modern Development*, Shefford, Bedfordshire, after 1896]

St Francis's church is certainly the best Catholic building in the county, although the Holy Child Jesus, Midland Road, Bedford, 1872 is slightly earlier. Small in scale, but rich in detail and interest, it was designed by the architect S. J. Nicholl, who had already created the Boys' Home next door. The foundation stone of the church was laid on the Feast of St Francis, 4 October 1882, and as Collis commented 'the seven hundredth anniversary of the birth of this great saint'. It was consecrated on 3 July 1884 and opened on the 8th in the presence of Mrs Lynes Stephens. Mrs Lynes Stephens is herself worth more than a passing comment as she is one of the most unusual of Bedfordshire's benefactresses. She began life in France as Mademoiselle Duverny, the brilliant and talented ballet dancer in the reign of Louis-Philippe, the toast of Paris and the admired object of William Makepeace Thackeray. She appeared in London, but a subsequent crisis of faith and marriage with a millionaire turned her into a paragon of rectitude and good works. It is not recorded what she thought of her church, but she is memorialised in the stained-glass window facing the street, where she appears presenting the model of the church to the patron saint.

XI
Victorian Expansion

In July 1841, the young Queen Victoria and Prince Albert made their first visit to Bedfordshire following their marriage, in fact their first country house visit as a married couple. In the privacy of her journal, the Queen described her arrival in the county. 'We changed horses at Dunstable, where the people were very civil but rather boisterous in their demonstrations of loyalty. From here the 11th Hussars escorted us, but numbers of farmers all rode with us too, & it was very funny to see the pushing and jostling; they nearly smothered us in dust.' The reception at the Abbey was rather formal and elderly and Lady Lyttleton describes the Queen as like a schoolgirl, looking very young and too frightened to ask questions. Three days of dinners and drives followed, visits to the hothouses and the gardens, the Queen enjoying the sensation of Prince Albert reading to her and of watching him play tennis! The Queen notes that she drove through the town of Woburn 'crowded with people who again rode and ran with us'. The following day she 'Bought some pretty Bedfordshire lace'.

This description of the royal visit does not read very differently from that of other royal visits down the centuries. The Queen arrived by carriage, she exercised in the park, she received loyal addresses and purchased local artefacts. But change was only just around the corner. The steam railway had already crept into a corner of the county at Leighton Buzzard, the Penny Post had begun to make its impact the year before and only eighteen months earlier, the magistrates had passed a motion to establish a rural constabulary force. Towns were already beginning to grow in size at an unprecedented rate and industry was arriving in a hitherto largely agricultural area. In a word the 'Victorian' world was to alter the lives and aspirations of thousands of people dramatically and to transform both the structures of society and the appearance of the landscape.

The great improvement in the roads during the Regency, partly the result of the turnpike trusts and partly the diligence of surveyors, completely revitalised passenger transport and the efficiency of the waggon trade. The establishment of the Post Office in 1786 also encouraged the improvement of roads, for although it had no legal authority to do so, the ever extending network of postal towns led to a healthy rivalry in good communications and good services. The golden age of the mail coach and privately run conveyances was probably in the 1820s, when increased competition resulted in record runs and faster equipages. The traditional routes northwards on the Watling Street and the Great North Road were improved by bigger and better inns and posting houses with an efficient staff that could turn round a team of horses and have the mail ready again for the road in a question of minutes.

Although Bedford itself did not lie on the principal routes, it continued to have a considerable cross-country importance and many of the crack coaches halted there. Of these the more significant were the *Eagle*, Birmingham and Cambridge coach, *The Wonder*, Oxford and Cambridge coach, *The Peveril of the Peak*, Manchester to London, and the *Leeds Mail*. The traveller had a considerable choice of local coaches to London: the *Bedford Times*, which ran through Hitchin from the Swan Inn; the *Civility*, which ran through Luton to London from the Red Lion in the High Street; the *Pilot*, which took the same route from the Fountain; and the *Umpire* which went by Hitchin from the Rose. Many of these left Bedford in the early morning, returning to Bedford the next day, but the *Bedford Times* left the Swan at 8.30 a.m. and returned from London at 8.30 p.m. the same day. The journey took between four and a half and five hours and the *Times* was the longest running of the coaches, surviving from 1825 until 1846. The vehicle was driven by the brothers John and George Crow, who, as there was no guard, had the full responsibility for luggage and the valuable bank parcels that were delivered along the route.

These rapid journeys were not always acccomplished without mishaps. In the 1830s, the *Times* coach ran into heavy snow between Shefford and Bedford and had to be dug out three times, the postilions riding several miles to bring back fresh horses. In

1836, the *Peveril of the Peak* coach, descending the hill before the Falcon at Bletsoe, overturned, killing one passenger and breaking the leg of another.

It is fascinating to note that James Wyatt (1816–78), the first editor and owner of the *Bedfordshire Times* newspaper, was the son of a coach-proprietor of Hemel Hempstead. Perhaps Wyatt realised that this occupation was on the wane, for instead of following his father, he became a journalist and arrived in Bedford in 1838 as correspondent of the *Hertford Mercury*. In 1843, he married the daughter of a prosperous Bedford merchant and within two years had founded the county's first newspaper. The first four-page issues for October and November 1845 had column after column of advertisements devoted to the projected railways that were burgeoning all over England. They included the 'Great Leeds and London Direct Railway', 'The Tring, Cambridge and Newmarket Company', 'The Eastern Counties Extension', and many others. The age of steam had arrived with a vengeance. 'Railroads are the passion of the day', ran the leader in the *Bedfordshire Times*, 'and engross the capital, the energies, and the mind of the country.'

One occurrence with which young James Wyatt was linked before the railway age was the Corn Law agitation in the early 1840s. Wyatt was at this time a dedicated Radical Liberal and he espoused the cause of Free Trade in a markedly reactionary area. Richard Cobden (1804–65) passed through Bedford on the top of the *Peveril of the Peak* coach on his first visit to Manchester in 1831. His subsequent conviction that agricultural protection as laid down in the Corn Laws and Provision Laws was detrimental to this country and was putting a heavy burden on industry and the working population, resulted in the founding of the Anti-Corn Law League in 1838. Cobden and his friends received rebuttals from the Peel Tory government in 1842 and in 1843 the League was determined to bring the issues 'into the strongholds of the enemy . . .' A series of county meetings was planned and that at Bedford, on Saturday, 3 June 1843, was amongst the first. (This happened to be Cobden's birthday!) Cobden again arrived in the town by coach. 'At three the Castle Rooms were crowded to overflowing and the meeting was consequently adjourned to the cricket ground and a number of waggons obtained.' [*Beds*

Mercury, 10 June 1843] From this improvised stage, Cobden battled with the meeting for six hours at Peck's Close. Lord Charles Russell, a notable neutral, was in the chair and supposed to have the confidence of both Cobden and Bedfordshire farmers. Cobden was attacked verbally by Francis Pym of the Hazells who moved a resolution that 'to abolish that protection and further depreciate the productions of our own soil, will only end in the spread of inevitable ruin throughout the rural districts . . .' He was supported by Bennett of Luton who was concerned about the importation of cheap plaits. The opposing motion by Mr Lattimore was 'That in the opinion of this meeting the Corn Law, and every other law which protects one class at the expense of other classes, must prove injurious to the national prosperity'. The latter motion was carried by two to one.

According to Cobden's biographer, Henry Ashworth, Cobden swayed the meeting in favour of free trade by dividing the farmers from the landowners. The society formed shortly afterwards to oppose reform was entirely made up of small Tory landowners, that is to say the Orlebars, J. T. Brooks, T. A. Green, H. Stuart M.P., Lord Alford, Mr Astell, Lord St John and Lord Ongley. The Bedfords did not subscribe. Cobden must have been pleased to have Wyatt's support as the press tended to ignore the League. A week after the meeting, Cobden wrote to Wyatt to urge his support at Huntingdon and added: 'I should be glad to know what the good folks of Beds say of our late doings.' [Private Collection]. Wyatt continued to correspond with Cobden and was presented with a photograph in 1859. Wyatt's stature was such that he had correspondences with such varied figures as T. H. Huxley, Richard Owen and William Yarrell in succeeding years.

Cobden could have travelled by train to Leighton Buzzard because it had a railway station before any of the other towns, being served by the prestigious London and Birmingham Railway from September 1838. Naturally enough there was agitation among the Bedford tradesmen to be grafted into this profitable system as soon as possible, the outcome being the proposal of a branch line from Bletchley to Bedford, heavily sponsored and supported by the Duke of Bedford. On 17 November 1846, the Duchess of Bedford turned the first turf of the Bedford, London and Birmingham railway 'beyond Brogborough Hill, near the farm of Mr Turney, in the parish of Husborne Crawley'. Her Grace, dressed in black and with a satin scarf embroidered with gold, accomplished the task with a silver spade and a wheelbarrow of polished oak grown on the Woburn estate. Exactly a year later, the first train of thirty carriages and pulled by two 'powerful engines' conveyed the first six hundred passengers from Bedford St Leonard's station to Bletchley to the tune of a brass band and all the church bells ringing.

The period immediately before and immediately after the coming of the railway was notable for stagnation in the first instance and expansion in the second, so that the aims of the burghers were amply justified. Whether it was solely due to the arrival of steam is debatable, but it is probable that there was a greater pride and sense of confidence in the 1850s than there had been in the 1840s. Between 1841 and 1851, the population of the county town rose by two and a half thousand, the languishing wool fairs took on a new lease of life, a new Corn Exchange was built in 1849 and the prison completely rebuilt in that year by Thomas Smith of Hertford.

The new railroad was obviously a great benefit to the Bedfordians. The journey from Bedford to London took two and a half hours compared to four and a half to five hours by coach, it cost 5s 3d for a 3rd class ticket compared with a guinea on the coaches. In 1848, the stations listed by Bradshaw on the branch were Bedford, Marston, Lidlington, Ridgmont, Woburn Sands, Fenny Stratford and Bletchley, the station houses built in a delightful, half-timbered, gabled style reminiscent of the estate villages.

For the country landowner the new line was also an improvement. In May 1843, J. T. Brooks of Flitwick Manor records in his diary that he rose at 4 a.m. to get to the only existing station at Leighton Buzzard by 7 a.m. in order to catch the London train. In January 1847, he writes: 'Bass drove me to Ridgmont. We left home at 7 o'clock and reached Ridgmont Station 20 minutes before 8. Arrived in London a quarter past 10.' He was able to return comfortably the same evening 'after a very pleasant day in London'. [B.H.R.S., Vol. 66, 1987, p. 57.]

The railway boom brought benefits to the ordinary population as well, but was an exciting speculation for businessmen, landowners and share-holders. The proposal for a South Midland Railway was taken up in 1846 by various Bedford townsmen such as Alexander Sharman, the prominent solicitor, W. H. Whitbread and Isaac Elger. At an enthusiastic town meeting, the audience was addressed by George Hudson 'the Railway King'.

The attitude of landowners could be rather ambiguous at times. The Duke of Bedford was wholeheartedly behind the Bedford and Bletchley line because it did not interfere with his private residence. In 1847, the proposals for a Leicester, Bedford and Hitchin railway did not meet with His Grace's approval because the line would come too close to his retreat at Oakley. Lord de Grey was said to welcome a railway near his estate at Wrest – a possible Shefford to Clophill and Ampthill branch – whereas Mr Pym of Sandy was said to dislike extensions that interfered with his property. Lord de Grey had already benefited by building materials being brought from the railhead at Leighton for his house at Wrest.

The myriad private companies and haphazard extensions were further complicated by private interest, one company or landowner trying to thwart another because a convenient route might undercut a profitable one. The position in the 1850s and early 1860s, when rival companies were sharing lines and the Midland Railway's Leicester, Bedford and Hitchin route ran into the Great Northern system to King's Cross, was obviously unsatisfactory. This anomaly caused a fatal accident at Welwyn and resulted in the construction of the county's crack railway, the Bedford, Luton and St Pancras route.

Miss Louisa Moore of Maulden (1835–1933) recollected a garden party at Flitwick Manor when new railways were debated and 'all had thought it would spoil the countryside'. [Richardson Archives] It seems strange that this opinion should have been voiced at the home of J. T. Brooks, an inveterate railway traveller, but it is probable that the debate was in the time of his son, Major Hatfield Brooks, in the middle of the 1860s, when the projected Midland line through the county drove perilously close to his Flitwick estate.

The most important figure in Bedfordshire to see the benefit of the railways and give them his support and blessing was W. H. Whitbread M.P. (1795–1867), whom we have already encountered as an enlightened landowner and man of science. When the Leicester, Bedford and Hitchin route was first mooted in 1845, Whitbread, who was anxious to have it running through his estate, offered the Midland the land at only £70 an acre. In 1858–9. he was heavily involved with the Luton, Dunstable and Welwyn Railway, highlighting the extraordinary fact that until that date the prosperous manufacturing town of Luton had been totally left out of the system. Whitbread had also given moral support to the Bedford and Northampton Railway which ran through Turvey and which unfortunately he did not live to see completed. Because of Whitbread's loyal support, the Board of the Midland Railway erected an obelisk on the Whitbread estate to his memory. Travellers moving out of Southill station towards Shefford would have their eyes attracted by this monument. It read: 'To William Henry Whitbread Esquire For his Zeal and Energy in promoting Railways through the County of Bedford. 1864. Erected by Public Subscription.'

The Bedford to Hitchin line, which Whitbread had fought to have at Southill, caused a fierce argument in Bedford. The county had to have a new station, but where was the Midland Railway station to be situated? The Duke of Bedford had such a strong involvement with the Bedford to Bletchley line that he was adamant that any terminus of the Midland must be situated at St Leonard's (now St John's). There were long arguments within Bedford itself as to whether a station should be north or south of the river, the location being crucial to business. The alternative sites were in St Mary's, south of the Ouse, or on the north-west edge of the town known as Freemen's Common. This is where it was finally erected in 1858–9, perhaps because the strongest trade and the strongest lobbying came from north of the bridge.

This line was a great financial undertaking. To the north of Bedford, the railway crossed the Ouse seven times, and at Sharnbrook the foundations of the viaduct had to be sunk twenty-five feet below the clay. But the service was an improved one, especially from February 1858, when trains were permitted to run directly from Bedford to King's Cross without a change at Hitchin. It was the furious driving of this line that caused Charles Dickens to alight at Bedford and complain about it in a letter to *The Times* on 26 January 1867.

One of the most intriguing examples of private enterprise in the railway age was the construction of a line by the Peel family from Potton to Sandy in 1854–7. As well as providing a good indication of public spiritedness, it also introduces one of the most colourful figures of Victorian Bedfordshire. Although Sir Robert Peel was a Lancastrian, the Peel family had estates at Sandy and Eyeworth from about 1852, and the Prime Minister's third and fourth sons lived at the Swiss Cottage, a small house on the site of Sandy Lodge, now the Royal Society for the Protection of Birds.

The third son, Captain William Peel R.N. was a sort of schoolboy hero, the stuff of which adventure stories are made. Well-born, athletic and good-looking, he had had a meteoric rise in the Royal Navy from midshipman to commander, loved by his men and admired by his brother officers. A captain at twenty-four, he had seen service off the Syrian coast, in China, at the Cape of Good Hope and on the North American Station before 1849. In that year, he took leave to explore Central Africa, and, after learning Arabic, made a tour of the Holy Land and the Nile in 1852, writing a book about his expedition.

Peel took command of H.M.S. *Diamond* in the Mediterranean in 1852 and his ship formed part of the Naval Brigade in the Crimean War two years later. In October 1854, Peel, with a party of men, was landed at the Siege of Sebastopol and had the task of moving ammunition for the allied batteries. When a 42lb Russian shell landed right next to the gunpowder, Peel seized it with its fuse still burning and tossed it over the parapet. It exploded only yards from him without injuring anyone. For this and other acts of outstanding heroism, he was awarded the newly instituted Victoria Cross, becoming the first Bedfordshire man to win the honour. As a result of these exploits, in September 1856 Peel was given command of one of the most modern frigates in the Royal Navy, H.M.S. *Shannon*.

During his brief periods at home, Captain Peel was buying up land on his estate between Potton and Sandy in order to develop a line of his own which would connect with the Great Northern Railway. The four and a half miles of track was to be entirely on his own land, thereby obviating the need for any acts of Parliament to obtain permission. The line had a gradient of 1 in

100 at certain places but it only crossed over one main road on a small bridge. The Sandy and Potton Railway, which was expected to improve the trade in the small town of Potton and benefit the Peel estate, was opened by Lady Peel in November 1857 though it was apparently operative from June 1857. A small engine, named 'Shannon' after Captain Peel's frigate, was built by George England at a cost of £800 and drew two carriages, a goods waggon and a brake van. It ran successfully for about five years, closing after 1862.

Captain Peel lived to hear of the opening of his steam railway but did not survive to see it. Ordered to China in 1858, his command were diverted to India to help contain the Indian Mutiny. Characteristically, the gallant Captain distinguished himself during the Siege of Lucknow and was rewarded with the honour of a Knight Commander of the Bath. Sir William, as he now was, intended to return to England, but, somewhat ironically, contracted smallpox from travelling in an infected carriage. He died on 22 April 1858. His engine, 'Shannon', had a second lease of life at Wantage and is now preserved at the Railway Museum, Didcot.

The railway which was such an obvious outlet for manufactures and trade was also a considerable harbinger of recreations and broader horizons. For many ordinary folk in the country, travel had hitherto been impossible, but now cheap rate tickets to markets, fairs and race meetings offered an increased freedom. W. H. Whitbread, the railway pioneer, was very ready to allow excursionists into his park at Southill. In June 1861, the Volunteer Corps entrained from Bedford and drilled in the park at Southill, through his newly opened Southill station. In July 1866, trains brought two thousand passengers for a grand fête in the grounds, and in August 1868 the teachers of the Bunyan Meeting Sunday School travelled there. 'The party proceeded to the Park by kind permission of S. C. Whitbread Esq.' and was conducted through the beautiful gardens. Tea was prepared on the banks of the lake. "Innocent games were indulged in and then came a stroll to Warden church. The party returned on the 7.39 train to Bedford having enjoyed the rural picnic exceedingly.'

Sunday excursion trains were roundly condemned by many nonconformists and some Anglicans. In one of the

Bedfordshire chapels, probably at Stevington, an extraordinary poster was displayed entitled 'The Up and Down Line'. This piece of temperance propaganda showed a Sunday excursion train with all its trippers on board being swallowed up by the jaws of Hell.

It was typical of the rather haphazard way in which the system was evolving that the burgeoning town of Luton should lack a railway. Until now we have only witnessed Luton as a small market town with a magnificent parish church, the mere adjunct to the great estate of Luton Hoo on its southern boundary. In 1835, the German art historian G. F. Waagen visited Luton Hoo and left a brief description of the town. 'What a difference between that and the places of equal extent in Germany! In the principal streets there is a good flag pavement, such as but few of the largest towns in Germany can boast. Some shops, with all kinds of manufactures, are very elegant.' Luton at this time was the centre of an agricultural district, already well known for local straw plait work like its sister town of Dunstable, but essentially a middle-class trading community of handsome brick houses with less well appointed cottages and outlying farms. In 1810, the town was still sufficiently agricultural for George Street, the main thoroughfare, to contain eight or ten farmhouses.

The part played by Lord Bute in the transformation of Luton is an interesting one, for he appears to have been concerned to develop the town residentially to start with, later moving on to speculative housing. In the earlier period he evicted a tenant farmer from a house in the centre in order to build better quality houses for renting. However, after the disastrous fire at Luton Hoo in 1843, when the Adam building was gutted, the Butes seem to have lost interest in the estate and consequently in the ordered improvement of the town.

This date coincides with the alteration in the town's status from market town to industrial centre and the change from a basically middle-class population to a working-class one. Without a resident landowning family or a powerful Anglican presence, Luton became a deeply nonconformist community with a large floating population. It was particularly significant that the Anglicans did not attempt to levy a church rate after about 1830 as the nonconformists simply refused to pay it.

In 1808, the population of Luton was 3095, three-quarters of the men being employed in agriculture. By 1854 there were 12,000 inhabitants and by the 1860s nearly 17,000. Although celebrated for straw-plait from the eighteenth century, Luton was not better known than Shefford, Hitchin or St Albans and a great deal less well known than Dunstable, which had been famous for specialised straw work of a fine and intricate kind. William Bray reported in 1783 that 'Dunstable is remarkable for a neat manufacture of straw, which is stained of various colours, and made into boxes, hats, toys, &c.' These were sold to travellers at the inns. In *Pigott's Commercial Directory* for 1839 thirty-two straw hat manufacturers are listed at Dunstable, but they had already been overtaken by the thirty-nine at Luton. Sixteen of the latter were actually plait-dealers and some of these dealt in the highly prized leghorn straw.

It was clearly an absurdity that Luton had no railway. One story states that George Stephenson attended a meeting in the town in 1844 to promote such a link, but walked out because of dissensions. His plan had been to create a Luton, Dunstable and Watford line and, in his own words, 'reinstate Dunstable in its former position as an important town on the Great Northern thoroughfare'. Dunstable received its rail link with Leighton Buzzard in 1848: perhaps its greater status and bigger factories carried weight. Luton's manufactures had to be carted to the Dunstable railhead.

But despite this setback, Luton was booming in the 1850s because it was less stratified and more flexible. Straw-plait at Luton was largely a cottage industry, little businesses flourished, migrant workers came in and out while the work lasted and female labour was paid piece work. The conditions for such workers were appalling; wretched housing was run by the Butes and others and the population was crammed in without sanitation. Slums of this sort were an absolute breeding ground for vice and disease and Luton was to become notorious within a generation. There were outbreaks of cholera in Adelaide Terrace in 1853 and again in Tower Hill in 1854, when fifteen people died. In the 1851 census it emerged that sixty-five per cent of the population had Bedfordshire origins, just over nineteen per cent came from Hertfordshire and smaller percentages from

Buckinghamshire, Northamptonshire, Essex, Cambridge and London. It was part of the national trend for agricultural populations seeking work to move into the towns, but Luton's attraction was that its industry suited seasonal workers and women. In the 1860s, when the seasonal jobs dried up, there would be a thousand girls leaving the town a week. Such a work pattern gave no stability to a growing community and no investment in family life.

The town therefore was and remains quite unlike any other town in Bedfordshire. Richard Cobden called it 'the Manchester of Bedfordshire'. A boom town with a huge working-class population, it had a very small middle class of doctors, solicitors and clergy and a peripheral class of landowners who were aloof from it and its problems. There were never sufficient leaders among the hat-manufacturers and small shopkeepers to give the town a sense of civic pride and, without a real commitment to stay by them, there was very little continuity. In 1847, a town hall was constructed, in most towns a sign of civic importance, but here a sign of civic obligation in order to accommodate a county court. A clock was added to this basically classical building in 1854 to commemorate the Crimean War.

A good example of how Luton was struggling for an identity in the 1850s is the publication in 1855 of the first book about the town, *The History of Luton* by Frederick Davis, issued in thirteen parts. Davis was a self-made Lutonian, a shoe-maker of Market Hill and Stuart Street, who speculated in property and was more ambitious than most of his townsmen. The book is not rated highly today as a history, but a second edition in 1874 was opulently bound in blue morocco with seventeenth-century Luton trade tokens in gilt on the front cover. But Davis was no more a leader of society in this pilotless town than anyone else and so the town council was made up of cautious, self-educated men who adopted no grand schemes.

The most lively part of the community was among the nonconformists, and the most unusual among them was the Revd Henry Burgess (1808–86), minister of the Park Street Baptist Chapel in the 1840s. Burgess had qualities of leadership and learning that were rare in Luton and totally at variance with the flock that he led. He was a powerful preacher and a determined advocate for causes, but he was not interested in anybody else's views and he took no care of the church's funds. He was instrumental in starting the first newspaper in the town, in reality a monthly news-sheet called *The Wreath*, on 21 August 1846, and he was behind moves to begin a Mechanics' Institute and to ensure that the railway finally came to Luton. Burgess's single-minded approach and dismissive attitude to consensus rule (an important element of nonconformity) led him into trouble in 1848 when his congregation was split over his use of money and persuaded him to stand down with an honorarium of £250. Burgess joined the Church of England and went on to be a Doctor of Divinity and a Syriac scholar, but his departure caused a division in Baptist circles.

Chapels were already featuring as the main contribution to Luton's Victorian architecture, their bulky presences dominating the crossings of many streets. The Union Chapel in Castle Street was one of the best, a stuccoed Greek Doric building of 1836–44, as was the Wesleyan Chapel in Chapel Street, an Italianate structure of 1851–2 by W. W. Pocock. The most splendid was probably the King Street Congregational Church of 1865–6 by J. Tarring, built at that point where nonconformist prosperity flirted with the Gothic and built towers and spires. This chapel was attended by many of Luton's wealthiest hat-manufacturers and it frequently features in early photographs of Luton. The Anglicans built Christ Church, Upper George Street in 1854–66, an attempt at thirteenth-century Gothic but less 'High Church' than the Congregationalists.

The passion for chapel building was certainly the result of the town's squalor and deprivation in the mid-century. The small body of prosperous traders were concerned at the crime and prostitution that surrounded them: public houses and brothels had sprung up and there was little control. The temperance movement grew from the concern of the small traders rather than from the leaders of society, because they were more affected by lawlessness. In the late 1860s there were practically no Luton men on the magistrates' bench. The justices of the peace were made up of the nearby landowners, the Crawleys, Leighs, Adeys and Ames, who were far removed from the town's problems. Luton concerns had more of a voice when town newspapers arrived: the *Miscellany* in 1854, a *Luton Times* in 1855 and a first *Luton News* in 1861, followed by the still existing *Luton News* in 1891. With the opening of the Bute Street Station in 1858, the largest town in the county was at last recognised as a crucial rail link.

Charles Knight (1791–1873), the tireless worker for self-education, visited Luton in 1865 and his account is a classic picture of its teeming industry:

The Straw-plait market of Luton is held on every Monday throughout the year at eight o'clock from Lady-day to Michaelmas, at nine from Michaelmas to Lady-day. It has been described to me as a scene combining many features of the picturesque, such as a painter would delight in if he beheld it on a bright summer morning, when the crowds from the country would hilariously display the golden plait on stalls set out from one end to the other of a long street, and cheerful matrons and smart lasses would stand quietly on the pavement, each with their scores of plait hooped on their arms. It was my misfortune to see this assemblage on a morning when the rain came down with a settled determination that destroyed all the gaiety of the scene. Nevertheless the street was crowded with sellers and buyers and every gateway that could give shelter was filled with the poor women who brought their week's work to a certain market. All the curious organisations of the trade could here be followed out. At nine o'clock the market bell rings, and the traffic begins. My attention is first attracted by the dealers in straw prepared for plaiting. These come from the neighbouring hamlets, in which they are employed in the selection of straw from the farmers' barns; in sorting out into different degrees in fineness; in cutting it into a regulated length; in bleaching it by exposure to sulphur fumes; and in making it up for sale in little bundles. The straw-plaiters come to the market to buy this straw; as they also come to sell their plait. Those women whose goods have not been collected by a middle-man stand in rank, their small dealings being principally confined to the private makers of bonnets at their own homes, who chaffer with the plaiters for a score or two of the plait. The dealers are opening their bags upon the stalls. The commodity will sustain non material damage from the rain; and so the trade goes forward as if all were sunshine. The buyers here are the agents of the great houses. They rapidly decide upon the quality and price; enter the bargain in their note-book; the bags are carried to the warehouses; the loaded tressels are soon relieved of their burdens; and in an hour or two the street is empty. The scene reminds one of Defoe's description of the cloth market of Leeds at the beginning of the last century, when the High Street was covered with a temporary counter, to which the clothiers from the country came each with his piece of cloth, rarely with more; and the business was settled between the producers and the cloth-factors after a very few words. A straw plait manufactory employs no straw plaiters within its walls. There are huge warehouses in which every variety of plait is kept in spacious receptacles – English plait and foreign plait, dyed plait, and plait called 'rice', the white inner part of the straw being worked outwards. The variety of degrees of skilled labour is manifest in these productions. I was shown a bundle of plait of the most exquisite fineness, worked by a dame of eighty; as well as the commonest plait worked by very young girls, who sit at their cottage doors in the sunny days or wander about the green lanes, playing as it were with their pretty work. The bonnet-sewing and hat-sewing process is exhibited in spacious rooms, in each of which sixty or eighty young women are busily plying the needle. [*Passages From A Working Life*, 1865, pp. 200–2]

The coming of the London Midland line in 1869 coincided with the opening of the Plait Halls and the Corn Exchange, both signs of civic importance and expansion. The new buildings were opened by the Lord-Lieutenant, Earl Cowper of Wrest Park; that week 1200 women were treated to tea in the Corn Exchange by the hat-manufacturers. The Plait Halls were utilitarian buildings of not much architectural style, but they are remembered by many people with affection as the covered Luton Market, full of bustle and character. In the 1870s, the style of trading described by Knight began to change, plait was no longer a cottage industry and activity was concentrated in bigger and better factories. Gradually, other industries came to the town and hat-manufacturing was no longer predominant.

No greater contrast could be imagined between 'Strawopolis' in the south and the sedate county town of Bedford, twenty miles to the north. Bedford was a town shaped by its history, the legacy of a fine river, an ecclesiastical past and famous schools. In the nineteenth century, above everything else, the Harpur Schools created the tone and timbre of Bedford, even to some extent its architecture. It was a centre of professionals and pedagogues, many of whom were associated with the schools and were to go out into distinguished careers in the church, the services, missionary work and business in all the corners of Queen Victoria's Empire.

The early nineteenth century had seen the Bedford Grammar and Writing Schools begin to rouse themselves from their Georgian torpor. Bedford was not alone at the time in suffering from a poor standard of education, unsuitable schoolmasters and bad accommodation, but it was among the earlier institutions to improve itself. The master and usher of the Grammar School in 1800 were John Hook and Charles Abbott, both graduates of New College, but who regarded the posts as a sinecure. Abbott, as we have seen, was an able botanist, but when Hook died in 1810 he was unwilling to accept extra responsibility for boarders at a school that had dropped to six pupils! A committee appointed to examine the situation concluded that 'the children of this town do not derive those benefits from its establishment that were so evidently intended by the founders and the legislature, and . . . instead of having classical education gratis, are in fact sent to other schools at a considerable expense to their parents'. [Godber, *The Harpur Trust*, 1973, p. 60] The outcome was the appointment of the dynamic Revd John Brereton in January 1811.

The committee had originally looked to Rugby as their model; Brereton was a Wykehamist, but it is certain that in the forty-four years of his headmastership he intended to turn Bedford into the classic nineteenth-century public school. He came from a cultured clerical background and it was the all-round interests of the gentleman – astronomy, archaeology, music and gardening, as well as the classics – that he liked to inculcate in his pupils. His regime, where the emphasis was on boarders, was strict but kind, the food was ample, and on Sundays veal was dispensed to the boys by the doctor himself. Despite his sonorous Latin graces and demand for absolute silence during meals, he was genial enough to organise firework displays for the boys. Over the years, numbers steadily rose from fifty-three in 1817 to one hundred and fifteen in 1835 and one hundred and seventy-eight in 1850. In that year, Brereton's income was more than £1300 per annum and he was said to be the richest man in Bedford.

By the middle of the century, because of changes in the Harpur Trust regulations, there were far more day boys than boarders. The free education for Bedford residents combined with the growing status of the school was a great draw for non-Bedford families. These settlers, more rudely referred to by the inhabitants as 'squatters' increased in the 1820s and 1830s and greatly enhanced the interest of the town. When William Dawson climbed on to the leads of St Paul's church in 1833 to draw his memorable panorama of the town, he saw a basically Georgian townscape below him. Neat streets of eighteenth-century houses stretched away from the central square, their small gardens neatly partitioned off behind railings, the whole prospect punctuated by open spaces and trees. Some echoes of this small county town can still be seen in those best preserved of Regency thoroughfares, St Cuthbert's Street and Cardington Road, with their varied range of beautifully scaled houses.

On the periphery of Dawson's panoramic view, elegant middle-class enclaves were growing up, peopled by these settlers who were so impressed by Brereton's new school. They included some of the houses round St Peter's Green, the development of the New Town and The Crescent (1825), Pleasant Place (1825), Macqueen Place (1833, now demolished), Priory Terrace and Adelaide Square. The red brick of The Crescent was succeeded in the late 1830s by the fashionable stucco of the villas along Kimbolton Road, run up by the enterprising builder James Woodroffe in Gothic or Grecian mode according to taste. The 'Capital Cottage Residences' of about 1838–40 on the west side of Adelaide Square are even more genteel, one boasting a fretwork porch that is more Indian than Gothic.

In these elegant villas resided the temporary residents who had sons at the schools. A great number were naval or military men who, in the 1820s to 1830s, included Captains Griffith, Leech, Mitford, Home, Smyth, Haig, Howe, Scriven, Hasleham, Bell, Sparrow, Duval, Addington and Law, as well as a Colonel Hamilton and an H. P. Russell of the Bengal Civil Service. Most of these people tended not to be in the top flight of their services and they were generally slightly impecunious, but they could be very distinguished. Typical of these new Bedfordians was Mrs Catherine Young, afterwards Maclear, who came to Bedford in 1831 as a young widow to educate her son. A cultured and capable woman, she had to make her own way, but soon established herself in an ever widening circle of clergy, gentry and professionals. She played the harp and the piano and attended concerts, and was very soon receiving visits from admirers. Her personal diary records that on 26 April 1832 she 'took poor Willy to Dr Brereton's to commence school as a boarder' and later 'I took possession of our house' on St Peter's Green: 'precious confusion it was'. Catherine walked to the school often to 'have a long confab' with her boy and sent him 'a cake and some good advice' on his birthday. Willy came home to St Peter's for the holidays and brought friends with him. In longer vacations she accompanied her sons on horseback or hired a boat for them on the river. On 1 July 1835 the toll was removed from Bedford Bridge and the populace celebrated with 'fireworks and all sorts of gay doings in consequence'. [*B.H.R.S.* Vol. 40, *Some Bedfordshire Diaries*, 1960, pp. 144–62]

Among Catherine Young's Bedford acquaintances was Captain Smyth (1788–1865), the astronomer and man of science, who had come to No. 6 The Crescent in 1827 with the intention of researching and experimenting. He had become prosperous in the Navy as a result of taking prizes and, in the garden of his new home, he built an observatory to house his 'Bedford equatorial refractor telescope', made by George Dolland of London, and one of the first to have a clockwork drive. His observations were published as *A Cycle of Celestial Objects* (1844), and before he left Bedford in 1839 he was visited by all the leading astronomers of the time including Sir John Herschel and Sir George Airy, the Astronomer Royal. Smyth was advanced to the rank of Admiral; his son, Charles Piazzi Smyth, was Astronomer Royal for Scotland, and his grandson was Lord Baden-Powell. [Keith Sugden, 'Admiral Smyth and the Bedford Observatory', *Beds Magazine*, Vol. 18, p. 3]

In 1836, Catherine Young of St Peter's married the Revd George Maclear, a young widower with three sons and chaplain of the Bedford Penitentiary. The combined family moved to The Crescent and the second Maclear boy was also sent to Brereton's school. Maclear's brother was a brilliant young doctor at the Bedford Infirmary and, after taking up astronomy under the influence of Smyth, he left in 1833 for the Cape of Good Hope where he became Astronomer Royal and was knighted.

The success of the Grammar School in its rather cramped old building was mirrored by the advances of the Writing or English School, later Modern School. This had always been popular in the town for its practical application of skills required in commerce, but it needed a building of its own, with individual classrooms, to conform with the new teaching practices. The

Trustees valued the great legacy passed down from their sixteenth-century benefactor and were determined to give the foundation a fitting building. They had consistently bought up properties on the west side of Angel Street (Harpur Street) where the new building was to stretch from north to south.

Discussions about a new school were current in 1826, but it was not until 1828 that the Trust put an advertisement in *The Times* for a competition. The brief for this was 'a Commercial School, a Preparatory or National School with an Infant School annexed, a House and Offices for lodging, boarding and educating 25 boys and 25 girls of their Blue Coat School, a House and Offices for the residence of the Clerk to the Trustees, and hall for their General Meetings, with a Muniment Room adjoining . . .' It was specifically stated that the designs had to be in stone 'in the style of what may be called the Collegiate, Conventual and Domestic English Architecture of the period, comprising the reigns of Edward VI, Mary, and Elizabeth'. The Trustees were adamant that no designs should be submitted in the Grecian, Roman or Anglo-Italian styles. Architectural purity was beginning to become an issue in the provinces; the first published catalogue of the Bedfordshire General Library, founded in 1830, lists works on Egyptian architecture and the picturesque, as well as J. C. Loudon's *Village Architecture* and Rickman's *Gothic Architecture*. J. C. Loudon had visited Flitwick in 1829 to advise on the Manor grounds.

The competition of 1828 was questionable, because a committee of five set up to judge the entrants included two local architects who were entrants, Messrs Elger and Wing! By April 1829, designs had been received from Charles Purser (with Bedford connections), John Chessel Buckler, George Allen Underwood (a pupil of Sir John Soane), Lewis Vulliamy and Anthony Salvin. Vulliamy's surviving designs show that his entry was based on Elizabethan domestic architecture, a graceful compliment to Harpur. J. T. Wing, the Bedford boy, won the competition, but the committee was unhappy. Wing's design was more like a terrace of houses than a composite building and would have given little importance to the site. In March 1830, Edward Blore (1787–1879) was consulted and co-opted on to the design team of Elger and Wing as a consultant. He was appointed architect on 14 June 1830 and it was his collegiate building that rose in Angel Street, now Harpur Street and which survives as a façade today. The result was a harmonious if somewhat ponderous school, late Perpendicular in style, but in its Council Room and furnishing more Elizabethan, with heavy stall-like thrones for the trustees. Elementary Schools for Boys and Girls were added at either end in 1834 and 1840. The Harpur Trust dominated the scene sufficiently to insist that the new Assembly Rooms opposite the school should be in the classical style, failing this they would not make a contribution! Blore's appointment certainly set a precedent; after his success, major architectural schemes in Bedford were usually put in the hands of London architects for the next fifty years; the only exception being John Usher.

John Moore, the new headmaster, stepped into a virtually new school on his appointment in 1831. He was a charity scholar and had none of the advantages of Brereton, he was not as well supported or as well financed as the headmaster of the other school, but he was an outstanding man. He is believed to have suffered from ill health and was advised to retire in 1847 but continued to reign there until 1860. Moore expanded and improved the curriculum and he had a French master and a Latin master appointed in 1837 much to the irritation of Dr Brereton next door who thought only the Grammar School should teach Latin. In 1840, a Drawing master was appointed, Bradford Rudge (1813–85), who was to do so much to record the changing topography of the town and Bedfordshire at large. Rudge, the son of the Rugby drawing master Edward Rudge, who also worked in Bedfordshire, very soon had twenty-eight pupils and established a watercolour tradition in the area.

Bradford Rudge's splendid series of lithographs of Bedford at this time give a decidedly collegiate feel to the place. Grey buildings with towers dominate the scene, and figures in mortar boards scurry about with here and there a pupil carrying a bundle of books, watched over by an anxious mama. In a letter to the warden of New College in 1848, Dr Brereton wrote that he had 'devoted 38 years in raising the school and consequently the character of the town'. [Godber, *The Harpur Trust*, 1973, p. 44] Bedford citizens must have been well aware of this, but they were also aware during the 1840s of increasing conflicts of interest.

There were now four Harpur Schools, their scope was greater than ever before and the expenses were much increased. This added burden affected the welfare side of the charity, the provision of almshouses in the town and the paying of apprenticeships and marriage portions for poor people. In 1848, four hundred and thirty inhabitants signed a petition against economies on the welfare side to finance the education of the better off. Naturally, Brereton and the schoolmasters were against reducing the levels of education for which they had fought, while the townsmen, well represented on the Trustees, were jealous of their rights. That year the Trust, which had been overdrawn to the tune of £9000 since 1843, was denied any more advances by their Bedford bank, Messrs Barnard's. Proposals for a redrafted charity scheme went before the Attorney General in 1852 and the Lord Chancellor in 1853 and included a new system of appointing trustees. A compromise scheme was passed in Chancery in March 1853, but the whole legal procedure had cost £7000 and created much antagonism.

Moore's second in command, Wilkinson Finlinson, became headmaster of the Writing (now Commercial) School in 1860, reputedly on the strength of his beautiful handwriting! A story goes that the chairman of the committee said, 'Gentlemen, we 'ave 'ere the letters of some very learned persons. Please look at 'em. I 'ope you will be able to read them – I can't . . . What we want is that [our boys] should write a good 'and.' [Underwood, *The Eagle*, Vol. 39, No. 283, 1974, p. 374] Five years earlier, J. F. Fanshawe had succeeded Dr Brereton at the Grammar School. Both Fanshawe and Moore, though able heads, had very difficult acts to follow, the stature of their predecessors being almost larger than life. They were in turn followed by rather more major figures, Dr R. B. Poole and J. S. Phillpotts in the 1870s, heads who were to pilot the schools into the twentieth century.

Writing of Finlinson's first years at the Commercial School in the 1850s, F. W. Kuhlicke sets the scene of this time admirably.

It must be borne in mind that when Finlinson was appointed Bedford was just beginning to feel its growing pains; it was an era of expansion and development, the climax of the industrial revolution which had some effect upon the town. Trade, rather than industry, was its principal activity and this was stimulated by the opening of railway communication with London, the Midlands and Cambridge. The trading interests were well represented on the Town Council and consequently on the Board of Trustees, governing the Harpur Trust. To them the Grammar School with its classical and academic bias appeared less useful than the Commercial School. Though the wealthier tradesmen might send their own sons to the Grammar School they were anxious that the lower middle-class and poorer families should send their young hopefuls to the Commercial School, where, in a few years, they would master the 'three Rs' and be able to seek employment in the shops and counting houses of the tradesmen. [*The Eagle*, Vol XXVIII, Christmas 1951]

A new crisis arose in 1865, when the Charities Commission was set up to look into the practices of grammar schools. From the start they were biased against ancient endowments and local day pupils' interests; they felt fees should be charged, more boarders encouraged from outside the borough and schools started for middle-class girls. The Endowed Schools Act of 1869 made it necessary to have smaller groups of trustees, fewer from the Corporation and to break the link with New College. Elementary Schools had been the province of the Trust since 1815, but the Endowed School Act gave preferential treatment to secondary education. Even so, the Trust established an Elementary School south of the river in the growing district of Ampthill Road in 1876, and another mixed school in Clapham Road in 1893. Even after the Education Act of 1870, the bulk of elementary education in the town was funded by the Harpur Trust.

Bedford became an important educational centre for establishments outside the Harpur Charity. When the old Aspley Guise School closed in the 1840s, several gentlemen felt that there was insufficient choice in the county as Bedford Schools took no 'county' pupils. Their efforts to provide alternatives resulted in the founding of the Middle Class Public School in 1869, situated on Ampthill Road, Bedford, but in the parish of Kempston. It was designed by Frank Peck and survived until 1964–5. It was the perfect composition for a small public school, a central tower above a red brick Gothic building, with the headmaster's house to the right and the chapel to the left, both detached, and actually more enjoyable than any of the Harpur buildings. The Moravian School in St Peter's was still flourishing in the middle of the century, principally because it ran a boarding school for girls where no other existed. The strong Christian base of the school, and the reputation of the Moravians for morality, gained them a wide circle of pupils from the gentry in Bedfordshire and beyond. The newspaper columns of the mid-century are stuffed with advertisements for private academic establishments in the town which, like proverbial butterflies, flourished for a season and then vanished.

Even with these new schools and their splendid buildings, Bedford, like any historic town, was still a mixture of old and new, a meeting place of its agricultural past and commercial future. In Well Street (now Midland Road) there was a tumble-down farmhouse with sixteenth-century gables, and, just off Silver Street, were the ancient congeries of the Hawes Almshouses. In the parish of St John's there was a picturesque alley called Rope Walk, led by Langley Cottage, the home of the master rope-maker George Turner, whose business continued there till the 1960s. In St Cuthbert's the small estate of G. P. Livius brought the country into the town until its glades were laid out with housing in the 1860s and 1870s.

Bedford's civilised inhabitants did not have the problems of their fellows in Luton, but there were occasional lapses into serious crime. In May 1863, a Mr Frederick William Budd was attacked while walking home with his wife to Kimbolton Road. Budd was so badly injured that he died three hours later. Two men named Jordan and Craddock were apprehended and at their trial that July were found guilty of manslaughter and sent down with seven years penal servitude. The affair shocked quiet Bedford and the punishment was regarded as far too lenient.

The fact that this town of the educators and the educated did not turn wholly into a Bath or a Cheltenham was largely due to the commercial and industrial zeal of a few families. Chief among these was that of Howard.

The founder of the firm of Howards' was Mr John Howard (1791–1878), who, in 1813, established himself in an iron-mongers' business in Bedford High Street. He developed into a manufacturer of agricultural implements and gained the reputa-tion for making the best ploughs in the country. The strong puritan element, which is such a feature of successful

Bedfordians, was abundantly present in Howard and his wife, who were both strong Methodists. They were described as uniting in themselves 'patient industry, strong common sense, and unswerving uprightness' which was 'all through their lives so fine an example'. [Anonymous, *A Visit to Bedford*, p. 32]

Howard was an agricultural, manufacturing and inventive genius, a man who today would be termed a brilliant entrepreneur. At the first meeting of the Agricultural Society of England in 1839, Howard showed the first iron-wheeled plough to be seen in England, the prototype of many to be made throughout Europe. The judges commended the plough as 'of small size, with a mould-board or furrow-turner of excellent form, calculated to give the least resistance in turning over the furrow...' Two years later, Howard's son, James Howard (1821–89) exhibited another at the Liverpool meeting. 'A Bedfordshire lad, not yet 20 years of age, brought an iron plough constructed at his Father's Works from his own design, and which was an object of much curiosity. Finding no one to whom he was inclined to entrust the Implement he took off his coat, guided it himself, and secured one of the eleven prizes awarded.'

The younger Howard and his brother Sir Frederick Howard (1827–1915) were the guiding forces behind the development of this remarkable business which they moved to a new site at Caldwell Priory, across the river, in 1857. They recognised the unique position of this new ironworks, close to both the river and the newly opened railway. In 1857, the Howard brothers began a great transformation of the works, turning it not only into a most modern means of production, but a thing of beauty. A model factory was created in an Italian style by the architect F. T. Palgrave, production sheds forming a quadrangle of patterned brick buildings, the front finished with a handsome gateway, clock and entrance screen of iron railings. A contemporary account of the place quotes from Longfellow, a typical example of the romance that the Victorians found in their industry, and the motto over the gate, 'Whatsoever thy hand findeth to do, do it with thy might', reflects the strong biblical element in all this endeavour.

The Britannia Works, as they were called, had a web of tram lines to take small trucks from one department to another. This connected the Pattern Room, the Grinding and Polishing Shops, the Boiler Shops, Fitting Shops, Forging Department and Painting Department. The works utilised many Howard inventions such as a patent moulder.

> It is something like magic to see a lad sift a quantity of fine black moulding sand upon the top of a metal pattern, then ram it, and almost instantly withdraw the pattern by sinking it downward with the smooth no-tremulous motion of the patented machine, leaving the mould perfect and complete. This moulding is repeated over and over again without requiring any patching, and a skilled labourer can, with one of these machines, do many times more work than can be turned out by the most experienced hand-moulder. [ibid.]

Howards' had a display of all the ploughs in their stock and many special ones adapted for the Cape, Southern Russia, South America, Spain and Turkey. Also included was a collection of historic ploughs, a sort of museum and models of the firm's past prize winners. The Painting Shop was so extensive that James Howard used it on occasions as a tabernacle for the great preacher, the Revd C. H. Spurgeon when 3000 people gathered there. At other times it was the scene for meetings of the British and Foreign Bible Society under the presidency of the famous Lord Shaftesbury.

Howards', with their customary ploughs and a machine for grinding or pea-splitting, were extensive exhibitors at the 1851 Great Exhibition at the Crystal Palace. The firms of Elliott and Cooper of Dunstable and Connell and Brodie of Luton also sent their best hats and bonnets, and Thomas Lester of Bedford exhibited a Bedfordshire 'lace fall'. Excursion trips by railway were arranged for labourers but J. T. Brooks of Flitwick Manor clearly disliked this. On his third visit he commented on 6 October: 'The crowd of dirty vulgar people was most disagreeable, one hundred and one thousand people being in the building this day.' [B.H.R.S. Vol. 66, p. 152]

It is hardly surprising that the Howard works attracted a number of distinguished visitors, the most notable being General Giuseppe Garibaldi. He wished to see the process of ploughing by steam, and although only two days' notice was given, the town was specially decorated and a welcoming committee arranged. The General planted a tree, a sequoia, at the Britannia Works and signed the Visitors' Book. It is not easy to recapture the romantic image that Garibaldi struck among the British, but some flavour of the excitement is contained in a letter from Miss Starey of Milton Ernest Hall to her brother on 16 April 1864:

My dear Willie,

We had a great excitement yesterday about twelve o'clock we heard from Charles that Garibaldi really was in Bedford & that there was every chance of our seeing him if we went. So Mr Starey helped to work us up to a sufficient degree of excitement – as he wanted to see him very much – so we ordered the open carriage in a great hurry – had some luncheon & in half an hour were off. We were very well rewarded – just at the entrance to Bedford we met him driving at the head of a procession – consisting of every imaginable vehicle that has been invented since Adam. We stood by to let him pass – wh he did close by – bowing to us most politely. He looked extremely aimable and pleasant. He was in an open carriage with Mr Howard the Mayor & another lady & gentleman. We fell in with the procession & proceeded with them to Mr Howard's farm, wh is that one near the cemetry – you turn up to Mr Fitzpatrick's to get there. At the farm he inspected the stock including a fat pigg & a bull & then went on through a large field of wheat to the steam plough – fancy our carriage driving round a field of wheat! but they all did the same & it was great fun to see the antedeluvian flies tumbling about – We did not follow him down into the ploughed field – where he mounted a little pony & followed the plough for some time as well as a great many other gentlemen on horseback. We watched them from the next field & he seems to have taken a great interest in it – & quite got to the bottom of it. Then we preceded him back again to the road where we drew up so that he had again to pass us quite close. We got some more bows & he kissed his hand to *me* I say – the others say 'to us' – but I was the mascot & waved my handkerchief to him – so I am sure it was to me. Then we went home very well satisfied with our view. [C.R.O., SY107]

It may have been the presence of the Howard manufacturies and the strong agricultural interest that resulted in the Royal Agricultural Society holding its Royal Show at Bedford in July 1874. It took place on the old race-course ground between the Ampthill Road and the Midland line, where a special siding ran on to the show ground. It was attended by the Crown Prince and Princess of Germany and the Duke and Duchess of Bedford, and the *Bedfordshire Times* produced a daily edition for that week.

The Howard family had become notable landowners during the 1870s, building a large mansion at Clapham Park, whose outlying farm Garibaldi visited. James Howard had chosen as his architect a local man, John Usher (1822–1904), who had made his name as a designer of large villas, chapels and mills for the prosperous middle class. He extended the Britannia Works in 1869 and moved on to the angular Tudor house of their owner at Clapham in 1870–3. Usher's background – he was the son of a Blunham builder – meant that he took great care with materials and enjoyed experiments. His bizarre style of poly-chromatic brick and fanciful silhouette can be seen all over Bedford, as well as at Blunham Rectory and the Italianate Arnold House at Great Barford. His finest work was probably 'Hiawatha', Goldington Road, designed for himself in 1867, but sadly demolished. The best surviving work in the town is 'Holly Lodge' in The Grove, designed for Bedford's lace king, Thomas Lester, in 1869. Usher's strict Baptist background probably accorded well with the nonconformist Howards, but he eventually became a recluse, dying in his Gothic fantasy at the age of eighty-two.

Other businessmen who had no particular connection with Bedford found it a convenient place to settle. The Miss Starey who wrote so glowingly of Garibaldi was the daughter of Benjamin Helps Starey, a prosperous London linen bleacher. With Brontë-esque inevitability, the handsome Mr Starey fell in love with the governess at the house of an acquaintance. After a long and prayerful engagement, the religious young couple were married in 1838. Starey's small fortune enabled him to migrate to Bedfordshire where he bought the Milton Ernest estate on which he decided to build a house in 1854. It was fortunate that the governess's brother and now Starey's brother-in-law was William Butterfield (1814–1900), the leading church architect of his day. A country house was a new departure for Butterfield, and indeed Milton Ernest, the home he built for Starey, is his only complete example. The setting, in a tree-lined park near the Ouse, is striking, as is the view of the great Victorian house from the top of Clapham Hill, a scene from a nineteenth-century architectural drawing. However, the house is rather gaunt and ecclesiastical in appearance, the excitement deriving from the great pile of gable, chimney and juxtapositions, rather than from the scant ornament. The court by the main entrance and the glimpses from the former farmyard are very manorial and pleasing. The quality of the stonework and the build up of buttresses and walls make it the sculptural inspiration that it undoubtedly is.

The severity of the design is underlined in the ascetic remarks of Butterfield to his nephew, who was living here in 1890 and studying to be a parson. 'I am glad you are reading "Tracts for the Times." But why did you take in hand such a book as "Lux Mundi"? Leave modern books alone, & keep to the writing of proved men.' [C.R.O. SY103/5]

The Starey family was here for one hundred and five years, and as Butterfield was a bachelor, Milton Ernest was the repository for his archives and drawings. It is a fine house but hardly a jolly one, and I well recall visiting the late Captain Stephen Starey there one grey and dismal day. He was hunched up against the cold in one small room, Butterfield's drawings for All Saints, Margaret Street on the walls, while the rain fell outside.

As a town of Victorian prosperity, Leighton Buzzard comes second only to Bedford. We last saw it as a bustling eighteenth-century market town, a centre of Quakers and farmers. Its nineteenth-century development may have been the result of the railway, its proximity to London and its prime position adjacent to the Grand Union Canal. For about twenty years before the recession of 1872, it was a boom town, largely through banking and as an agricultural centre for grain and wool. The principal benefactors were the Bassetts, Leighton's own family of Quaker bankers.

In 1845, T. D. Bassett (1786–1878) was instrumental in building the Leighton Institute or Temperance Hall in Lake Street, a delightful stucco assembly room with an ionic order and pediment, the last of a tradition. Here, away from the temptations of drink, the populace could be lectured and educated. By the 1850s, the town could already boast buildings in the High Street equal to anything in the county town and, unlike most Bedfordshire towns, the street is wide enough to see them. The earliest palazzo in the county is the former London & County Bank building by Horace Parnell of 1856 (now the National Westminster Bank), very dignified and business-like, with as much plate glass as possible only four years after the window tax was repealed. The Church Square had already been laid out in urban formality by the Bassett family of bankers in 1855, when The Terrace was designed by the London architect, W. C. Read. In order to encourage the right type of purchaser, Bassett offered the six houses for sale with a first-class railway season ticket valid for twenty-one years! T. D. Bassett employed the same architect to build The Cedars, another handsome town house facing up the High Street, for his own residence.

Contrasting styles were employed for the Bassett Bank (now Barclays Bank) in the High Street. With a great deal of daring, they employed the young architect Alfred Waterhouse (1830–1905) to design a Gothic structure with a re-inforced steel shell and the most beautiful stone details. The Corn Exchange was built in 1864, a more bizarre building with an eighty foot tower, and when it became redundant in 1872 due to the corn slump, the Bassetts bought it back for the town. T. D. Bassett's son, Francis Bassett (1820–99), who was Liberal M.P. for Bedfordshire from 1872–5, built two large houses on the outskirts of the town, The Heath and The Knolls, the latter designed by Richard Norman Shaw. All the way along the road to Heath & Reach, there are substantial stucco villas of the mid-century, an indicator of the comfortable life style of Victorian Leighton.

XII
Edwardian Elysium

The years following the first jubilee of Queen Victoria in 1887 were ones of peace and prosperity for large areas of the shire counties. Edward, Prince of Wales, was emerging as a European figure and his nonchalant air and relaxed style of life were attractive and engaging to a new generation. His errant son, the Duke of Clarence, announced his engagement to the Princess May of Teck at Luton Hoo in 1891. Although the Duke subsequently died and Princess May married his brother, Prince George (later George V), the event captured on photograph gives the flavour of the moment. Frederick Thurston (1854–1933), the renowned Luton photographer, was called to the Hoo on 5 December to take these engagement pictures. The Duke sits languidly on a table, palm fronds around him and his betrothed at his side. She is mute and serene in the presence of her foxy-faced suitor while Thurston times the long exposure. The chapter of earnest work and deeply held beliefs seems suddenly to have slipped away into an era of decadence and extravagance.

Luton Hoo was by no means typical of the Bedfordshire estates. It was then the home of Madame de Falbe, the English wife of the Danish minister at the Court of St James's. It was the glittering focus for the great society gatherings favoured by this very rich and extremely snobbish couple. When the millionaire shopowner Sir Blundell Maple, who was living at Childwickbury, called at Luton Hoo he was snubbed by Madame de Falbe. The butler returned with his card and the message from the great lady: 'When I need carpets I will call in Tottenham Court Road!' Edward, Prince of Wales, heard of this and when he was next staying at Childwickbury, summoned Madame de Falbe to meet Sir Blundell. It was a command and she was humiliated. The Luton estate was now run on new money and investment interests rather than on the land. This was a pattern for a number of other houses owned by the commercial aristocracy, the Howards at Clapham Park, the Stareys at Milton Ernest and the Harters at Cranfield Court.

The older families were still in command of their inherited properties, but they were just beginning to enter a period of depression from which few of them would survive. In 1873, when statistics of land ownership were first compiled, it was found that half of Bedfordshire was owned by fewer than fifty persons. This included the Duke of Bedford with 33,589 acres, S. C. Whitbread, 13,257 acres, Countess Cowper (Wrest Park) 8,888 acres and J. S. Crawley (Stockwood) with 8,240 acres. Slightly below this were the Trevors of Bromham, the Page-Turners of Battlesden and the Thynnes of Hawnes, while a score of squires were in the 1000 to 2000 acre range, among them the Osborns, Orlebars, Alstons, Polhills, Pyms and Thorntons.

The agricultural depression began in the 1870s and lasted until at least 1896. The trouble had begun with the import of cheap American corn, the very commodity that had been flourished as a beacon of prosperity in 1846. At that date nobody had suspected that the imports would be so huge or that transportation would be so efficient and swift by steamship. From 1870 the price of homegrown cereals steadily declined, local mills could not compete with those at the ports and many closed. Many landowners and their tenant farmers turned to livestock and so workers were laid off, causing a slow haemorrhage of village life and a drift to the towns. Even this branch of farming was threatened by the invention of meat refrigeration in the 1880s and all branches were affected by the financial crises in this decade.

The landowners saw their profits and their rentals rapidly sliding and were unable to maintain their rent rolls, the workers attempted to get higher wages as their existence was only at a subsistence level. Labourers near Bedford asked for a wage rise from 13s to 15s a week and were refused, so they went on strike. Some of them joined the Agricultural Workers' Union and formed a crowd in St Paul's Square, Bedford to hear Joseph Arch speak in 1874. The tenant farmers often went bankrupt, the landowners simply had to retrench, selling off outlying parts of their estates, or in the case of the Thynnes, the Page-Turners and others, letting their mansions to wealthier merchants.

Colworth House was one of those let during the Regency after the end of the direct Lee Antonie line at Sharnbrook. The new tenant in 1827 was Hollingworth Magniac (*c*.1787–1867) a millionaire art collector who had been an early partner in Jardine Mathieson of Hong Kong. Magniac purchased the Colworth estate in 1857 and bought lavishly and well for the remainder of his life, so that Colworth became one of the major Victorian collections of Renaissance art. Magniac was a benevolent patron of modern art as well and patronised sporting painters such as Henry Alken and Benjamin Robert Herring. This brilliant self-made man succeeded in grafting himself into the county of his adoption very successfully. He was Liberal M.P. for St Ives, Bedford and North Bedfordshire and his son, Charles, married the granddaughter of Lord Ossory.

Even such seemingly water-tight arrangements as this could go wrong in the 1880s and Charles Magniac M.P. got into serious difficulties. He had employed the architect William Burges to design a mausoleum for his father at Sharnbrook in 1867–8, but by 1882 he was heavily indebted to the family firm. He died in 1891, but the collection was sold the following year in a massive sale at Christie's. It was not enough to settle the family debts and in 1893 his son Herbert, who had married a daughter of the Duke of Grafton, was declared bankrupt.

Late Victorian Bedfordshire therefore was not ideal for the traditional landowner, the wealthy speculator or for the agricultural worker, but it was a very pleasant place for the middle classes. Increasingly, it is these men and women of note who make their mark upon the county, ruling on the bench, in the newly formed urban districts or County Council, or teaching in the major schools. The floating population of Bedford, which had always seen a vortex of interesting families attending the Harpur Schools, threw up some astonishing figures at this period. Bedford appeared on the surface to be a sedate backwater for aspiring or expiring colonial servants. E. M. Forster has his character Tibby in *Howards End* (1910) say 'I'll live anywhere except Bournemouth, Torquay, and Cheltenham. Oh yes, or Ilfracombe and Swanage and Tunbridge Wells and Surbiton and Bedford. There on no account.' But things were not always what they seemed. The tree-lined roads of the county town, as well as the quiet manor houses further afield, produced a rich crop of heroes and eccentrics.

Colonel Frederick Gustavus Burnaby (1842–85) is just such a one. Burnaby was born at Bedford in 1842, the son of the Revd Gustavus Andrew Burnaby, rector of St Peter's from 1835–66. After being educated at Bedford Grammar School, Harrow and in Germany, Burnaby began on a dashing career as an army officer and adventurer. He was a pioneer balloonist and astonished Bedfordshire in June 1866 by making a balloon trip from Windsor to Bedfordshire, he and his companion eventually landing in a field at Bletsoe. Burnaby later travelled to South Russia, Spain and the Sudan, and made a memorable trip from Kazala to Khiva in 1875. All his exploits were set down in fascinating and readable travel books which Burnaby as a fluent linguist and writer had no difficulty in compiling. His devil-may-care attitude to life is magnificently set down in James Tissot's celebrated portrait of him, where he reclines on a sofa, his immensely long legs stretched out before him, smoking a cigarette. Although approaching retirement age, Burnaby attached himself to the Egyptian Expedition of 1884, mainly with the intention of relieving his friend General Gordon, and he was killed by a spear at Khartoum in 1885.

Another late Victorian figure of distinction was Sir John Montagu Burgoyne, 10th Baronet of Sutton Park. We have already met him, dozing in his chair during divine service at Sutton church in extreme old age. As a younger man he had two remarkable experiences which mark him out as unusual and courageous. At the age of twenty-two, Burgoyne was sent out as a young Captain in the 3rd Bn. of the Grenadier Guards to fight in the Crimean War. From February to October 1854, Burgoyne kept a diary of his impressions, including the conditions of the troops and the newly arrived nurses. He was severely wounded in the Battle of the Alma and invalided home.

Sixteen years later, Burgoyne was involved in another dramatic episode while sailing in his yacht, the *Gazelle*. In the last week of August 1870, Sir John left his anchorage off Ryde to sail to Deauville in Normandy to meet his wife, who had been holidaying in Switzerland. It was an ominous time to be travelling: Napoleon III had just been defeated by the Prussians at the Battle of Sedan, and the whole of France was in a state of disruption. Lady Burgoyne reached Deauville on the afternoon of 7 September with the news that a revolution had broken out in France and the mob was on the rampage. Although Burgoyne was anxious to leave, the wind was unfavourable and his skipper advised him to delay his departure.

Meanwhile the Empress Eugénie had escaped from the Tuileries Palace with her lady-in-waiting and was being escorted across France by the Imperial dentist, Dr Evans. She refused to disguise herself as she was resigned to her fate, but simply wore a spotted black veil and black dress. It was a terrifying ordeal: it took her four days to reach the coast and several times she was in danger of being apprehended. At one point a coachman said that he would like to get his hands on the Empress! At another time, a stationmaster pushed her roughly but prevented the public from entering her compartment; when they were not looking he kissed her hand.

At Deauville, the Empress was put into lodgings while Dr Evans tried to obtain passage to England. On hearing that Sir John Burgoyne's yacht was in the harbour, he immediately approached him and asked him if he would convey the Empress across the channel. Burgoyne was uncertain at first, but finally agreed to do so if his wife agreed. 'You can submit the matter to Lady Burgoyne,' was his comment. Lady Burgoyne assented at once and Burgoyne then met the doctor in the lumber-yard of the railway station to make plans. He stressed that he could not have the Empress on board until just before they cast off. This proved to be a good move as the French police searched the boat at eleven o'clock that night.

The Empress recounted her side of the story to Sir James Reid twenty years later:

It was not safe for us to go together: so Madame le Breton and Dr Evans went together a round way by the surburbs, and I went all alone through the town to the *plage*, where it was arranged Sir John Burgoyne was to meet me. He did not know me, nor I him, so it had been settled that in order to recognise each other he was to say to me: 'Is that you, Lizzie?' or some such name. I said 'Yes', and then we walked on together, he talking and laughing in a chaffy way, so as to disarm the suspicion of anyone we met and make it appear we were enjoying ourselves. Then when we got on board his yacht, he knelt down and kissed my hand. [Michaela Reid, *Ask Sir James*, 1987, p. 268]

In a letter to Colonel Ponsonby, Burgoyne says that 'the Empress was very much agitated and sobbed bitterly, and on my saying to her, going over the side, "*N'ayez pas peur, Madame*," she replied in English, "I am safe with an English gentleman." '

Burgoyne put to sea in the most appalling conditions and it took over twenty hours to make Ryde Roads off the Isle of Wight where they dropped anchor at 3.35 a.m. on 8 September. The Empress never forgot her Bedfordshire friends; she entertained them at Farnborough, and after Lady Burgoyne's death and a second marriage, the baronet received a tea and coffee set as a present. When the Empress died, she left a drawing by Greuze to her rescuer in memory of 'the chivalrous way in which he came to my assistance on the 6th September 1870'.

Two Bedfordshire brothers who had a vision and obeyed it were the Polhill-Turners of Howbury Hall, Renhold. C. H. Polhill-Turner (1860–1938) and A. T. Polhill-Turner (1862–1935) were the sons of Captain Frederick Polhill-Turner, M.P. for Bedford from 1874–80. While at Cambridge they came under the influence of the evangelists Moody and Sanky and decided to give up everything for the Christian mission field. They joined some other Cambridge friends, including the famous cricketer, C. T. Studd (whose mother came from Bletsoe), to go out to China for the China Inland Mission. Known as 'The Cambridge Seven', they included the two Polhills who were army officers, and M. Beauchamp, the son of a baronet. The Seven left for China on 5 February 1885 and reached Shanghai on 18 March. They were among the first to identify totally with the Chinese, adopting Chinese dress and being shaved and pigtailed. Cecil Polhill worked in Shansi, but gradually moved towards Tibet where he became acquainted with the Dalai Lama. Although he inherited Howbury Hall in 1903, he made seven further missionary pilgrimages to China, often accompanied by his wife. Arthur Polhill lived principally in Pachow and remained in China during the Boxer Rising of 1900 and the Revolution of 1911. He returned to England in 1928 and became a parish priest in Hertfordshire.

Of a slightly later generation were two intrepid polar

explorers. Commander Frank Wild (1874–1939) spent his childhood at Eversholt where his father was the schoolmaster, who later settled in Ampthill. Wild travelled to Australia in the *Sobraon* in 1889 at the age of fifteen, already showing a spirit of adventure. He joined Captain Scott in the *Discovery* expedition of 1901–4, which broke all previous records of endurance, and followed this with expeditions to Antarctica with Shackleton in 1907–9 and with Mawson in 1911–13. In the first of these, the party came within one hundred miles of the South Pole, the nearest approach before Amundsen. He then enlisted with the Imperial Trans-Atlantic Expedition in 1914–16 with Shackleton and others. On this occasion he very nearly lost his life, as he and his men were trapped on Elephant Island for a whole winter and only survived through Wild's resolution and leadership. For this, Wild was awarded a silver Polar Medal by King George V with the inscription 'Antarctic'. Wild wrote down some of his experiences in his book *Shackleton's Last Voyage*. Apsley Cherry-Garrard (1886–1959) was born at Linden Road, Bedford in the house of his grandfather. After education at Winchester and Christ Church, Oxford, he became a prominent sportsman and eventually an explorer. He was a member of the fateful British Antarctic Expedition of 1910–13 and took part in some memorable sledge journeys, as well as editing *The South Polar Times*. Cherry-Garrard's career did not continue after the Scott expedition, but he was able to set down his impressions in his famous book, *The Worst Journey in the World*, which has become a minor classic.

Burnaby, Wild and Cherry-Garrard were not actually products of the Bedford Schools, although these institutions were sending out a steady stream of young men to garrison the Empire. A typical example of this new breed was George Farrar (1859–1915) who was a nephew of the ironmaster, James Howard, and was educated at Bedford Modern School from 1870–5. After a brief apprenticeship at the Britannia Works, Farrar left for travel and adventure in South Africa in 1879. Eight years later, he settled in Johannesburg and became the founder of the enormously successful East Rand Proprietary Gold Mine Company. Farrar became active in South African politics as a member of the controversial Reform Committee and was imprisoned at Pretoria on the orders of President Kruger. He was one of the members sentenced to death in 1896 but the sentence was commuted to a heavy fine. When the Boer War broke out in 1899, Farrar organised an irregular corps of non-Boers to support the British army. Farrar took part in the relief of Wepener in April 1900, was awarded the Queen's medal and the D.S.O. in 1901, and was knighted in 1902. He went on to become the leader of the Progressive Party in opposition to President Botha and his work for the Union resulted in him being given a baronetcy in 1911. Appropriately enough, Sir George's South African estate was called Bedford Farm, although he kept up his connections with the real Bedford town and leased the Chicheley Hall estate on the Buckinghamshire border. In his funeral address at Chicheley in June 1915, he was described as 'a man eager for adventure, quick in resource, strong of will, dauntless in courage' – a list of public school qualities that any of Bedford's headmasters would have gloried in.

At a rather different level, Henry Ryland (1856–1924) escaped from the family drapery business in Biggleswade to be an artist in London and Paris. He had been born in the High Street establishment of the east Bedfordshire town, the son of John and Elizabeth Ryland, who were well respected trades people. The family later moved to No. 1 Market Place, which was known as 'Ryland's Corner' because it was on the angle of the town square, and finally to Hitchin Street. Henry Ryland's precocious talents as a draughtsman and painter led him to the Government School of Design and on to the Ateliers Julian and Cormon in Paris in about 1888–9. He later recalled the Atelier Julian: 'The noise and extreme uncleanliness, physical and moral, affronted me as well as many others.' Ryland developed a rather dry, classical style of painting of Roman and Grecian subjects which had great popularity with late Victorian collectors.

Ryland's great claim to fame was that he shared a studio, albeit unwillingly, with Vincent Van Gogh. Ryland and his friend, A. S. Hartrick, had a studio together in Montmartre and the listless and misunderstood Van Gogh moved in there for hours at a time. Hartrick later wrote: 'I would return from going up and down in Paris, to find Ryland, who suffered from sick headaches, with his head wrapped in a towel soaked in vinegar and looking a sickly yellow, while he wailed: "Where have you been? That terrible man has been here for two hours waiting for you and I can't stand it any more!" ' [A. S. Hartrick, *A Painter's Pilgrimage Through Fifty Years*, 1939, p. 51.] It is odd to think of the Biggleswade draper's son and the red-bearded genius from Holland sitting together in such an awkward juxtaposition!

Just as Bedfordshire men and women were moving further afield, the county was also receiving a greater number of residents from outside its boundaries. This had always been true of Bedford, with its schools and families seeking to educate their children, but was not so true of the county at large. Now the railways gave easy access to the capital and the age of commuters had begun, particularly in the southern parts. The earliest Bedford commuter is supposed to have been Mr McDowal, the husband of the first, short-lived headmistress of the new Bedford High School, in 1882. From the 1880s the town guides emphasise this accessibility and increasing numbers must have followed the pattern.

The Bedford brewers had always played an important part in the life of the town, from the days of Sir William Long (1756–1841), the only Bedford mayor to have been knighted in office. An interesting late nineteenth-century brewer was Lewis Jarvis (1845–1900), who inherited his father's brewery, the second largest in the town, in Gwynn Street. The Jarvis family came from Eaton Socon and, some time in the 1840s, Thomas Jarvis moved into the town, where all his sons were born and subsequently educated at the Bedford School. Lewis Jarvis developed other talents apart from brewing: he was also a gifted amateur artist, and a noted collector of Hispano-Mauresque ceramics and contemporary art. Jarvis had married in 1876 Miss Maud Vesey-Dawson, a red headed Irish girl who was a cousin of the Earls of Dartry and of the influential Magniac family of Colworth. In 1877, the newly married pair moved into their first country home, The Orchard, at Blunham.

It was Lewis Jarvis who was responsible for introducing to the county one of the more exotic birds of passage, the American artist James McNeil Whistler (1834–1903). Jarvis may have become acquainted with Whistler through the collector W. C. Alexander in the 1870s when the Bedfordshire brewer was having lessons at the Slade school. It is certain that the friendship blossomed, possibly as a result of Whistler's admiration for the good looks of Mrs Jarvis. The American was witty, cutting and easily annoyed, so that it was a great tribute to Jarvis's tact that he won the painter's confidence. Even more surprising was Whistler's acceptance of several invitations to the country and of the rural weekends that he so much disliked.

In May 1879, Whistler won his famous law case against John Ruskin but was immediately declared bankrupt with liabilities of close on £3000. He appealed to Jarvis to help him to the tune of £50, a modest enough sum, but one that Jarvis found difficult enough to meet. Although in charge of a brewery, he had never been a wealthy man and both his present house at Blunham and the next one at The Toft, Sharnbrook, were rented. Moreover, he had expensive tastes and a family of seven sons and several daughters. A bargain was struck that Jarvis would supply the money if Whistler were to paint a portrait of Ada Jarvis. The sitting took place in the summer of 1879 and the completed portrait was despatched to Blunham, followed shortly afterwards by the artist.

Whistler then made a carriage drive to Sharnbrook to view The Toft and advise on its decoration. He subsequently attempted a colour scheme with his own hand which survived for many years. In 1880, Whistler left for a debtor's exile in Venice and did not return to Bedfordshire till 1881. After a visit in that year, he wrote to Jarvis 'I am thinking of the charming little dinner last night, and of the pleasant evening afterwards – though I fancy I owe Mrs Jarvis an apology for bringing late hours into her house!' The fine portrait of Ada Jarvis was sadly sold by the family in 1907 and now hangs in the Smith College collection at Northampton, Massachusetts, a fitting memorial of this friendship.

Two other men of distinction who came to the county for a short time chose to live in South Bedfordshire, where the railway links were even better.

Arnold Bennett (1867–1931) was a successful journalist with one novel to his name when he came to Hockliffe in January 1900. He had sufficient means to rent a property and as his commitments as editor of *Woman* and as a staff member of *Academy* and *Hearth and Home* meant a daily attendance in

London, he was able to commute from Dunstable or Leighton Buzzard. His choice of house was typical of the man: a yellow brick farmhouse, Trinity Hall Farm, bleak and uncompromising with its back to the village and its face to the outside world. Bennett had immense fun with it, negotiating the tenancy with its Bedfordshire owner, J. J. R. Adams, and choosing the art wallpapers from Messrs Essex & Co. It was the first time that Bennett had been in command of a household and he rather enjoyed preparing the place for his elderly parents and his sister, Tertia. The Bennetts were installed by the summer and the novelist soon settled into the house with its orchards, stables and trees, and its writing room with bay windows facing southwards to the Chilterns. One writer who visited him there in 1902 described him as a man in transition. 'At Hockliffe Bennett was between two worlds,' recorded Wilfred Whitten, 'the one he had not quite left and the one he had not quite entered.' Bennett relished his first taste of country life and this brush with nature is faithfully recorded in his journals.

Thursday, January 3rd [1901]

As we drove through Battlesden Park this misty moist morning, Kennerley and Tertia in front, and Sharpe and I cramped and pinched behind, I had a sense of a constantly unrolling panorama of large rounded meadows, studded with immense bare cedars, also of a formal and balanced shape; bulls and sheep all of fine breeds wandered vaguely about; sometimes a house; often a gate to be opened, and Spot gallivanting tirelessly around the trap; in one distant clump of trees, we saw a rook perched on an invisible twig on the top of a high elm; in the mist he seemed enormous, an incredible motionless fowl; at length he stretched his wings slowly, sank gently forward, and beat heavily away into the distance. Everything was a vague green and dark grey in the fog, everything except the red hips and the staring white of Spot's coat.

On the way home we called for a dead snipe that had been given to us: the first snipe I had ever seen; I was naively astonished at its small proportions, and the impossible length of its thin bill. [*The Journals of Arnold Bennett 1896–1910*, p. 106]

Bennett greatly enjoyed his country neighbours and recalls their banter in various pieces of dialogue in his journal:

Willison, the man who combines the function of tailor and horse-dealer, told me a story of old Adams, now over eighty, and still a 'character'. It was an early-morning dialogue between Adams and an old farm-hand.

Adams. What's this mean, Dick? It's a quarter past six, and you but just come.

Man. Yes, but I was late last night; it was nigh on eight before I left this yard last night.

Adams. Oh! Ah! But it's a quarter past six, Dick. I won't have this. You can go home Dick.

Man. (surprised). Go home?

Adams. You can go home, Dick. Go to hell, Dick.

Man. (recovering himself). If I do go to hell, damned if I don't tell your old father how badly you're farming his land. [*ibid*. p. 109]

Arthur J. Willison was the main source of Bennett's information and acceptance by the village. Willison's diaries still survive and show how much he was running errands for the family, buying them a dog, persuading them to order a trap and driving to fetch a nurse from Dunstable during old Enoch Bennett's final illness. Bennett immortalised Willison in the character of 'Mr Puddephatt' in his only Bedfordshire novel, *Teresa of Watling Street* (1904).

Bennett succumbed very early to the romance of this road which practically ran across his doorstep. 'Just recently,' he writes in an early essay,

> I had tracked it diligently on a series of county maps, and discovered that, though only vague fragments of it remain in Kent, Surrey, Shropshire, Cheshire and Yorkshire, it still flourished and abounded exceedingly in my particular neighbourhood as a right line, austere, renowned, indispensable, clothed in its own immortal dust. I could see but patches of it in the twilight, but I was aware that it stretched fifteen miles southeast of me, and unnumbered miles northwest of me, with scarcely a curve to break the splendid inexorable monotony of its career. To me it was a wonderful road – more wonderful than the Great North Road, or the military road from Moscow to Vladivostock. And the most wonderful thing about it was that I lived on it. [*Sketches for an Autobiography*, 1979]

Bennett's Bedfordshire novel *Teresa of Watling Street* is a far from satisfactory book, but it does contain local colour and topography. It is in reality a detective story, although its subtitle is 'A Fantasia on Modern Themes'. The setting is Trinity Hall Farm, renamed Queen's Farm, and the novel concerns the strange goings on of the Craig family, a mysterious London banker, his daughter and their henchmen. The Craigs are definitely outsiders in the village and it may have been this sense of being foreign and different that struck Bennett when he first arrived at Hockliffe.

Like Bennett, the detective character, Redgrave, makes friends with the villager, Puddephatt, and it is this country type who gives the story body and some credibility. The bizarre tale unfolds and includes a circus, a mysterious visit to a chalk pit (very common around Dunstable) and features motor cars, probably the earliest in a Bedfordshire novel.

But Bennett was also undertaking more serious work at Hockliffe. He published his *Anna of the Five Towns* while living there, probably wrote the short story 'Nocturne at the Majestic' in the house in August 1902, and certainly wrote *The Truth About An Author* there. The death of Bennett's father, Enoch Bennett, took place on 17 January 1902 at Trinity Hall farm after a protracted illness. It was a profound moment in the novelist's life and he must have mentally recorded every moment of the passing in the upstairs room. It was all faithfully reproduced some years later in *Clayhanger*, where the sequence appears as the death of the architect's father. The funeral took place at Chalgrave church a mile or two away and the novelist raised a handsome stone to his father's memory, probably designed by Edwin Rickards, the original of Darius Clayhanger.

Four years after Bennett's departure, another giant arrived. Joseph Conrad (1857–1924) leased the remote farmhouse of Someries at Hyde near Luton. Both Conrad and his wife were used to life in Kent, so that Bedfordshire did not appeal very strongly, although it was convenient. Conrad confessed to John Galsworthy: 'I've known not a single moment of bodily ease since we got into this new house', and to Mrs Ford Madox Ford: 'You have no idea of the soul corroding bleakness of earth and sky here when the east wind blows'.

Conrad had come with a sense of despair; his two novels *Nostromo* and *The Secret Agent* had not met with the acclaim he had expected and he was now struggling with *Razumov*, which was later to appear as *Under Western Eyes*. His most remarkable achievement at Someries, however, was the founding of *The English Review* which took place in November 1908. Conrad assembled for the weekend Ford Madox Ford, Douglas Goldring, the journalist, and a number of assistants, plus vast quantities of manuscripts, proofs and publisher's dummies. The writers devoured quantities of food and Conrad was still penning words at 2 a.m. when the lamplights were fading. The *Review* was born in December and Conrad received the first copy, with its contributions by Tolstoy, Hardy, Henry James, Wells, Galsworthy and W. H. Hudson, in his farmhouse. Early the following year, Conrad made his escape from Someries, but not before the ubiquitous Luton photographer, Thurston, had captured the whole family on his negative, standing in the brier-hung doorway of their temporary home.

Bennett's writings on the area certainly suggest that he dipped into books by local authors. The county had always been well served by historians, from Samuel Lyson's scholarly volume of 1806, through the detailed works of Thomas Fisher, 1812–16, and Thomas Parry, 1827. William Marsh Harvey's extensive *History of the hundred of Willey* appeared in 1872–8, dealing with the northern parts of the county, but all these books were antiquarians' researches. A different type of book made its appearance at the turn of the century, the readable romantic history, basically factual but with a glaze of subjective impressions and encounters. The Revd Albert John Foster (1843–1918) was the most prolific of these authors and was rector of Farndish from 1875 and vicar of Wootton from 1880 till his death. Foster launched into print in 1889 with his *A Tourist's Guide to Bedfordshire*, after which there was no stopping him. He published *The Bunyan Country* in 1890, a guide to Hertfordshire in 1891, the same year as *The Ouse*, then *Round About the Crooked Spire in North-East Derbyshire* in 1894, and *The Chiltern Hundreds* in 1897. His *Bunyan* was illustrated by himself and was the book for which he was best known outside the county. Foster's attempts at fiction were more questionable: *The Robber Baron of Bedford Castle*, published by Thomas Nelson in 1893, is a highly romanticised version of the exploits of Fulke de Breauté. His second novel, *Ampthill Towers*, was set in the Ampthill of Catherine of Aragon although it contained such local characters as Sir Hugh Conquest and Sir John Gostwick. These books were the ideal Sunday School prizes, but unfortunately they were regarded as gospel truth by their recipients and have entered local folklore as such!

A more reliable local writer was the Revd Charles Frederick Farrar (1860–1931), brother of Sir George, who was headmaster of the Elstow School. He wrote two large works, *Old Bedford* (1926) and *Ouse's Silent Tide* (1921), which has become a classic. Although his book on the town has been outmoded by history, it is still a good read, and his book on the river, recording a voyage down its length with his son, is a superb evocation of leisurely summers before 1914.

Bedford was also the town in which H. H. Munro, 'Saki', (1870–1916) grew up to write his weird stories and in which Christopher Fry grew up to write 'The Lady's Not for Burning'.

The gradual extension and improvement of Bedford had proceeded apace in the 1870s and 1880s giving the town that predominantly late Victorian look that it still has today. Those bosky streets, squares (Linden Road) and circuses (Rothsay Gardens) were largely raised at the bidding of the worthies who were mayors and aldermen of the town. Among these could be mentioned Joshua Hawkins, five times mayor, who speculated in land and developed estates of villa residences, George Hurst, an antiquarian alderman, Thomas Jobson Jackson, a builder, and the Revd John Jukes, who promoted discussion. Some of these were local men with a civic pride, and their efforts came to fruition in the creation of De Parys Avenue and the Park, laid out from 1881 and opened in 1888 with a neat lodge and 'handsome gates, richly covered with intricate scrolls and foliage . . . entirely the product of manual labour with forge, anvil and hammer'. [Anonymous, *Bedford Town and Townsmen*, 1896, p. 146] A focal point had already been created on St Peter's Green with the unveiling of the Bunyan statue by the sculptor Sir Edgar Boehm in 1874.

The creation of the new Bedford School building by E. C. Robins on a site to the north of St Peter's in October 1891 certainly opened up this area as an important residential district, and it was also a notable event. T. G. E. Elger, a former mayor, noted in his diary: 'October 29th 1891 A lovely summer day, though somewhat cold. Bedford Grammar School opened at 12-30 by the Duke of Bedford. Edith, Mrs Helmsley & Mrs Whyley went together & I walked with the Civic procession which was preceded by all the boys in the School 4 abreast. There were about 800 of them . . . The new Hall, though far from finished looked very handsome.' [Diary, University Library, Cambridge]

A contemporary writer refers to the 'imposing class of

residences' facing the Park and Kimbolton Road where 'a number of new streets named after Saints have been recently formed'. Miss Joyce Harding, the daughter of the Bedford musician, Dr Alfred Harding, who herself lived to a great age, told me she remembered when all these houses looked on to fields and the open country came right into Bedford. The same writer continues: 'Various handsome clubhouses have been built, and the social life of the place is full of animation and attractiveness.'

The Corporation had steadily bought up property adjoining the river, so that by 1890, it was possible to embank the Ouse and create an area of recreation, a stone balustrade to match the bridge being in place by 1895. St Paul's Square was also opened up at about this time and the magnificent bronze statue of John Howard with its remarkable *art nouveau* base by Sir Alfred Gilbert was unveiled in 1894. Such moves showed a vision and foresight sadly lacking today. The High Street was definitely the centre of attraction, the late Charles Linnell recalling that in the 1890s there was a daily parade of elegant gentlemen and fashionably dressed women up and down the street. 'Every morning between 11 and 12.30 there was a regular parade of admirals, generals, colonels and other officers with their ladies up and down the High Street between the Swan and St Peter's; and never was there such a doffing of hats and caps and so much bowing and saluting as friends and acquaintances met one another.' [*Beds Magazine*, Vol. 7, p. 80] The smart shops with their new plate-glass frontages included Charles Hart, Cook, Pastry Cook and Confectioner at No. 100; E. P. Rose for Millinery, Mantles and Costume; and the shining establishment of John Bull & Co., Goldsmiths and Jewellers, at No. 49. Above this shop was a large bull clock, still in place, and below it a bar that dropped at 12.00 noon to give Greenwich Mean Time. All the Bedford gentlemen set their watches by it! About twenty years later, my mother would drive by trap from Ampthill to Bedford with the local doctor and stable the horse at The Swan Hotel. After shopping, it was fashionable to go to Norman's at No. 5 High Street for a sherry and a biscuit. Walking to school in the mornings from the station, she would notice that every middle-class house had a housemaid cleaning the brass of the front doors, street after street of them.

As in the period of Edward Blore's Grammar School, the creation of the new High School and Modern School for Girls by Basil Champneys (1842–1935) stamped its character on the town in a remarkable way. The provision of private female education of this standard had been mooted since 1873, but was quite progressive in the country as a whole, let alone in Bedford. Champneys designed a pretty Jacobean building in blushing Henlow brick for the combined schools, with a lively silhouette on to Bromham Road and a screen of wrought iron gates and piers, leading on to a forecourt. It was formally opened by Lady Isabella Whitbread on 20 July 1882 and is really the most distinguished of Bedford's late Victorian buildings if one discounts the slightly earlier Shire Hall. The Shire Hall was designed by Alfred Waterhouse R.A. in 1879–81, in his typical red brick and red terracotta style, and is interesting for still containing all its original, quirky, high Victorian furnishings. This building only slightly pre-dated the setting up of a County Council in 1888 and rural district councils in 1894.

Despite this feverish building, the individual parts do not match up to the flavour of the whole; the lay-out of late nineteenth-century Bedford is intriguing, the separate houses are not. The one exception to this monotonous uniformity is the delightful villa in De Parys Avenue designed by A. N. Prentice for Miss Alison Collie, headmistress of the High School in 1900. These unexciting residences are surprising since, as from 1884, Bedford was the home of an important Arts and Crafts firm, founded by John Parrish White. White, who had been apprenticed at Biggleswade, first bought the business of the builder, Hull, in Hassett Street, Bedford and then acquired land to the west of the Midland Railway, starting the Pyghtle Works for the manufacture of architectural joinery. Subsequently, the Pyghtle Works established a masonry shop and a metalwork shop, specialising in garden ornaments, and issued expensive catalogues of their wares. It may have been the presence of such a prestigious business, so close to the railway, that attracted a number of celebrated architects to the area in around 1900. White's products were beginning to achieve a national reputation and the woodwork from the factory was used in the development of Letchworth Garden City, then being planned by Sir Ebenezer Howard.

The most famous of these young architects was Mackay Hugh Baillie-Scott (1865–1945) who moved to Bedford in 1901 and set up an office at 4 Windsor Place, St Cuthbert's Street. He was already well known as a designer of William Morris-inspired houses but had not published his important book, later to be written at Bedford. He is now seen as a pioneer of the modern movement almost on the level of his great contemporaries Charles Rennie Mackintosh and Charles Annesley Voysey. The Pyghtle Works very soon produced an illustrated catalogue of Scott furniture designs, all superbly crafted, but letting the woods and the inlays speak for themselves in simple *art nouveau* ornament. Scott may have hoped for a great response from the people of Bedford, but none came. He was something of a bohemian in a very traditionalist town; he preferred casual clothes, bicycling around the countryside, and he was not interested in possessions – definitely not pukka! His unprogressive neighbours were insulated against changes. T. G. E. Elger, attending a debate on the enfranchisement of females in May 1892, wrote in his diary: 'a lively debate, all spoke against it'.

Scott's furniture designs did, however, capture the imagination of the Germans, and his Pyghtle-made pieces were despatched to the Grand Ducal Palaces of Darmstadt and the residences of Mannheim, even if they were not appreciated in Bedford. White's were also making furniture for the architects Sir Raymond Unwin, Barry Parker and C. H. B. Quennell. Scott's one Bedford client was the musician, Carl St Amory, who asked him to design a house for an artistic person in 1895. St Amory, who taught music at Bedford School, had many ideas but no money, and so the half-timbered cottage was never built. Perhaps sensing that his work was not wanted, Scott moved out to the Manor at Fenlake on the Ouse in 1902 and remodelled it for himself. [P. D. Kornwolf, *M. H. Baillie-Scott and the Arts and Crafts Movement*, 1972]

By the later Edwardian years, prosperous Bedfordians were beginning to move into the villages on the edge of Bedford rather than inhabiting its suburbs. Such places as Biddenham, Bromham, Elstow and Moggerhanger were popular, and Scott and his friends built a few artistic houses out of town. The first was probably King's Close, Biddenham, for Miss Steele in 1907, followed by The White Cottage, Biddenham, for Miss Street in

1909 – idiosyncratic, vernacular creations with low doors and sweeping roofs. C. H. Mallows (1864–1915) was another Bedford architect who created a number of Arts and Crafts residences in Biddenham, notably Three Gables and King's Corner, of about 1900. Another of this circle was the great dry-point etcher, F. L. Griggs A.R.A., who designed the Biddenham war memorial.

Bedford's musical tastes were rather more definite than its architectural ones. A Bedford Amateur Musical Society had been in existence since January 1867 and concerts were held first in the Assembly Rooms and then in the new Corn Exchange, opened in 1874. From 1890, the town had a budding opera season, and in 1895 Carl St Amory commissioned Mallows to design an *art nouveau* opera house for his productions, a further scheme being made in 1898. Like all of St Amory's schemes, it failed. The Royal County Theatre, however, a far less prepossessing building, was opened at Midland Road on 1 April 1899.

The tradition of high quality art teaching, which had been a feature of the Bedford schools since the days of Edward and Bradford Rudge, continued later in the century. Three of B. Rudge's pupils, R. W., G. W., and G. G. Fraser, gained distinction as watercolourists of the Ouse in the 1880s. A number of younger artists were making headway at the turn of the century. A. C. Cooke (1867–1951) was the son of a Luton solicitor who showed promise as an artist while at the Bedford School. He went on to St John's Wood Art School and the Academy, achieving some success as a narrative painter. His early works of social realism were based on the country life of the villages on the fringe of Luton. He used Bedfordshire cottages to relate the hardships of these people in such canvases as *Widowed* and *The Poacher*. His soft approach made him a good portrayer of the country child but he soon left his ruralism for more lucrative work.

A somewhat different vision of the county was given by the watercolourist Henry Sylvester Stannard R.S.A. (1869–1951), the son of an artist, who was brought up in Bedford and educated at the Modern School. Trained at South Kensington, Stannard was a born teacher and devoted his life at Bedford and Flitwick to taking pupils. He trudged round the countryside of middle Bedfordshire, capturing the cottages, homesteads, village ponds and muddy roads that were shortly to be engulfed by tarmac and jerry building. It is a very gentle vision of the country: besmocked workers pitching hay into carts, horses waiting patiently to be shod, villagers idling, and poultry and ducks aplenty. He is inclined to romanticise, but to locals, a leafy Edwardian lane or an overgrown stile will suddenly produce that shock of recognition. [*Beds Magazine,* Vol. 21, pp. 12–16]

Stannard's Bedfordshire is definitely one seen through the artistic presentation of a carved frame and a gilt mount. The reality could be much harsher. At exactly the time that Stannard was painting his most roseate views, an old friend of mine was growing up in a cottage at Millbrook in the 1900s. Her parents were grindingly poor, but managed to keep a pig, a status symbol at the time. The father could keep six children on a farm labourer's wages and everything was bearable until the mother died. At this point my friend, a little girl of twelve, had to take her mother's place with the five younger children. After a year, the father had had enough and disappeared, leaving the young girl responsible for the whole family, the only breadwinner being the brother aged ten who now worked as a ploughboy on a nearby farm. A search was made for the father in every pond and river within miles, but it was years before he was discovered, happily remarried with another family. Somehow this Millbrook family survived before all the girls had to go into service in the country houses at the age of fourteen. Such a story would be impossible today and yet it is easily within living memory.

A slightly more modern exponent of the arts than Stannard was Amy Kathleen Browning (1882–1974), the daughter of J. D. Browning of Bramingham Hall, Streatley. Her father farmed at Kitchen End, Pulloxhill, from the 1890s and it was there that the young girl developed as an artist and set up a studio in about 1900. She left home to train at the Royal College of Art and in Paris, but constantly returned home to paint figure subjects and flowers. She married the portrait painter Thomas Cantrell Dugdale R.A. (1880–1952), who also worked at Pulloxhill, and who produced exquisite portraits and character studies there that are the equal of Sargent or Munnings. Rural paintings of Bedfordshire by A. C. Cooke (1867–1951) are in the Luton Museum and watercolours by Stannard in the Cecil Higgins Art Gallery, Bedford.

The age of the country house building was very nearly over, but not the age of creating gardens. An interesting arrival at Pulloxhill in 1877 had been Captain Edward Jekyll (*d*.1921) and his German wife, who built a small country house, Higham Bury, on the edge of the village. Jekyll was the elder brother of Gertrude Jekyll the noted horticulturalist and garden designer and it was she who laid out the garden for Higham Bury, perhaps the first she undertook. She continued to visit Pulloxhill until the First World War and later designed a garden for Ickwell House. Very little of her lay-out survives at Pulloxhill, although the summer-house must be hers and the mature trees were probably planted with her approval.

At Ampthill, the Jekylls' friend, Anthony H. Wingfield of Ampthill House, established a private zoo for the amusement of his family and friends. This included camels and llamas, but also cheetahs and boars, which were quite tame. Wingfield's keepers saddled zebras, ostriches, guanacos and zebus for riding, and it was not an uncommon sight before 1914 to see Wingfield's footmen, riding through the town on a llama to deliver a letter to the post office!

Where the *belle époque* touched the county, it was confined to a few glittering families in the country houses, mostly newcomers who had little to do with the old landed squires or the ordinary people. In 1896, the elderly and frail Madame de Falbe let her country home, Luton Hoo, to the South African mining millionaire Julius Wernher for £3000 a year. Wernher, from a German merchant family, had travelled to South Africa in the 1880s and become the partner of Alfred Beit and a close associate of Cecil Rhodes. Wernher returned to this country with unbeliev-able riches and, with his young wife, had moved into Bath House, Piccadilly, where he at once spent £100,000 on furnishings.

Luton Hoo was finally acquired by the Wernhers in 1904, with 5218 acres of land, and it became the family's principal home, where its art collections could be displayed and Edwardian houseparties given a suitable setting. Although they did not rebuild the main house, they reconstructed it under the super-vision of the French architect, C. F. Mewes, in a lavish Parisian style. Louis XVI interiors were all the rage in the high society of Edward VII's *entente cordiale* so that marble, boiseries and ormolu mounted furniture abounded in this *fin de siècle* palace. A last minute adjustment in costs resulted in the old chapel being retained, so this masterpiece by the Victorian architect, G. E. Street, survives with its alabaster east end and its ceiling paintings. It is now a Russian Orthodox Chapel and dedicated as a shrine to the murdered Tsar Nicholas II and his family.

The works at the Hoo were enormous and the cost so prodigious, that there was criticism in the popular press. It was difficult, even in 1904, to spend one's own money privately, and both Joseph Conrad at Someries Farm and Beatrice Webb on a visit, burst out in vitriol against such extravagance. The work force lived under canvas in the park, while marble insets, woodwork, plasterwork and gilding were undertaken by craftsmen from London and as far afield as France. The final bill was £147,000, but it did not include the great undertakings outside: the creation of an Italian garden with pavilions by the landscape architect, Romaine Walker, the draining and cleaning of the Capability Brown sixty-acre lake, and the restocking of it with 11,000 trout. [Trevelyan, *Grand Dukes and Diamonds*, 1991, pp. 165–7]

The Wernhers' purses allowed them to stop at nothing, so the collection included Beauvais and Gobelin tapestries woven for the French royal family, paintings by Francino, Filippino Lippi, Watteau and Reynolds, and, in 1904, the acquisition of Altdorfer's 1520 masterpiece *Christ Taking Leave of His Mother*. The completion of the interiors was marked by a visit from King Edward VII in February 1907 when the King was delayed for two hours by a burst tyre on the royal motor car. He was believed to have used the occasion to get tips on South African investments from Sir Julius, to whom he had already given a baronetcy. Wernher was still an immensely powerful figure in the mining world; he had personally launched the London Diamond Syndicate in 1903, was consulted by politicians, and he was well respected in South Africa. He made an extensive tour of his mines in 1903, but was widely criticised for advocating the use of cheap Chinese labour, which Europeans considered tantamount to slave labour.

Luton Hoo is today still the best place to catch a glimpse of that Edwardian England, where a leisurely life could be combined with art and opulence. Sir Julius's family were already friendly with some of the Russian exiles with whom they were to intermarry. Before 1914, the dashing young son, Harold Wernher was getting to know Countess Zia, the daughter of Grand Duke Michael of Russia, whom he was eventually to marry and bring home to Luton Hoo. With this connection, the old house became the resting place for her astonishing collections of Russian art and Fabergé, for which it is still famous.

An arrival on a similarly grand scale in 1905 was The Hon. Whitelaw Reid (1837–1912), the American ambassador to the Court of St James's, who took a lease on the Wrest Park estate. This followed the death of the owner, Lord Cowper, whose nephew, Lord Lucas, was not anxious to live in the house. Reid was a journalist and a sportsman, so Wrest became the scene for his extensive shoots, houseparties and riding. There was no electricity in the mansion, a disaster for an American, but Reid simply relied on oil lamps and the services of forty-four indoor servants. He was probably the first landowner to travel wholly by motor car, cutting the train journey time by an hour. In July 1909, Reid entertained Edward VII at Wrest and a vast concourse of people stood by the Park gates to see the King pass. His Majesty could be seen in the back of his motor car, raising his hat to right and left at the populace. Reid had a large party staying, including the Austrian, Spanish and Portuguese ambassadors, and the celebrated Countess of Dudley, to intrigue the susceptible monarch. The royal party dined to the strains of Casano's orchestra. The King attended church at Silsoe next day and visited Flitton in the afternoon.

A slightly more altruistic approach was adopted by the remarkable couple who had taken over the reins at Woburn Abbey. Herbrand, 10th Duke of Bedford (1858–1940) had succeeded his brother unexpectedly in 1893. While serving in India, the Duke had made an unusual marriage in 1888 to Mary Tribe, daughter of the Archdeacon of Lahore. Her wide interests and vitality injected a new life into Woburn, where he was to preside for over forty years. Like his ancestors, the Duke was passionately interested in agriculture and created an experimental fruit farm at Woburn and a Farm College at Ridgmont for boarding students. Both the Duke and Duchess were keen zoologists and introduced rare breeds to Woburn Park, including the famous herd of Père David deer and bison. A less popular import was the European grey squirrel which eventually escaped from Woburn to infest the country!

In 1898, the Duke appointed the writer and academic, Rowland Prothero (1851–1937), to be his Agent-in-Chief for the Russell estates, not only in Bedfordshire but in Cambridgeshire, Devon, Dorset and Cornwall. Prothero was given the superb riverside mansion, Oakley House, to live in rent free, with three indoor servants, seven gardeners, three keepers and a plentiful supply of milk and cream from Woburn. Prothero devoted his spare time to Oakley village, forming a cricket team and giving lectures in the village hall. It may have been under his influence that the Bedfords built splendid new tile-hung cottages at Woburn and in the estate village of Oakley, designed by the architect, C. H. Holden. Prothero was adopted as the Unionist candidate in Northern Bedfordshire in 1907 but was defeated in the 1910 election as 'the pampered pet of a noble duke'. He was returned for Oxford University in 1914 and, after serving as President of the Board of Agriculture under Lloyd George, was created Lord Ernle.

Mary, Duchess of Bedford, was an unconventional woman who preferred an active life to sitting about at the Abbey and performing the usual duties expected of a duchess. Interested in painting, photography and bird-watching, these hobbies were not sufficient to satisfy her questing mind, and in about 1898 she decided to devote her life to nursing. With ample resources available, it was no problem for her husband to build and equip a small cottage hospital for her in 1904. This handsome building on the western edge of Woburn was also designed by C. H. Holden. The enterprising Duchess was trained as a theatre sister and a radiologist, even performing small operations herself.

The county had been in the forefront of the bicycle craze in the 1890s and guide-books were produced with the cyclist in mind and small shops opened in every town to cater for these intrepid flyers. It had the effect of liberating a new class of educated young people who hadn't the money for other forms of travel. But old habits die hard and J. D. Browning's farm labourers at Kitchen End, Pulloxhill, never had bicycles and continued to walk to work. The growing mechanisation of the country at the end of the century meant that many young men of promise seized the opportunity to invent new machines in backyards and workshops all through Bedfordshire.

The first was Dan Albone (1860–1906), the bicycling pioneer, who could turn his hand to almost anything. Albone was born on 12 September 1860 at Biggleswade, where his mother kept the Ongley Arms public house. Bicycle construction was at a formative stage, so Albone began to manufacture 'Penny-farthings' behind the Ongley Arms. He was successful enough to be able to expand to bigger workshops on the banks of the Ivel in 1886, marketing a special safety racing bicycle at the Ivel Cycle Works. The sport of the time was road cycle racing and Albone's pub (he had succeeded his mother as landlord) became the 'Mecca' of the London cycling clubs, particularly the Anfield Cycling Club, the North Road Club and the North London. He officiated at the time trials with stop-watch in hand and one of his young enthusiasts in the 1890s was A. E. Richardson, later Sir A. E. Richardson of Ampthill.

Albone invented a tandem bicycle in 1886, and in 1887 the most revolutionary of machines, a lady's bicycle. In order to publicise this, he persuaded a young Biggleswade lady to pose on it for a photograph and in so doing scandalised the neighbourhood. By the early 1900s, he had moved on to motor tricycles and an Ivel motor car, of which very few were made. Before his death in 1906, he had produced an armour-plated car which the Army were invited to fire at while he drove and a motor tractor which was sold throughout the Empire; a surviving example is in the Science Museum.

Only two or three miles from Albone's home at Biggleswade, on the west side of Girtford Bridge, is a memorial garden. It is a triangular space between poplar trees where the old North Road joins Shefford Lane, once a busy junction. The sundial and memorial are to F. T. Bidlake, 'the father of Road Sport', who knew Albone and instigated cycle racing in the area.

Across the county at Kempston, another young Bedfordshire man, H. P. Saunderson, was experimenting at 70 Bedford Road. In the winter of 1894, he constructed a sleigh to cross the frozen River Ouse from Kempston to Bedford with passengers, much to the fury of Bedford Town Council. A Saunderson car, developed in 1896, was of a wagonette type and, although it ran well, it had an engine under the passenger seats, resulting in over-heating! From 1900, he had a factory at Cow Bridge making 'Universal Tractors' for ploughing, mowing, binding and threshing. His machinery found favour all over the world, especially in South America, and in the 1914–18 War soldiers from the Bedfordshire and Hertfordshire Regiment came across Saunderson tractors in Palestine. In about 1909, Saunderson developed a small aircraft, the 'Mayfly', which had trial runs at Wickey Farm, Little Staughton, with Saunderson at the controls. It was later entered for the *Daily Mail* Air Races at Leagrave and Blackpool.

At Ampthill, A. E. Grimmer (1877–1960) opened a cycle repair shop in Bedford Street in 1895 which gradually became a manufactury. Although under twenty years of age, Grimmer could see the possibilities ahead for the motor car and, despite opposition from his cycle agents, began to experiment. In 1902, he built the county's first steam car and made trial runs to Bedford, Chelmsford and London. Teething troubles included a steam burst on the Ampthill hill which sent them into the ditch and a stripped gear that resulted in a night in the open. This car was eventually sold for £150. Mr Grimmer later became an early aviator, piloting a Blériot plane and a Deperdussin from fields at Flitwick, Houghton House and Bedford polo ground in 1912. Both of his planes are now on display at the Shuttleworth Aircraft Museum, Old Warden.

The authorities were remarkably ill-equipped to deal with these new vehicles, as was shown by the tragic death of the distinguished Indian judge, Sir William Rattigan (1842–1904), in July 1904. Sir William's sons, including the father of the playwright Terence Rattigan, had been staying with the Revd Alfred Houfe, vicar of Pulloxhill, and his brother Charles Houfe, who were *in loco parentis*. Sir William, Unionist M.P. for N.E. Lanark, was passing through the county when his hired Darracq motor car came off the road. 'The car,' as the *Bedfordshire Times* reported, 'which had a glass front, was approaching an awkward turn in the road at Langford, at the rate of ten miles an hour, when the car was overturned. Sir William was thrown against the glass screen in front of the car and Lady Rattigan and the chauffeur were imprisoned beneath the glass screen. Some labourers rushed forward to render assistance and found Sir William was dead. They extricated Lady Rattigan, who was suffering from cuts and shock.' The body was taken to The Boot public house and the Coroner's Inquest was held a few days later at the Corner House, Langford. The court was not asked to discuss the roadworthiness of the car but whether anyone was culpable. It emerged that the motor was sent out by Messrs Rawlings of Gloucester Road, London, despite having been in an accident with a coal cart. A verdict of Accidental Death was returned, for although 'the car was not in a fit condition to be sent out on a journey, the driver acting under the instructions of his masters is duly exonerated from all blame'. The *Daily Mail* of 5 July, imagining that the cause was a tyre burst, urged the Automobile club to 'authoritatively' state whether tyre bursts were dangerous or not.

XIII
The New Order, 1914-39

The Great War came imperceptibly upon the county in August 1914. A large part of Bedfordshire still moved at the pace of the horse, a majority of its workers were employed on the land, and in a score of country houses the same families resided and ruled that had done so since 1700. The High Sheriff still had a resplendent carriage and four horses to take him to official functions, and Mr Anthony Wingfield of Ampthill House still had a butler, housekeeper, five footmen, six chamber and kitchen maids, a hall boy, a chef and several keepers. The Duke of Bedford still changed cars on his journeys from Woburn Abbey to London because the coachmen had traditionally changed horses and the town criers were a familiar sight on the streets of Bedford and Luton. There was no hint in those summer newspapers full of flower-shows and regattas that this way of life was facing a watershed and leaving a past to which it could never return.

Bedford could face the declaration of war in August 1914 with the discipline of a military town. It had been an army centre since 1881, when the Bedfordshire Light Infantry Militia and the Hertfordshire Militia were brought together with headquarters there. It was the Bedfordshire Regiment that fought in the Great War, but afterwards the name was changed to the Bedfordshire and Hertfordshire Regiment. The massive castellated barracks on Bedford Road, Kempston, (part of which survives) had been built in 1875–6 at a cost of £50,000. It must have been in this building that Reginald Hind was medically examined in 1914.

It is long ago, but I am not likely to forget my first examination in the Bedford barracks. Escorted by a corporal, I was marched off to room 13 and ordered to strip. For a moment I flinched. The room itself – already stripped – needed examination more than I. It had no hangings, only cobwebs. The bare boards were carpeted with a quarter of an inch of dust. The windows which had not known a cleaner for months, looked gloomily out on a range of latrines. The walls, distempered who knows how many years before, were pictured with pencilled caricatures of officers and N.C.O.s, with many a ribald rhyme scribbled insultingly below. As I undressed I gazed about me in despair. There was no hook on which to hang my clothes. No chair on which to sit. Not a stick of furniture in sight. But I am wrong. There *was* just one piece. It was a bottle placed, so as to attract attention, in the centre of the mantelpiece. And it was labelled *Poison*. [*Confessions of an Uncommon Attorney*, 1945, p. 190]

The Bedfordshire Regiment served with distinction in the Great War; large numbers were lost in the trenches of France, some saw service in Gallipoli, but they were also in Italy, and one battalion was with General Allenby for the capture of Jerusalem in 1917. It was to supply new recruits for this regiment that the Duke of Bedford set up a camp at his own expense in Ampthill Park at the commencement of hostilities.

The camp at Ampthill was particularly well appointed and was intended to attract Bedfordshire lads into the service, where they could be taught drilling, physical training and exercise before being sent abroad. Wooden huts were built across the park and a drill ground was cordoned off near the Catherine Cross. Because of the money lavished on it by the Duke, the camp, which eventually contained about two thousand men (almost the population of Ampthill), had an entertainments hall and a kinema driven by a petrol dynamo. There was eventually a women's section, set up after the first year or two. The Duke funded his own band and the men came to be known as 'The Duke's pets'. They were even given the command by the sergeant-major when they landed in France: 'Fall in, the Duke's pets!' Hubert Bennett of Lidlington remembered that he earned 1s 9d on his first day in the camp and five shillings in his first week. He recalled that the Duke liked to drill the troops himself but had a gruff voice which they couldn't understand. Each soldier had a wire bed and mattress, unheard of luxuries, and they were supplied with venison from Woburn Park. When the trained soldiers were ready for France, they were marched to Ampthill station and personally seen off by the Duke. Captain Kenneth Hope recorded that the Duke gave every departing officer a pistol, a pair of field-glasses and an electric torch.

The Great War was the first occasion when the civilians on the Home Front felt themselves to be fully involved. As early as 10

August 1914, there was a disturbance in Dunstable over a grocer who had put up his prices in the belief that there would be shortages. But in the country it was different. The Lawson-Johnston family at Bletsoe Cottage was happy and healthy despite shortages, and were very nearly self-supporting, living on the fresh, home-grown produce from the garden, fruit from the orchard and eggs from the chickens they kept. Mrs Lawson-Johnston learned to bake her own bread and bought a tub churn to make 7 or 8lbs of her own butter a week. It certainly denoted a change in the old order when the grandchildren of Lord St John were learning to milk their own cows by hand! [Olive Lawson-Johnston, 'Bletsoe During the 1914–18 War', *Beds Magazine*, Vol. 17, pp. 13–14]

The excitement of the Royal Artillery coming to Stopsley in 1914 with horses, mounted men and guns, enthralled the young A. B. Allen of Stopsley House. He was allowed to ride the major's horse and, by scrounging among the soldiers, obtained for his friends many forage caps and belts for their own war games. He noted how the countryside changed as the war progressed; the younger women disappeared to work in the munitions factories of Luton and were replaced by middle-aged or even elderly women in the fields. The villagers bought chocolate and cigarettes each week to send off to the local boys at the front. A. B. Allen wrote: 'The letters we received in acknowledgement were all posted in the hall so that all could read them. But it was not until George, our gardener came home with the loss of an eye that we began to realise that war was something more than flags and songs and fascinating maps.' [A. B. Allen, 'War comes to Stopsley', *Beds Magazine*, Vol. 14, pp. 203–4] Nearby at Leagrave, Mrs Maurice Hewlett's Omnia Works were manufacturing aeroplane parts amidst the smell of dope and plywood.

Luton and district had some 25,000 troops in the immediate vicinity during the war, there were camps at Biscot Mill and the Hoo Park, and a military hospital at Wardown House (now Luton Museum). The engineering factories turned over their production to war work and, with an increasing work force from the Midlands and the North, trades unionism became a dominant force in labour relations. Luton experienced its first strike of munitions workers in 1917.

In August 1914, the Duchess of Bedford was better equipped than almost anyone to prepare herself and her house for the reception of wounded soldiers. Wrest Park was made available by the public-spirited Lord Lucas and the Duchess was keen that the facilities of the Woburn Cottage Hospital should be fully utilised. The outbuildings, Riding School and enclosed Tennis Court at the Abbey were turned into a base hospital for the reception of troops straight from the front. She wrote to her sister on the 11 August 1914: 'I have had 1500 applications to join my corps in 24 hours, and I am told may expect double the number in the next 24 hours. I am fitting my hospital for 24 beds and my idea is, if it is used, to draft recovering cases to be nursed by the trained amateurs. I have six trained London-Hospital nurses and a trained district-nurse with many years experience . . . I am going to do practical work at my Cottage Hospital from 7 a.m. to 9 a.m. daily till I have learnt something.' The following day she wrote: 'I went to the War Office with a surgeon yesterday to see the Director of the Army Medical Corps who assured me the Cottage Hospital would not be forgotten . . . They say the wounded are coming into London fast . . . Also many people offer their empty houses to the Red Cross to get the Cross put on so that they won't be shot at!!' [John, Duke of Bedford, *The Flying Duchess*, 1968, p. 57]

The Duchess was desperate to get going but was frustrated by the rigmaroles of bureaucracy. 'Please do not suppose I want to go to the Front and use my rifle,' she wrote to her friend Dr Long, 'I only "kick against the pricks" . . .' She informed him that she had an operating theatre, an X-ray, a motor ambulance, six trained nurses and five surgeons. To her delight, the hospital became official a month later. She confided to her diary on 7 September 1914: 'Admitted the first soldiers from Bedford to my Cottage Hospital. I little thought when we built it ten years ago, that we should ever see the Red Cross flag flying over it.' She had as her director, the distinguished surgeon from Guys Hospital, Brydon Glendinning, who stayed on after the war. Surviving photographs show the considerable degree of comfort in the Abbey hospital, where the high ceilings and expanses of white wall were softened by potted plants and low hanging lights.

During the five years and seven months of its existence as a military hospital, Woburn received in its one hundred and twenty beds a total of 2,453 serving soldiers. As well as Bedfordshire, the hospital served five other neighbouring counties and the Duchess personally superinted the arrival of forty-five convoys from the main station at Ampthill. On 1 May 1915, a train of wounded soldiers, its sides painted with red crosses, arrived there at 1.30 a.m. Volunteer stretcher-bearers were at hand to convey the wounded to the various houses in cars. The week before, most of these wretched men had been the gallant defenders of Hill 60.

The Duchess worked in the hospital throughout the war, only taking a break for three weeks, but her increasing deafness must have been a great trial to her and awkward for her staff. She had some trouble with V.A.D. nurses, who were not up to the job, and 'lady' servants, who arrived powdered and painted, were unpunctual or simply wept at the sight of a difficult task.

The hospital at Wrest Park had two hundred and twenty beds and the sanitary arrangements had already been improved and temporary electric light installed. Lord Lucas was there to welcome the first batch which arrived in the middle of September, the wards being superinted by his sister the Hon. Nan Ino Herbert. As the *Bedfordshire Times* reported: 'The heroes of Mons left the General Hospital, Whitechapel, soon after 2 o'clock in motor cars and omnibuses, and arrived by instalments. They were expected about four, but the first did not put in an appearance until some time after that hour. The last did not reach their destination until 6.30, and as the motor bus, from its height, could not proceed beyond the gates, the majority of the soldiers had to walk the length of the avenue.'

The newspaper went on to describe the bandages and slings of the walking wounded and added: 'It is needless to say that crowds awaited the arrival of the gallant fellows, and the latter thoroughly appreciated the cordial reception. Few of the working men were, of course, able to be present, but women and children waving Union Jacks and cheering lustily brought a smile from the dust-stained khaki-clad visitors.' Wrest was well liked by the soldiers with its grounds and double tennis courts. The newspaper reported that the boys were confident that a decisive battle in France and a rebellion in Berlin would end the war soon.

While Wrest and Woburn were the principal hospitals, the smaller country houses acted as convalescent homes to the wounded who were recuperating. One of these was Ampthill House, made available by Anthony H. Wingfield and remembered in the reminiscences of his butler, Charles W. Cooper. The Tommies came over from Wrest Park in batches of six, eight or ten in their official hospital uniforms of blue suits and red ties. Ampthill House had sixty in all. 'Most of them had been in the first expeditionary force known as the Old Contemptibles, several were married and had families, and were of the poorer class,' Cooper recalled. 'The reader can imagine how their faces lit up and how grateful they were for the huge joints of English meat, with liberal allowance of ale.' Cooper, the butler, had agreed with the visiting medical officer to serve twice the prescribed quantity of beer, four glasses a day instead of two! Cooper (who soon had to leave for war service himself) got them to do household tasks and the surviving household joined in. 'We played all sorts of card games and other amusements were provided,' Cooper remembered. 'At times I would arrange a musical evening and get an hour's extension for them from the sister; these evenings they thoroughly enjoyed, but one by one their wounds healed and they got well enough to be sent home to their families.' [*Town and County*, 1937, p. 174] Wingfield provided packets of tea for his own men who were serving abroad, and clothing for the young convalescents, who often had very little.

Cooper described the regime at Wrest Park as stricter and more disciplined under Dr Beauchamp, the first director, then Dr Kirkwood. In June 1916, a fire broke out in Wrest and the wounded soldiers had to be evacuated along with paintings and furniture. The smaller houses were very popular as convalescent homes because of the family atmosphere. At Hinwick House, Mrs Faith Orlebar made all the soldiers welcome and they became firm friends with her young children, who arranged games and recreations for them. Mrs Orlebar recorded a letter from Private H. A. C. Clark in June 1915, one of scores, written from Wrest. 'This morning I couldn't say much; but I think you know, Mrs Orlebar, how I appreciate your kindness to me, & to all the soldiers that are fortunate enough to be sent to Hinwick – My stay has been to me pleasantest and most profitable I have ever spent – My own home is a thorough Christian home, & when I tell them how beautifully each day is started at Hinwick they will be delighted.' Mrs Orlebar added: 'He means family prayers in the hall, in which all the soldiers are invited to join.' [C.R.O. OR 2343/24]

Ampthill Park House was put at the disposal of the convalescents by the Dowager Lady Ampthill. As a noted Germanophile before the war she had had to be careful. She removed all the portraits of German royalty from her walls except for one painting of the Kaiser. This she maintained was surety in case the Germans should arrive and would be used to bargain for the lives of the people in Ampthill! British and Empire soldiers who stayed at Park House were able to buy small china ornaments commemorating their stay. They depicted a soldier in bed and a nurse at his side with the inscription 'Ampthill Park'.

Bedford and Luton became centres of recruitment, Bedford became the host to the Highland Regiments and Luton became host to an expanding engineering industry that was to stay. Rumours were rife in the late autumn of 1914 that the Scottish regiments were to be stationed at Bedford, and on Sunday, 16 August, they arrived. Trains kept coming into the station and disgorging thousands of Highland Territorials; the 4th, 5th and 6th Seaforth Highlanders; the 4th Cameron Highlanders; the Gordon Infantry Brigade; the Gordon Highlanders and the Argyll and Sutherland Highlanders. They were billeted in blocks by street, some living in the Harpur Schools and some under canvas at Renhold. 'Soon they were thronging the streets and the promenades, many wearing in their caps the bonnie purple heather they had brought from their native heaths, and singing "The Land o' the Leal" in the land of Bunyan, and the "Bonnie Banks of Loch Lomond" on the banks of the bonnie Ouse.' They were extremely popular visitors, made friends with the children and, as a newspaper reported, 'there has been a boom in trade ever since'. On New Year's Eve 1914 the town provided them with a Hogmanay supper in eighteen public halls and welcomed two distinguished visitors, the Provost of Aberdeen and the Editor of the *Aberdeen Journal*. In January 1915, the town received a visit from Harry Lauder, whose son was stationed there. In February, Princess Louise came to inspect the Argylls and shortly after this the town built the troops a swimming-pool fed with hot water from the Electrical works. They gradually moved out by Easter 1915, but not before many local marriages had taken place!

Another sign of the times was the influx of refugees, mostly Belgians, into the county. At Shefford, the families of Cromber, Asperlagh and Diennsart were reunited after being separated in the flight from Antwerp. This reunion was largely due to the efforts of the vicar of Shefford, Revd E. Dakin. The Belgian musician, Mr de Reyghere of Bedford, gave a hundred concerts in the county to raise money for the poor of Bruges.

One of the signs of the war at Luton was the number of young women who were walking about with orange-yellow faces from the chemicals. They were employees at the big shell filling factory at Chaul End, where a temporary station had been opened. The hat industry continued its work and rather surprisingly managed to obtain spare parts for its sewing-machines from German agents, but the difficulty in obtaining raw materials and the loss of the foreign markets in wartime made engineering and chemicals more attractive occupations. Gradually the work force drifted away to these better paid jobs and the hat industry never regained its nineteenth-century dominance.

The Armistice of 11 November 1918, which brought a halt to the unpopular and unnecessary carnage, had some odd repercussions in this industrial town. The Versailles Peace Conference of June 1919 was a time for celebration and Luton Council's ill-judged festivities were scheduled for 19 July that year. Although the councillors made provision for street decorations, children's parties, and processions with five bands, there was no actual ceremony of thanksgiving. This brought protests from ex-servicemen's associations who planned rival events. But the Council banned their use of Wardown Park. With much unemployment about and a great deal of discontent, the scene was ripe for confrontation. The procession was halted in front of the Town Hall and the Mayor's speech drowned in the jeering of a hostile crowd. At midnight the crowds invaded the Town Hall, threw out the furniture and set the place on fire with petrol from a nearby garage. When the fire brigade arrived their hoses were cut and shops began to be looted. While the Town Hall burned down, a requisitioned piano was used to accompany 'Keep the Home Fires Burning'. Troops were called out from Biscot to defend the town centre property but, fortunately, they were well received by the populace. They were kept on hand for several days, however, due to the threats of the ringleaders to fire other buildings in the main streets. It was a miserable affair which made headlines in the nation's papers, but the judge at Bedford Assizes took a lenient view on those arrested, giving it as his considered opinion that they were provoked.

The most surprising arrival in the county during the Great War was not in a town but in the country. In 1916, an airship base was established at Cardington under the auspices of the Admiralty. Cardington was chosen because it was within reasonable distance of London, had good rail links and was supposed to be inaccessible to German spies landed by submarine! From a technical point of view, it was in a broad and flat situation, in a plain running east to west and out of range of German aircraft flying from Belgium. Some of the land belonged to the Whitbread family; another part, belonging to J. Armstrong of Bedford, was purchased for £110,000.

In January 1916, the Admiralty's Rigid Airship Committee decided to construct hangars at Cardington, and Short Brothers were given the contract to build two 23-class airships of Admiralty design. Work began on a giant hangar that year: concrete foundations were being laid by Edmund Nuttall of Manchester and the girder work being undertaken by A. J. Mayne of Glasgow, who were specialists in this field. The immense structure was built by gantries and steam cranes, Shorts being allowed to take possession just before completion. One hangar was completed in 1917 and extended in 1927, the other hangar designed specially in 1927. At one time they were the largest buildings in the British Empire, and they still stand to inspire and amaze passers-by. They are great monuments to the industrial age and still dominate this corner of the county, being visible for ten miles. At the same time, below them, the attractive little industrial village of Shortstown was created for the workers with its classical, brick, headquarters building.

The Admiralty ordered an airship 594 feet long by 64 feet in diameter, but before this was completed British Military Intelligence had obtained German engineering drawings from a Swiss engineer, Herr Muller. Further information was obtained from the wreckage of the German zeppelin L33 which had been brought down at Little Wigborough, Essex on 23–24 September 1916. As a result of this, the original ship was abandoned and a new R33-class airship, based on the German prototype, was planned. Experiments were made with various gas-bag systems and the construction was to be in re-inforced plywood.

This airship, the R31 Schutte-Lanz design, had six Sunbeam engines in gondolas suspended from the hull and was capable of a top speed of 70 m.p.h. It was launched in August 1918 and had a second flight on 16 October 1918. On its maiden flight, on 6 November 1918, the production girls from the top shop all came down to help open the massive doors, singing First World War songs as they took the strain. These girls, like the other workers, had to labour in highly dangerous conditions with much escaped hydrogen vapour hanging about in the top of the hangar. After the maiden voyage it was discovered that she had some cracking caused by deficient glues and she had to be withdrawn.

Shorts' had two other airships on the production line: the R32 and the R37. The R37 was abandoned as early as September 1918 because Germany was on the point of capitulation. It was recommenced in January 1919 as a possible civilian airship and again abandoned in 1924 when it had cost £320,000. In August 1918, the Admiralty planned scouting airships for Light Coastal Forces; these were Admiralty 'A' design craft with a range of 3000 miles. Shorts' won the contract for these. The R32 was a fairly successful model and had its maiden flight on 3 September 1919

With the end of the war, the Admiralty proposed to order one new airship a year from the contractors Armstrongs', Beardmores' and Shorts'. But Shorts' were already finding their link with the Admiralty very restrictive, for they could not develop commercially when one berth had to be kept empty for service requirements. This uneasy relationship came to an end in 1919 when, to the fury of Mr Short, Cardington was suddenly nationalised.

From 1 April 1919, Cardington became the Royal Airship Works, the focus of much national attention on the airship industry. The first major airship to be launched after the change was the R38 which had been designed by Commander Campbell. It began trials in 1921 and on 23 August 1921, while over the

Humber, it broke in two and many experts, including Campbell himself, lost their lives. An official enquiry concluded that there had been 'structural weaknesses' and that Campbell's design had never been checked by naval architects.

The next projects were the R100 and the R101, the latter more closely associated with Cardington. These airships were more gracefully designed than the First World War giants and were to be important passenger carriers across the empire, with a greater range than aircraft. The R101 made her first flight in October 1929 over the centre of London, followed by a fourteen-hour test over the Isle of Wight and a thirty-hour test over the British Isles. On the occasions of her departures, the roads around Cardington were jammed with sightseers.

On Saturday, 4 October 1930, the R101 left Cardington on its maiden flight to India. The Government had been pressing to open up this air route and the airship, now beautifully appointed with a saloon, cabins and promenade deck, was filled with government officials including Lord Thomson and Sir Sefton Brancker. Early in the hours of Sunday morning, the airship ran into bad weather over Northern France, drastically lost height and nose-dived into the hills at Beauvais. Only eight people survived, seven of them crew members.

It is perhaps difficult to appreciate the pitch of national grief after the disaster of the R101 crash. The nation was deeply stunned and national pride deeply affected. With no large-scale civilian airliners then flying, the impact of forty-eight people being killed simultaneously was devastating, and the tragedy was treated as a national disaster by the government and the media. Plans were made for a lying-in-state in Westminster Hall, a mark of respect reserved till then for sovereigns. The forty-eight coffins, draped in the Union Jack, were placed side by side in the dim medieval splendour of the great building, while thousands of mourners filed past. At one point the queue stretched from Vauxhall Bridge to Westminster and back, a distance estimated to be two miles, and the doors did not close till 1 a.m. The memorial service at St Paul's was attended by the Prince of Wales, all the foreign Air Ministers, and the relations and friends of those that had perished, many of whom came from Bedfordshire. During the service, the charred flag of the R101 was draped over the altar. All the London papers brought out special editions and the B.B.C. broadcast the St Paul's service from its special Chelmsford station. The bodies were interred beneath a large memorial at Cardington and the tattered flag was raised in Cardington church. The whole scene was captured on film.

The epitaph on the R101 was one of misplaced hurry and government expediency in the preparation for the voyage. The *Bedfordshire Times* in the first week of October 1930 had more to say than most: '. . . the brave company, believing in the work of their brains and hands, had proved their faith in it by entrusting their lives to it. But there are two ways at least of doing that; And we Bedfordians refuse to believe that some form of duress was not imported into the proceedings. And that duress could be applied from one source only – the Ministry of Air.' It was the epitaph on the whole airship industry for sixty years.

The demands and the need of a country at war were to accelerate changes that were already apparent before 1914. In the years between 1900 and 1930, Bedfordshire was to see alterations in its structure, economy, social mix and traditions, greater than any in the thousand years of its history. At first, the most noticeable changes were on the land, its management and its ownership having remained static for more than a hundred years. The great agricultural estates had never recovered from the malaise of the 1880s, and although some of them lingered on into the Edwardian years, few could sustain the body blows of the Great War, the continued agricultural recession and, later, the depression. The war certainly took its toll among these families, but some had begun to move away before the conflagration of 1914.

The Haynes Park estate of the Carterets and the Thynnes came to an end with the death of F. J. Thynne in July 1910, the historic contents of the mansion were put up for auction in May 1911 and the farms and land sold by lot in 1914. Battlesden Park had been demolished by the Bedfords thirty years earlier and been absorbed into Woburn Park. The Bedfords were not much affected by the slump, but they sold their Covent Garden property before 1914 and put the proceeds disastrously into Russian bonds. Their other house on the Ouse at Oakley was sold in 1920.

The most serious departure was from Wrest Park, where the Greys (now Lucases) left in 1917 after more than six centuries of ownership. The house had belonged to Auberon, Lord Lucas since 1905, but he had let the mansion and hardly ever lived there before it became a hospital. He was an unusual figure, part intellectual, part individualist, happier in the company of men of action than sitting about in a country house. He had embarked on a governmental career and become Under Secretary of State for the Colonies in 1911, a Privy Councillor in 1912 and President of the Board of Trade in 1914–15. His death in the Royal Flying Corps while piloting a plane near Baupaume in 1916 sealed the fate of Wrest. His only sister felt unable to cope with the vast problems of her unexpected inheritance.

Maurice Baring wrote of Lucas:

Bron was a wanderer by nature; his heart was above all things adventurous, and he went on seeking and finding adventures in spite of every handicap, in spite of circumstances, till he met with his last adventure fighting in the sky on his last errand. At Oxford he had rowed two years in the 'Varsity boat. He went out to the South African War as *Times* correspondent, where he was wounded. The wound, although not serious in itself, was followed by disastrous consequences and complications, and finally he was obliged to have his leg cut off, and for many months he was seriously ill. One would have thought this was the end of active out-of-door life and physical adventure as far as he was concerned, but not at all. [Maurice Baring, *The Puppet Show of Memory*, privately printed]

The treasures which the Greys had acquired over five hundred years were dispersed in a series of sales between 1917 and 1922 when priceless volumes, French furniture, master paintings by Van Dyck, Claude, Lawrence, Reynolds, Turner and Bordone were sold for knock down prices at an unpropitious moment for the art market. Even the set of tapestries specially woven for the mansion was dispersed.

There was a similar break in continuity at Luton Hoo. One of the Wernher sons was killed in the war and at Woburn, the Marquess of Tavistock became a conscientious objector, causing a ruction in his family that lasted for thirty years. The son of Viscount Peel of Sandy, an acting chaplain to the forces, was killed in 1917. Such events were not helpful in families that relied on continuity.

The remorseless roll of losses was to continue for the next thirty years. Cooper, the Ampthill House butler wrote: 'What a pity it is to see in the newspapers every now and again that some stately mansion and estate has to be sold, or else abandoned to the care of caretakers; what a wrench it must be to these good old families. I'm afraid many do not give a thought until they lose their own houses.' [*Town and County*, p. 177)

Odell Castle, the home of the Alstons for two centuries, was burnt down in 1931, the estate already encumbered by debts. Ickwell Bury, the home of the Harveys, was destroyed by fire in 1937 but rebuilt. Chicksands Priory, the scene of so much history, was to pass out of the Osborn family in 1935, acquired by the Air Ministry, a fate rather worse than death. Cranfield Court and Pavenham Bury were demolished. The Peel family had left Sandy Lodge by the 1930s. Richard Ormonde Shuttleworth, the heir to Old Warden Park, was killed in the Second World War and the mansion became a college just as Wrest became a research institute. Lord Melchett left Colworth, which was never to be privately occupied again, and, with the death of the 18th Lord St John in 1934, Melchbourne Park was sold, some of its famous pictures being bought by American art galleries. Stockwood Park, the only important eighteenth-century house in the environs of Luton, was demolished in 1964 on insufficient evidence of incurable dry-rot. Stratton Park, Biggleswade and Ampthill House, both substantial seats, were also demolished at this time. Where the houses remained, their fates were mixed: Ampthill Park House became a factory store, Clapham Park a convent, Milton Ernest lay empty and Oakley House became an antique shop!

Even the smaller properties were not exempt from this period of callous destruction. The Rectory at Houghton Conquest was used to sty pigs, Wootton and Sandy rectories were pulled down, and Goldington Bury was demolished. The Hasells, after being used as a mental hospital, became derelict. There was a sense of hopelessness and a conviction that such places could never be used again; without contrary legislation they were just erased from the landscape. The most tragic part of this was that their collections and records went with them: the portrait galleries and libraries that spelled out the whole history of an area. Fortunately, Dr G. H. Fowler (1861–1940) had begun the Bedfordshire Historic Records Society in 1912 and a Bedford Records Committee in 1913. This resulted in one of the earliest County Records Offices in the country, where these priceless documents could be kept.

Bedfordshire was still a very attractive place for the city man or academic to retire to for relaxation. Professor A. E. Richardson, afterwards Sir Albert, who was Professor of Architecture at University College, London, moved to Ampthill in 1919 and created his own coterie of writers, artists and collectors. Brendan Bracken, later Lord Bracken and Churchill's Private Secretary, settled at Lynch House, Kensworth at about this time, and E. W. Sursham, the paper manufacturer, had bought Markyate Cell, the Jacobethan house just inside the county. A more controversial figure was Sylvia Pankhurst, who came to Eggington House in 1927 to recuperate after the birth of her natural child. An artist who had become a feminist and a communist, she was a listless and difficult character in a country village where there was not enough to distract her powerful mind. Many of the northern and western villages remained remarkably rural and a sense of this can be caught in the novels of H. E. Bates, some of which are set in the area around Sharnbrook, where he grew up.

The exploits of the Duchess of Bedford were great headline catchers in the late 1920s and 1930s. She was still running her Cottage Hospital at Woburn, but suffering increasingly from deafness and the intolerable isolation that came with it. She was greatly troubled by a perpetual buzzing in the ears and she was told by a friend that flying relieved it! She therefore made her first flight in 1926 at the age of sixty-one. After this, there was no stopping her, and in January 1928 she made an attempt to fly to India with Captain Barnard, acting as his assistant. The newspapers loved it and crowded to the airport to see her off. They had a forced landing at Basra and eventually got to Karachi, but not in time to beat any records, which was what was uppermost in the Duchess's mind. By 1929, the Duchess had bought a Fokker plane which she called *Spider* and was preparing for another Indian trip. She and her pilots made the round trip to India and back in eight days, not a record but a sensational journey for an elderly woman and one that delighted the press. She recorded in her diary: 'It was . . . a tremendous surprise to find a big crowd waiting to receive us both inside and outside the aerodrome and on the roofs of the surrounding buildings. A perfect hornet's nest of reporters and Press photographers swarmed upon us and, almost overwhelmed by this avalanche, a little party of our own personal friends.' From then onwards she was affectionately known as 'the Flying Duchess'.

The next flight in 1930 was to the Cape, when the Duchess was employed sitting at the back and pumping petrol into the wings. Then, in 1931, she bought a Puss Moth and engaged Flight Lieutenant Allen as her personal pilot. This was a very happy time for her; the flying brought relief for her deafness and Allen proved to be a perfect companion although it was strictly an employer and employee relationship, every airborne message prefaced by 'Your Grace'. She flew to Constantinople with him, then explored Palestine and Egypt before returning home. This idyllic period was brought to a tragic end in 1933 when Allen was killed at Lidlington while trying to land the plane at Woburn Abbey.

In January 1934, the Duchess engaged the services of Flight Lieutenant Preston, and with her new pilot she was determined to conquer the Sahara Desert. This was another successful venture although they were forced to land in inhospitable country and spend the night in the open. The Duchess had been flying her aircraft for some years and by 1937 she had an 'A' licence and had nearly reached her two hundred hours of solo flying. On Monday 22 March 1937, the Duchess took off from the Woburn hangar to complete her two hundred hours; she had only fifty-five minutes to complete, and Flight Lieutenant Preston had suggested a round trip to Buntingford. By 4.30 p.m. that afternoon a heavy snowstorm set in and the Duchess and her de Havilland Gipsy aeroplane were never seen again. A fortnight later, a strut from the aircraft was washed ashore at Yarmouth. It is not known what happened to this intrepid, elderly aviator. Was it an accident? Was it suicide? It was known that she had become increasingly depressed about her deafness and the Duke's determination to close her hospital and save money. Perhaps she felt this was the simplest way out. A memorial window was dedicated to her memory in Woburn church depicting the flowers and birds that she loved. Her sitting-room can still be seen at the Abbey, just as she left it, but with the strut of her aircraft in one corner.

By the middle of the 1920s, most of the great firms that were to make the names of Luton, Dunstable and Bedford had already arrived. The Bedford firms, in particular, were to be geographical choices rather than ones connected with historical industries. W. H. Allen saw the thirteen-acre site at Bedford from the window of his train and decided to start an engineering works there in 1894. Similarly, W. H. A. Robertson created an engineering works there because it was midway between Birmingham and the ports. The Igranic Electric Co. came in 1913, the same year as Meltis chocolate.

Luton was a more powerful industrial base because of its huge resident work force, previously engaged in hat making. Early arrivals were Commer Cars in 1906, Bagshawes of Dunstable in 1906, Davis Gas Stove Company in 1907, George Kent's in 1908 and S.K.F. Ball Bearing Company in 1910. The most celebrated, Vauxhall Motors, came in 1905, but was then largely a company producing hydraulic pumps. It manufactured cars as a sideline and this resulted in a separate company in 1907 under Leslie Walton and Percy Kinder. Vauxhall produced large luxury touring cars for the Edwardian market, notably the Prince Henry tourer, which became a legend before the First World War and led the field in events and trials. After the war, the car market changed radically from the production of luxury cars to the production of small, economic, family cars. Vauxhall did not adapt to this new format and so was taken over by General Motors in 1925. Basing its marketing on Henry Ford's practices, the company gained a reputation for mass-produced cars with a bit more quality than most. This success led them through the slump of the 1930s with little difficulty under the direction of Sir Charles Bartlett. Bedford firms survived too during these difficult times, although a sad casualty was the closure of the Britannia Works in 1932

Luton, like Bedford, had one major brewery, J. W. Green's, which had developed from a number of smaller breweries. These included Burr's brewery which had been taken over in 1857 by Thomas Sworder of Hertford. He bought up inn after inn and continued to expand until he met a rival, J. W. Green of the Phoenix Brewery. Green was a brilliant businessman and succeeded in outwitting Sworder and eventually bringing him down. Green acquired the whole Sworder empire in 1897 for £139,000. At Bedford, most of the small breweries had disappeared and were replaced by Charles Wells, ably administered by Sir Richard Wells, M.P. for Bedford, Chairman of the Harpur Trust, and a product of the Harpur Schools. He was that rare twentieth-century phenomenon, a local man representing his home town, for since 1900 the parliamentary candidates had been chosen by party organisations rather than local cabals of the ruling gentry.

The middle part of the county, where Oxford clay was most abundant, had enjoyed a small brick industry from the seventeenth century. This only developed commercially in the nineteenth century and became an industry in the twentieth century. There was a brick works at Arlesey from 1852, making the yellow bricks of the Cambridge type frequently seen in east Bedfordshire, and Forder's had works at Elstow, Harlington and Wootton Pillinge. It was the chairman of this company, Sir Halley Stewart, who succeeded in taking over the other companies and establishing the London Brick Company which gained a national reputation by 1936 under Sir Malcolm Stewart.

The characteristic tall brick chimneys and the long trails of grey smoke have been a familiar part of the Bedfordshire landscape ever since, although not one always welcomed by the inhabitants. The London Brick Company's Bedfordshire headquarters was Wootton Pillinge, renamed Stewartby, where a model village was designed in the shadow of the tall, thin, brick chimneys. This was laid out with greens and trees and has a village hall built in 1928–30 by the architect Vincent Harris, and a Secondary School by Oswald P. Milne in 1936. The old people's homes and hall were designed by Sir Albert Richardson in 1955. Stewartby is the only sizeable industrial village in the county.

One of the last railway lines to be built was created at Leighton Buzzard in 1919 to transport sand from north of the town to the L.N.W.R station. It was later taken over by enthusiasts and still runs as the Leighton Buzzard Narrow Gauge Railway from Page's Park Station.

Entertainment had switched from the bandstand and the concert hall to the cinema. Bedford's first cinema, The Picture-drome (1910), was right on the banks of the Ouse, providing added excitements in times of flood. It was owned by the Blake brothers, who became prominent members of the Kodak

Company. This was followed by The Palace (1912), The Empire (1912), The Plaza, on the Embankment (1919) and the Granada, St Peter's Street (1934), which was far the grandest both on account of its architecture and its facilities: a neo-Regency extravaganza with a touch of Art Deco, a true temple of the talking picture! The total cost of the building was £48,750 and it accommodated 1690 people and had a stage that could be adapted for plays. One of the great features in the early days was the Wurlitzer organ which was occasionally heard on the B.B.C. under the fingers of the genius of the keys, Reginald Dixon. In 1928, Luton had five cinemas, the Empire, the Gordon Street Electric Pavilion, the Picturedrome, Park Street, the Wellington Picture Palace and the High Town Electric Theatre.

A new venture which provided much excitement in the early 1930s was the opening of Whipsnade Zoo. This was a far-sighted move by the Zoological Society of London to create an alternative to a city zoo, high on the Dunstable Downs but within easy reach of tourists. The brainchild of Sir Peter Chalmers Mitchell, the secretary, it became reality when a derelict farmhouse and five hundred acres were purchased in 1927. Four years were spent in fencing the site against foxes and providing access roads across Whipsnade Common as well as in building restaurant facilities. The zoo opened on Whit Monday 1931 and a crowd of 40,000 people visited the park. Sir Anthony Wingfield of Ampthill House was an enthusiastic patron and gave many rare species to the zoo. These animals were then ponderously led across the county to start their new life. In 1932, the Zoo purchased all the animals from Bostock's Circus and these were walked up to Whipsnade from Dunstable station. The great symbol of Whipsnade, however, was the lion cut out on the hillside in the white chalk and visible for miles.

Stevington Windmill, dating from 1770, the only working example of a post-mill to survive in the county, was totally restored in 1921 with wood from the Oakley estate, donated by Lord Ampthill. It went out of production in 1936 and was taken over by the County Council in 1951. In the mid 1920s, attempts were made to save Houghton House from demolition and this was achieved in 1931 when it was taken over by the Board of Works. Another milestone was passed in the 1930s when the

Willington dovecote became a property of the National Trust, its importance having been canvassed to the Trust by Mrs Orlebar, the vicar's wife, early in the century. These years also saw the first borough museum in the county. In 1931, Luton Council voted to turn the empty mansion of Wardown into a Luton Museum and this was begun with a good collection of local artefacts from the earlier library collection. It became a focal point of local history, specialising in the history of hats and lace. Its success was largely due to the unbounded drive and energy of its curator from 1936, Charles Freeman (1906–65).

In the late 1930s the Bedford born brewer, Cecil Higgins (1855–1941) began to consider the possibility of founding an art gallery in the old home of the Higgins family at Bedford. Cecil Higgins had not lived there since his boyhood, but he still owned it and its position behind the castle site and close to the river was ideal. Higgins, who lived in London, had devoted his life to art collecting, pictures and furniture, but principally European ceramics. When he died in 1941, Bedford became the fortunate beneficiary of a porcelain collection of national importance, although it could not be displayed until after the Second World War. His dream was not realised until 1949 when the Cecil Higgins Art Gallery opened its doors to the public. A general museum collection already existed in the town, the Modern School Museum which had been established early in the century. This was to form the basis of the Bedford Museum, opened on the Embankment in 1960 and finally in the Castle Works building beside the Art Gallery in the 1980s.

With this mixture of cultural improvements and urban advances, the county approached the period of the Second World War. Its most enduring visual symbol was the ribbon development, beloved of inter-war builders, that frog-marched Bedford and Luton into an unsuspecting countryside. Roads were lined with neat semi-detached houses of 'By-Pass Tudor' stretching out from Bedford to Goldington and Elstow, most of them without garages. Luton, which had always had a ring of satellite hamlets, swallowed them all up one by one.

Postscript

Events in the past fifty years have occurred with such rapidity that it is almost impossible to record them as history, more as a continuing tidal wave. Time cannot be expected to stand still anywhere, let alone in a county that lies in close proximity to the capital and in the most prosperous and expanding corner of England, the south-east. But it is equally unthinkable that a county with such a history should be wrenched away from its roots, or be allowed to forget its origins and traditions in a miasma of grey, twentieth-century conformity. It is absolutely right that its sons and daughters should know something of this past and be aware of the villages and the landscapes in which their grandparents grew up. Sadly, it is only necessary to compare the quality of newspaper reports of seventy years ago with those of today, to recognise the woeful ignorance of history in our ostensibly better educated society.

The Second World War and its effects on Bedfordshire almost warrant a book in itself. Suddenly, peaceful villages became a centre of activity as aerodromes were created for the R.A.F. at Cranfield, Podington, Tempsford, Thurleigh and Little Staughton. At the last named place, the creation of the base resulted in the destruction of three ancient inns, the Georgian Baptist chapel and about half the village. Tempsford was particularly connected with the Allied drops into occupied France and some of the most famous resistance workers were trained there. The two Special Duties squadrons of the R.A.F. were part of the Special Operations Executive and their work was extremely secret. From Tempsford, Flight Officer Yvonne Baseden was parachuted to the Toulouse area in March 1944 and Wing Commander F. Yeo-Thomas was dropped into occupied France on three occasions. It was also from this base that two planes left for Dijon to bring to Britain twenty senior Frenchmen including the future president, Vincent Auriol. Both King George VI and Queen Elizabeth visited the airfield and other distinguished visitors included Marshal of the Royal Air Force Lord Trenchard. Of all these airfields, only Tempsford reverted to agricultural land again after the war.

Little Staughton was used by the United States Air Force and Bomber Command, and among its hundreds of bomber pilots two were awarded the Victoria Cross. Woburn Abbey became a base of Military Intelligence and Rudolf Hess, Hitler's deputy, was interrogated there after his dramatic flight to Scotland in 1941. The late Harold White of the White Crescent Press, Luton, had to prepare a dummy newspaper, to be given to Hess, in the hope that its contents would provoke him to talk.

A more pleasurable invasion was provided in 1941 with the arrival of the B.B.C. Music Department at Bedford. A staff of two hundred were accommodated, and studios and concert halls provided throughout the town. Sir Adrian Boult moved to Bedford with the B.B.C. Symphony Orchestra and lived for four years at Woodlands, Clapham with his wife. He records in his memoirs the meandering loops of the Ouse on its slow progress from Clapham to the county town and the pleasant strolls he took into Bedford for his concerts. Performances and broadcasts were held in the Corn Exchange and in the Bedford School Hall with a mixed audience of townspeople, troops and schoolboys. In 1944, the Proms were performed from the Great Hall of Bedford School with Sir Henry Wood conducting his very last season.

A musician of a rather different cut arrived in Bedford in 1944, Glenn Miller of the 'Big Band' sound. His American Band was stationed in Bedford and Miller himself lived in Waterloo Road and gave concerts at the Corn Exchange and at Twin Woods Farm, north of Bedford. It was from the tarmac of the training station at Twin Woods that Miller took off for France on that fateful day, 15 December 1944, and was lost over the North Sea.

Bedfordshire had its influx of wartime visitors: evacuees living with the rural population, landgirls working on the fields vacated by men in the services and prisoners of war in camps up and down the county. At Ampthill Park, many of the German prisoners were talented musicians and gave concerts of a high standard in their hall. Both Winston Churchill and General de Gaulle stayed in the county at various times. There were all the upheavals that had marked the First World War. Large houses were commandeered, offices and military headquarters set up, and road and direction signs taken down. There were also additional problems, not a part of that earlier conflict; the finest of the county's Georgian ironwork was seized by the Ministry of Supply for scrap, despite protestations. It was never used!

The confident decade following the war saw considerable changes in a county of small agricultural holdings. A booming farm industry, coupled with the break up of many old estates, resulted in the regrouping of land into slightly bigger farms. Mechanisation increased rapidly and fertilisers and phosphates turned the management of the land into a highly scientific operation. Bedfordshire became a centre of agricultural and scientific research with institutes at Wrest Park and Cranfield, and colleges at Silsoe and Old Warden, as well as Unilever's headquarters at Colworth House. A growth in the brick industry in the middle of the county and the development of light engineering companies at Bedford resulted in many displaced persons being employed in Bedfordshire. This led to a large Polish community in Bedford, followed by a large Italian one and migrants from the Commonwealth, thus giving the town a cosmopolitan atmosphere it had not had in earlier days. The Polish community established their own church in the redundant St Cuthbert's and the Italian community have their own church of St Francesca Cabrini, off the Bromham Road, and their own consulate.

The Welfare State had brought undreamed of advantages in health, education and working conditions for many people. Both urban and rural districts indulged in a spree of building schemes for schools, council houses and hospitals, and new estates and new roads sprang up overnight. The private sector of education also prospered and the Harpur Schools benefited from the increase in value of their London properties.

A good example of the leopard changing its spots can be found in the roll of the country house owner. In 1951, the 12th Duke of Bedford, persuaded by an over zealous agent, demolished the east front of Woburn Abbey containing the Holland Riding School. Horrified architectural societies called Sir Albert Richardson in as consultant to restore what was left. When the 13th Duke of Bedford succeeded in 1953, he and his Duchess were forced to become the first stately-home owners to go public! They imported fair ground attractions, roundabouts, dodgems, pets' corners and gift-shops to make their home and its park a going concern. In the mid 1950s they had performances of 'Son et Lumière', one of the first houses in the country to do so. The Duke was mercilessly lampooned in *Punch* and other weeklies for his showmanship at Woburn. Writing twenty years later, the Duke said: 'What I did in the early days and was regarded as scandalous I find the sons of my erstwhile competitors doing as something completely normal. I started out as the *enfant terrible* of the stately home business and today I am the grand old man (retired); it's a strange sensation.' [*The Destruction of the Country House*, 1974, p.162]

The opening of the M1 in 1959 spelt out a new era of communication for Bedfordshire. Up to that time the journey to the capital had been a two-hour grind through all the towns along the North Road and the Watling Street. Suddenly, London and the Midlands were an hour away, although the sight of traffic seering through the countryside above once peaceful and remote lanes was a visual shock. No motorway planner ever envisaged the changes in transport and the volume of traffic that would result from this new highway. Within a few years the carriage of freight was being moved to this new road and the railways, already in decline, lost their dominance.

Railway stations were starting to close in the 1950s but whole lines were axed under the murderous policies of Lord Beeching. The first to suffer was the old Bedford to Hitchin line on 1 January 1962, followed by the Bedford to Northampton line on 31 March 1962 and the Dunstable branch in July 1962. The Luton, Dunstable and Welwyn railway with its station at Bute Street, Luton, was closed in April 1965 and the county's most important easterly link, the Bedford to Cambridge line, was shut down on 1 January 1968. With hindsight, it can be appreciated how hasty these decisions were. More and more traffic was pressed on to unsuitable roads, and villages and small towns on east-west routes were shaken by intolerable noise as Midland traffic roared to the East Coast. Local demands for relief from protest groups resulted in by-passes, but these in turn often divorced the village from its countryside and wildlife. Ironically, the great *cause célèbre* of the 1960s was the A6 murder, committed at Deadman's Hill, Clophill in 1961. The subsequent conviction and hanging of James Hanratty at Bedford Prison was the finale of one of the longest trials in legal history, and the verdict still causes many famous legal heads to wag in disapproval.

The 1950s was also the decade of the new town and the 'overspill' creating new communities from urban areas in the virgin countryside. Uncompromisingly awful homes were built without any attempt to enhance the landscape or use local materials. In the case of Houghton Regis, a village of considerable historical interest was nearly obliterated by estates, its ancient church standing today in streets of cheap shops and warehouses. In the countryside, the prosperous farming of the fifties became the intensive farming of the sixties, with hedges grubbed out and trees left to wither and die. The beautifully laid hedges of my childhood were replaced by savagely machine-cut hedges or arid ditches with no greenery in sight. In recent years an attempt has been made to turn back the clock, but there is a long way to go.

With the advent of the superstore in the 1970s, shopping itself changed and customers were lured to huge retail establishments away from the small towns and villages. The result has been the demise of personal shopping and the disappearance of the small family businesses and corner shops that gave life blood to a community. The shops of my childhood that were so full of character, filled with goods and busy with people, are now replaced by the dead windows of estate agents. A few small towns like Woburn have a thriving tourist trade, but no butcher! Few of the smaller villages sustain anything bigger than a post-office stores where half a century ago there were a dozen small businesses.

The principal towns, with the exception of Luton, have retained something of their dignity. Bedford remains the traditional county town along its river, although its axis has shifted westward from the High Street. This is partly due to the removal of the Bedford Modern School from its Blore building to a site on the Clapham Road in 1974. The old buildings are now a

Gothic screen for the Harpur Shopping Centre, although the Harpur Trustees still meet in the tower of the old gatehouse. It is a pity that a similar sensitivity could not have prevailed in Luton, where the old bones of the town were torn out to make the Arndale Centre. The centres of Potton, Ampthill and Leighton Buzzard would be recognisable to anyone returning after an absence of sixty years, but their peripheries are slowly being built up and their green spaces filled in.

With today's demands for change, higher expectations and refusal to accept anything that is not purpose-built or conforming to European standards, the advance of urbanisation is acute. In the decades since the war, planning control, the listing of buildings and the designation of areas of scientific or landscape value should have protected the county's heritage from the developer. But the scale has tipped in the developer's favour. Forty years ago, a developer was usually local and his fight with conservationists was at a village level; today's developers are huge national consortiums who can afford endless tribunals and enquiries regardless of expense. Far removed from local opinion, superstore directors or development partnerships can wear down district councils and ride rough-shod over the feelings of ordinary people.

Mineral extraction has always been a problem and in Bedfordshire, licences to extract clay, gravel and fuller's earth, granted forty years ago, are still valid though not conforming with today's standards. In this way, out-dated legislation still threatens villages and green field sites. One of the finest tree-lined roads in the county, running between Woburn Sands and Woburn, has recently been obliterated to satisfy an outstanding fuller's earth claim.

Earlier planning decisions remain to haunt us. The dominating presence of the modern hotel on the south bank of the Ouse at Bedford is a case in point, its barbaric materials and huge scale being at variance with all its surroundings. Hardly less surprising at the Swan Hotel opposite, is the manner in which Henry Holland's original interiors have been swept away in a welter of hotelier pastiche set somewhere between 1700 and 1920.

A more positive side to the county in the last few years is the increasing use of the countryside for recreation, education and leisure. Country parks have been created at Harrold and Stockgrove, nature trails and woodland walks have been laid out and a community forest has been set up in the middle of the county. The Greensand Ridge Walk is followed by hundreds of people every year and gardens such as Wrest Park and the Swiss Garden at Old Warden are more accessible than ever before, while the Bird Garden at Stagsden offers a variation on the same theme. Preservation societies and conservation groups have mushroomed, and bodies like the Bedford Society are actively consulted over new buildings in the town. Bedfordshire has gained one or two institutions of national significance: the headquarters of the Royal Society for the Protection of Birds at Sandy is one and the international Woburn Golf Course is another. The major airport at Luton has developed as an arm of London Airport.

It is popular today to say that 'nothing can be set in stone'. But if our predecessors had not had the pride and foresight to care about their county we should not have inherited those riches from the past that give us our identity. The plea from these pages is that we should care for what we have been given and hand it onwards, augmented but intact, to future generations.

Bibliography

Ailesbury, Thomas Earl of *Memoirs*, 2 Vols, 1890
Annals of Agriculture, 1799–1800
Anonymous, *A Visit to Bedford*, 1913
Aubrey, John *Brief Lives*, 1949
Bagshawe, T. W. *Apollo*, Vol. 29, 1939
Bedford, John Duke of *The Flying Duchess*, 1968
Bedfordshire Historical Record Society, Vol. 27, 1948 [Dyve];
    Vol. 30, 1950 [Rogers]; Vol. 34, 1954 [Williamson]; Vol. 35,
    1955 [Okey]; Vol. 36, 1956 [Gostwick]; Vol. 37, 1957
    [Astry]; Vol. 38, 1948 [Dyve]; Vol. 40, 1960 [Salusbury];
    Vol. 42, 1963 [Luke]; Vol. 50, 1971 [Whitbread]; Vol. 57,
    1978 [Russell]; Vol. 66, 1987 [Brooks]
Bedfordshire Magazine, Vol. 8, [Bloomfield]; Vol. 17, [Bletsoe];
    Vol. 20 [Sunday Schools & Underhill Robinson]; Vol. 21
    [Stannard]
Bedfordshire Notes & Queries, Vol. 1
Bell, Patricia *Belief in Bedfordshire*, 1986
Bennett, Arnold *The Journals 1896–1910*, 1930
Blundell, J. H. *Toddington, its annals and people*, 1925
Buck, Anne *Thomas Lester, His Lace and the East Midlands Lace
    Industry*, 1981
Burgon, J. W. *Letters from Rome*, 1862
Burgon, J. W. *Twelve Good Men*, 1891
Byng, Mrs *Political and Social Letters*, 1890
Cardigan, The Earl of *The Life and Loyalties of Thomas Bruce*
Colvin, H. M. *Biographical Dictionary of English Architects,
    1660–1840*, 1978
Conisbee, L. R. *A Bedfordshire Bibliography*, 4 Vols, 1962–78
Cooper, Charles W. *Town and County*, 1937
Creevey, Thomas *Memoirs*, 1904
Croese, *History of the Quakers*, 1696

Defoe's Tour Thro' Great Britain, 1761 Edition

Dony, Dr John G. *Flora of Bedfordshire*, 1953

Elliott, Sir Gilbert *The Life and Letters*, 2 Vols, 1874

Gentleman's Magazine, 1845 [Pembroke]

Garrett, Mattingley, *Katherine of Aragon*, 1942

Godber, Joyce *The History of Bedfordshire*, 1965

Godber, Joyce *The Harpur Trust*, 1973

Godber, Joyce *Friends in Bedfordshire & West Hertfordshire*, 1975

Hare, Augustus J. C. *The Story of My Life*, 1900

Harrison, F. M., *John Bunyan*, 1928

Hartrick, A. S. *A Painter's Pilgrimage through Fifty Years*, 1939

Hind, A. *Confessions of an Uncommon Attorney*, 1945

Houfe, Simon *Through Visitors' Eyes*, 1990

King, H. E. *Ancient Catholic Mission and Its Modern Development*, c.1896

Knight, C. *Passages From A Working Life*, 1865

Kuhlicke, F. W. *The Eagle*, Vol. 28 [Modern School]

Nichols, J. *The Progresses of Queen Elizabeth*, 1788–1821

Nichols, J. *Progresses of James I*, 1828

Parry, E. A. (Editor) *The Letters of Dorothy Osborne*, 1888

Parry, J. D. *History of Woburn*, 1831

Piggott, C. *The Jockey Club*, 1792

Reid, Michaela *Ask Sir James*, 1987

Russell, Lady Rachel *Letters*, 2 Vols, 1853

Simco, Angela *Survey of Bedfordshire: The Roman Period*, 1984

Steward, William, *A Bedfordshire Village*, 1898

Sundon Memoirs, 2 Vols, 1847

Torrington Diaries, Ed. by C. Bruyn Andrewes, 4 Vols

Trevelyan, R. *Grand Dukes and Diamonds*, 1991

Underwood, Andrew *A Goodly Heritage*, 1976

Underwood, Andrew *The Eagle*, Vol. 39, [Modern School]

Victoria County History, Bedfordshire, 4 Vols, 1904–12

Walpole, The Hon. Horace *Letters*, 1906

Watson, W. J. H. *Community Libraries of Bedfordshire 1830–1965*

Young, *Countess of Pembroke*, 1912

Young, Arthur *Six Months Tour through Northern England*, 1779

Young, Arthur *Autobiography*, 1898

Index